Psychoanalytic Criticism

Psychoanalytic Criticism
A Reappraisal

SECOND EDITION

Elizabeth Wright

Polity Press

First published in 1998 by Polity Press
in association with Blackwell Publishers Ltd

Editorial office:
Polity Press
65 Bridge Street
Cambridge CB2 1UR, UK

Marketing and production:
Blackwell Publishers Ltd
108 Cowley Road
Oxford OX4 1JF, UK

ISBN 0–7456–1965–7
ISBN 0–7456–1966–5 (pbk)

A catalogue record for this book is available from the British Library.

Typeset in 10$\frac{1}{2}$ on 12pt Times
by Graphicraft Typesetters Limited, Hong Kong
Printed in Great Britain by M.P.G. Books, Victoria Square, Bodmin, Cornwall

This book is printed on acid-free paper.

For Ella, Maya and Louis, who may never read it

Contents

Contents

There was once a red-haired man who had no eyes and no ears. He also had no hair, so he was called red-haired only in a manner of speaking.

He wasn't able to talk, because he didn't have a mouth. He had no nose, either.

He didn't have any arms or legs. He also didn't have a stomach, and he didn't have a back, and he didn't have a spine, and he also didn't have any other insides. He didn't have anything. So it's hard to understand whom we are talking about.

So we'd better not talk about him any more.

Daniil Kharms *Ministories*

Preface

In preparing a new version of this book, I have had to make some difficult decisions: what to retain, what to revise and what to add. I posed myself certain questions and it might be useful to answer them in terms of guiding the reader of the first edition, who might wonder where to look for the updating. The question I first asked myself was whether I had dealt fairly with the key figures, psychoanalysts and critics, whom I took to represent this field.

I decided that my presentation of Freud was still useful as far as it went, since one can only revise Freud through the readings of others, this being where the changes are to be found. Looking at his distinguished followers and the apostates, I decided I had done less than justice to Jung, Klein and Winnicott, and more than justice to Deleuze and Guattari. I dealt with this both by adding new material and by shifting points of emphasis, in some cases making substantial revisions (Jung, for example). I have also revised the chapters on classical and post-Freudian criticism, where the old material was no longer sufficiently relevant and has been overtaken.

The second question for me was what to do about Lacan, since I had largely focused on Lacan up to the mid-sixties, where the main emphasis was on the determining force of language rather than on that which causes language to fracture. Since these two aspects of Lacan are in dialectical relation rather than one displacing the other, I decided not to change the Lacan of the Imaginary and the Symbolic, but instead to allow the Lacan of the Real to dominate some of the later additions to the book (in particular sections 9.2 and 9.3, but also parts of 10).

As a consequence, the greater part of the new material is in the second half of the book, where I have turned to those psychoanalytic critics who have cast a suspicious eye on artistic productions high and low. Here psychoanalytic criticism moves into the realms of dance, music and popular culture. For example, the remarkable work of Slavoj Žižek is only just beginning to be placed in a psychoanalytic context, psychoanalysis having been slow to incorporate his findings into its domain. Finally, I have now included a part specifically assigned to feminist psychoanalytic criticism in order to give due place to its pioneering endeavours and complex trajectories. The feminist critique of the cinema, for instance, documents the particular struggles of women inside the constraints of representation.

I hope that in making these revisions and additions I have extended the range of my explorations in a way which includes the whole book. For it seems to me now that all psychoanalytic theories, from whatever ideological direction they come, are about the symbolic appropriation of that which is heterogeneous, inexpressible, unrepresentable, radically other. Even more than before, it is important to suspect the functions that art is performing within the culture, including popular culture. In this respect the notion of aesthetic ambiguity, confined to a humanist perspective in some portions of the book, can become a new dialectic constantly wary of rigid colonization from any quarter, thus calling for an aesthetics of suspicion.

Introduction

The purpose of this book is to give a critical overview of what has become an ever-wider field: the relation of psychoanalytic theory to the theories of literature and the arts and the changes in critical practice that developments in both domains have produced. This practice now takes place in an end-of-century milieu in which attitudes to psychoanalysis have sharpened into oppositional stances: on the one hand, over the last ten years there has been a spate of virulent and visible attacks on psychoanalysis, and Freud in particular; on the other hand, paradoxically, studies informed by psychoanalysis have burgeoned and thrived in the academic institutions. The political status of psychoanalysis is thus a controversial issue with broad implications. This new edition endeavours to include the insights of psychoanalysis itself that would contribute to the understanding of these shifts in ideology.

Psychoanalysis addresses itself to the problems of language, starting from Freud's original insight regarding the determining force within all utterance: he draws attention to the effects of desire in language and in all forms of symbolic interaction. The language of desire is veiled, does not show itself openly: to read its indirections, to account for its effects, is no simple matter. Political life is no exception: it does not all take place at the level of the newspaper headline. What is at issue?

Psychoanalysis explores what happens when primordial impulse is directed into social goals, when bodily needs become subject to the demands of culture. Through language, desire is constituted and 'subjects' come into being, yet this language cannot define the body's experience accurately. What is of peculiar interest to psychoanalysis – some would say peculiar in both senses, 'special' and 'bizarre' – is that aspect of being which is ignored or prohibited by the laws of language. Words fail to catch it but it is real none the less. The energies of this desire become directed outside conscious awareness, attaching themselves to particular ideas and images which represent unconscious wishes; *Wunsch* in Freud's terminology has this special sense, as desire associated specifically with particular images, memory traces which take on the form of indestructible fantasies.

Only through its effects do we come to know the unconscious: through the logic of symptoms and dreams, through jokes and Freudian slips, through the structures of children's play, and, most crucially, in the mutually affective relationship which human beings develop as a result of their past total helplessness and dependence on another person. These feelings, revived in the analytic situation, may be taken as evidence that no experience the body has is ever totally obliterated from the mind. In the unconscious the body does not take the social mould, and yet the conscious mind thinks it has. On the basis of clinical experience psychoanalysis has built up a theory of how this divergence comes about. It hypothesizes that there are certain recurrent stages of socialization each of which has its own problems of invasions from the unconscious. The joint re-creation on the part of patient and analyst of the patient's life-development graphically reveals that no phase is ever totally outlived, no early satisfaction wholly surrendered. The distress and suffering which bring human beings to the consulting room symptomatically speak of the mismatch between bodily desire and sexual-cum-social role.

None of this can be scientifically proved, despite the efforts of the founder. If science is given a positivist definition, psychoanalysis cannot count as one of the physical sciences. What psychoanalysis has to offer therefore cannot be assessed without raising the problem of what a science is or can do. It is through its implicit questioning of traditional philosophical theories of knowledge that psychoanalysis makes its most distinctive contribution. Attacks on its scientific status continue to take for granted that it must situate itself in relation to other modes of knowledge and to 'common' sense, and that therapy alone is the yardstick by which the theory has to be measured. On the contrary, psychoanalysis is a theory of interpretation which calls into question the commonsense facts of consciousness, which it maintains can only be grasped after the event. To this degree psychoanalysis is itself a theory of knowledge in which the notion of a plain objectivity susceptible to a true–false analysis is open to question. Science may continue to be reliable without our necessarily accepting that labelling and measuring can do justice to what they are applied to. Its progress has been marked by revolutionary changes in the understanding of concepts, leading to definitions that are incompatible with those they replace, not merely falsifications of them. At the most fundamental level of science, quantum physics, the problem of interpretation emerges irrepressibly. Science itself is a highly interpretative activity, and it is as a science of interpretation – that is, in part as a science of science – that psychoanalysis is to be regarded. Which is not to say that the theory must be accepted uncritically.

This book tries to show in what way Freudian theory has been and still is part of an ongoing debate, although it is taking a much less decorous form than hitherto. Aside from the foregoing attacks on it as a theory and clinical practice, there is also considerable controversy within the psychoanalytic institution about certain endemic issues, which the book treats in historical sequence. Should psychoanalysis concentrate on uncovering the energies of the drive in its pursuit of its aim (instinct- or id-psychology)? Should it strengthen that part of the self capable of social integration (ego-psychology and its off-shoot, object-relations theory)? Should it focus on the division of the subject in language (structural psychoanalysis)? Should it openly serve a revolutionary purpose by opposing and accusing social institutions (anti-psychiatry)? All these positions are traceable in the changing scene of modern critical theory. Finally, and this was absent from the first edition of this book, what can psychoanalysis reveal about collective fantasies and their historical determinants, as evidenced in literature, the arts and popular culture? In particular, feminists have looked to psychoanalysis – even if not necessarily with an approving eye – for a theory of the subject that would release them from the constriction of patriarchal representations. This crucially involves an intensifying of the suspicion of that view of art which wants to regard it as entirely separate from other social practices, having a privileged language of its own.

If there is a single key issue it is probably the question of the role of sexuality in the constitution of the subject and, crucially, how this sexuality is to be defined. This raises the question why we should still concern ourselves with psychoanalytic theories of sexuality in the context of the arts. Critics from Kenneth Burke and Lionel Trilling onwards have warned against linking art and neurosis while at the same time hallowing the ingenious mechanisms of the unconscious within the creative process. This kind of attitude usually betokens the wish to protect the arts from the intrepid psychoanalytic critic who would ineptly perpetrate psychobiography and all manner of vulgar Freudianisms on the innocent art-object. But this does not take into account that author and reader are both subject to the laws of the unconscious and the fantasies it encodes. To concentrate on mechanisms without taking account of the energies with which they are charged is to ignore Freud's most radical discoveries: it is precisely the shifts of energies brought about by unconscious desire that allow new meanings to emerge. A desexualized application of psychoanalytic criticism, an attempt to confine it solely to the mechanisms of language – whether as an example of the plenitude of ambiguity (New Criticism and its off-shoots, the 'work' of an author) or as a set of shifting ambivalences (deconstruction, the 'workings' of language in a text) – does not engage the full explanatory force of psychoanalytic theory.

Psychoanalysis brings out the unconscious aspect of language through its concentration on the relationship between sexuality and social role. Clinical practice has borne out to what extent sexuality in its wider Freudian sense is the component of intention, how all utterance is concerned with the demands of bodies which have been socialized. The literary text, the art-object, the works of popular culture are forms of persuasion whereby bodies are speaking to bodies, not merely minds to minds. The plays of Samuel Beckett graphically present us with images of bodies or parts of bodies, comically and desperately struggling to channel their desire through speech. Conversely, the theatre of Antonin Artaud assaults us with the images of the body's violent refusal to become entrapped in language.

This emphasis upon the bodily aspect of art poses a problem for psychoanalytic criticism because the public and the social are thereby neglected. Psychoanalytic aesthetics intermittently battles with this problem on two fronts: first, how the work of artistic merit is to be distinguished from the 'work' involved in the construction of dreams or fantasy; second, how the work as text is to be regarded, now it is no longer the property of a single author but produced in a network of social relations. Each of these questions is concerned with the part consciousness (whether true or false) plays in the creative process, and the way ideology situates the reading and writing of texts. The language of desire has both a private and a public aspect and that is why the literary and artistic work is a 'text', the proper reading of which is no simple matter.

Although in the past psychoanalytic criticism has been irresistibly drawn to those texts that are classified as literature and art, it has not come up with an adequate theory of aesthetic value, but then neither has any other approach. It contributes rather to an understanding of the creative process at the point of intersection between language and being, and this has implications for aesthetics. Beginning with Freud, this account deals with those psychoanalysts and critics who have been the main contributors to the criticism of literature, the arts and popular culture. Included also are theorists (Derrida, Foucault) who have made an impact on psychoanalytic criticism.

The outline follows a historical course, though like Freud's sequence of sexual maturation, no stage totally supersedes another. On the contrary, in recent times French psychoanalysts (for example, Kristeva) have tried to merge an id-centred approach focusing on the affect attached to the sexual drives, with a linguistic one taking off from structural psychoanalysis. Tracing out a sequence of development in chronological order does not therefore imply that there is a necessary logical order. Such a method merely enables me to give as clear as possible an exposition of the field while still leaving room for critical appraisal. The aim will be to show how psychoanalytic theory and practice, not always working in concert with each other, have infiltrated the theory and practice of criticism. There are four variables here, which makes for a complex set of interactions. At the same time I shall be suspicious of the ideological assumptions that underlie successive developments in both theory and practice.

My criteria derive from a three-fold scheme: first, I see psychoanalytic criticism as investigating the text for the workings of a rhetoric seen as analogous to the mechanisms of the psyche; second, I argue that any such criticism must be grounded in a theory which takes into account the relations between author and text, and between reader and text; and third, I argue that these relations should be seen as part of a more general problem to do with the constitution of the subject in the social as history proceeds.

PART I

1
Classical Psychoanalysis: Freud

1.1 Theoretical principles and basic concepts

Though the summary of Freudian theory given here cannot but be selective, it aims to indicate what sort of knowledge psychoanalysis has to
contribute to the understanding of literature and the arts. The same mechanisms which Freud shows as determining in normal and abnormal behaviour
come significantly into play when we are engaged in aesthetic activities
of any kind. The theories which follow offer various explanations of how
the unconscious functions in the production and consumption of the arts.
This section will introduce the main concepts of psychoanalytic theory:
the models of the psyche, the concept of repression, the role of the sexual
instincts – their nature and place in Freud's theory of the unconscious,
and the phenomena of transference.

Sigmund Freud (1886–1939) gives a genetic explanation of the evolu-
tionary development of the human mind as a 'psychical apparatus'. He
regarded such an explanation as providing a scientific basis for a theory of
the unconscious, by which he relates it directly to the needs of the body.
He looks at the mind from three points of view: the 'dynamic', the 'economic' and the 'topographical' (see Freud, XX, pp. 265–6 for a brief
summary). These are not mutually exclusive interpretations but emphasize different aspects of the whole. All three are evidence of Freud's
attempt to derive the mind from the body.

The 'dynamic' point of view stresses the interplay of forces within the
mind, arising from the tensions that develop when instinctual drives meet
the necessities of external reality. (The German word for these drives is
Triebe, translated as 'instincts' in the *Standard Edition*, but because, as
will be seen, they are to be distinguished from instinct in animals, it is
now more usual to translate *Triebe* as 'drives', particularly when the

notion of pressure is at stake. Owing to this rivalry of translations I have had to make use of both terms.) The mind comes into being out of the body. What is necessarily given at the start is the needs of the body itself: these are inseparably connected to feelings of pleasure and pain.

From the 'economic' point of view pleasure results from a decrease in the degree to which the body is disturbed by any stimulus. Unpleasure results from an increase in disturbance. In the interaction of the body with the external environment a part of the mind Freud calls the 'ego' evolves to mediate the actions of the body so as to achieve the optimal satisfaction of its needs. In particular the ego is concerned with self-preservation. This of its nature implies that there has to be control of these basic instincts if there is to be an adjustment to reality. Under the economic model this is viewed as a struggle between the 'reality principle' and the 'pleasure principle', in which the body has to learn to postpone pleasure and accept a degree of unpleasure in order to comply with social demands.

The third point of view is the 'topographical' of which there are two versions. The psychical apparatus is here conceived of in a spatial metaphor as divided into separate sub-systems, which together mediate the conflict of energies. In the first of the two versions Freud sees the mind as having a three-fold division, conscious, preconscious and unconscious. Consciousness he equates with the perception system, the sensing and ordering of the external world; the preconscious covers those elements of experience which can be called into consciousness at will; the unconscious is made up of all that has been kept out of the preconscious–conscious system. The unconscious is dynamic, consisting of instinctual representatives, ideas and images originally fixated in a moment of repression. But these do not remain in a fixed state; they undergo a dynamic interplay in which associations between them facilitate the shift of feeling from one image or idea to another. In Freud's terminology they are regulated by the 'primary process', a type of mental functioning where energy flows freely by means of certain mechanisms. These mechanisms, of crucial interest for psychoanalytic criticism, will be explained later in this chapter in the sections on dreams and art, where their function as strategies of desire will be discussed. The second version of the topographical scheme was introduced by Freud in 1923, when he came to view the mind as having three distinct agencies: the 'id', a term applied retrospectively to the instinctual drives that spring from the constitutional needs of the body; the ego as having developed out of the id to be an agency which regulates and opposes the drives; and the 'superego', as representative of parental and social influences upon the drives, a transformation of them rather than an external agency. This model of the psyche is often called the 'structural' model and is the one drawn on by ego-psychologists.

With the appearance of these agencies, the picture of dynamic conflict becomes clearer. The id wants its wishes satisfied, whether or not they are compatible with external demands. The ego finds itself threatened by the pressure of the unacceptable wishes. Memories of these experiences, that is images and ideas associated with them, become charged with unpleasurable feeling, and are thus barred from consciousness. This is the operation known as repression: 'the essence of repression lies simply in turning something away, and keeping it at a distance from the conscious' (XIV, p. 147).

Unfortunately this theory, what there is of it, is far from simple. If the notion of there being unconscious mental processes is to be seen as the key concept of psychoanalysis, it has of necessity to be linked with the theory of repression, 'the corner stone on which the whole structure of psycho-analysis rests' (XIV, p. 16). Freud makes a distinction between two senses of the term. 'Primal repression' initiates the formation of the unconscious and is ineradicable and permanent. Although the forces of instincts are experienced before socialization, such experience is neither conscious nor unconscious. Freud cannot account for how such forces find representation in the mind. He has to hypothesize that these instincts have become bound to thoughts and images in the course of early (pleasure/pain) experience. Primal repression consists of denying a 'psychical representative' (that is an idea attached to an instinct) entry to the conscious: a fixation is thereby established, splitting conscious from unconscious. Without these initial imprintings the later entrance into language that establishes personhood could not be achieved. For Freud primal repression marks a prelinguistic entry into a symbolic world. Lacan, on the other hand, reserves the term for the second stage of symbolization, the entry into language (for further discussion of this problem see Weber 1982 on Freud, pp. 39–48; see also Laplanche and Leclaire 1972, on Freud versus Lacan, pp. 155–63).

The term 'repression' in its second and more generally known sense is used by Freud to designate repression proper or 'after-pressure' (XIV, p. 148): it serves to keep guilt-laden wishes out of conscious experience. The symptoms, dreams and parapraxes ('Freudian slips') that turn up in the course of this process represent the 'return of the repressed', a mechanism that marks both the emergence of the forbidden wish and the resistance to it. Within the unconscious, the flow of energy becomes bound up with certain memory-traces, developing the character of unconscious wishes that strive continually to break through against the counterforce exerted by the ego. Where the primary process allows the psychical energy to flow freely, the 'secondary process' transforms it into 'bound energy', in that its movement is checked and controlled by the rational operations of the ego. The censorship of the ego can be subverted, however, precisely because of the free shifting of energy in the primary process. The drives or wishes can get through in disguise, as the so-called 'compromise formations' of the return of the repressed. It is the nature of these disguises that has occupied classical psychoanalytic criticism. Where the earlier 'instinct-psychology' emphasizes that which gets through the disguise, that is the content of the wish, the later 'ego-psychology' concentrates on that which 'controls' the wish, the work's formal devices.

Freud's theory of the instinctual drives was dualistic throughout his work; he always opposes one drive with another. It is with the earlier theory that we are concerned for the moment; the opposition of the sexual instincts to the instincts of self-preservation. The sexual instinct plays a major role in psychical conflict precisely because it is always opposed by another instinct. This is invariably forgotten when Freud is accused of 'pan-sexualism', tracing all action to the sexual instinct; his radical notion of sexuality is confused with the popular understanding of the term. He calls the total available energy of the sexual instinct 'libido', and it is essential to realize that it is not solely directed towards sexual aims *per se*. Sexuality is to be understood as not specifically limited to the process of reproduction: 'Sexual life includes the function of obtaining pleasure from zones of the body – a function which is subsequently brought into the service of reproduction. The two functions often fail to coincide completely' (XXIII, p. 152). The prime example is the infant, who gets the pleasurable stimulation of the region or 'zone' around the mouth, hence called an 'erotogenic' (eros 'love'; -gen- 'create') zone. The infant later, in sucking its thumb, is fantasizing the repetition of that sensual pleasure in the absence of nutritional need:

> The baby's obstinate persistence in sucking gives evidence at an early stage of a need for satisfaction which, though it originates from and is instigated by the taking of nourishment, nevertheless strives to obtain pleasure independently of nourishment and for that reason may and should be termed *sexual* (p. 154).

The concept of what is sexual is thus greatly extended and complicated. Freud is showing that sexuality is not a mere matter of a biological urge but involves the production of fantasies under pressure of external circumstances. There is then a disjunction between mere physical need and mental satisfaction. In Freud's view human sexuality is to be understood as what in 1910 he came to call 'psycho-sexuality' (XI, p. 222).

The libido is checked when it comes up against the environment and can only achieve partial satisfaction. In the course of an infant's development those instinctual drives which Freud came to designate sexual or 'libidinous' in nature are channelled into zones. At each stage the infant has to give up a part of its bodily satisfaction: the breast, the faeces – its first product – and the unconditional possession of a penis. Its selfhood will depend on its assumption of a sexual identity, not merely anatomically determined, but psychically constructed. Until this is achieved the infant's sexuality is 'polymorphous': it is at the mercy of the 'component instincts', functioning independently and varying in their aim, their object and their source (*Three Essays on the Theory of Sexuality*, in VII, pp. 191 and 167ff.). Only gradually and with difficulty do they become organized into what our culture considers to be adult sexuality. The match of biological sex with the sexual role determined by society is thus achieved, not given.

For Freud this matching is accomplished via the combined workings of the Oedipus complex and the castration complex. It is impossible in this short introduction to give an account of how Freud's theory of gender evolved from the *Three Essays* (1905) through to his lecture 'Femininity' (1933) (XXII, pp. 112–35). The development of his theory has been of particular import to women (see Chasseguet-Smirgel 1981; Mitchell and Rose 1982), since it started out with the notion that until puberty the little girl sees herself as a little man. The account that follows can be no more than a summary of Freud's later position, given on the most general lines.

Freud sees the child's relationship with its parents as critical for the achievement of its proper sexual identity. The difficulties begin with the child's dependence on the nurturing mother. Not only are there problems specific to the very formation of a self-concept in the initial separation from the mother's body, but the love of the mother remains dominant in the early formative years. Inevitably, according to Freud, a perception of the father as rival in this love becomes insistent for the boy-child to the point where he is drawn into fantasies of the killing of this rival and of possessing the mother. This is the Oedipus complex. The way out of it is provided by the fears of the castration complex. The father is experienced as the source of all authority, all direction of desire, and thus as capable of castrating the boy-child, who unconsciously believes this to be the reason for the absence of the penis in the girl. The boy thus abandons his love for the mother and moves towards identification with the father, with the understanding that he too can in time occupy such a position of power.

The trajectory for the girl-child is not so straightforward. In her case the complexes work in reverse, and the castration complex ushers in the

Oedipus complex. She interprets the absence of a penis as a failure in provision on the part of the mother. Under the influence of this disappointment she turns away in hostility from her mother, but in the unconscious the wish for a penis is not abandoned: it is replaced by the wish to bear the father a child. Hence the girl becomes the rival of the mother for the father's love. Freud saw the fading of the Oedipus complex in the girl-child as a more uncertain process, because the identification with the father's law, facilitated for the boy-child by the anticipation of power, is not so secure. Nor has he an adequate explanation of how the girl overcomes her jealousy of the mother and attains identification with her.

The Oedipus complex is for Freud the nucleus of desire, repression and sexual identity. Its residue is a life-long ambivalence towards the keeping and breaking of taboos and laws. As the complex declines, the superego is formed and becomes part of the topography of the psyche. The struggle to overcome the complex is never quite resolved. It is the cause of neurotic illness and *raison d'être* of the psychoanalytic process, where the patient is offered a chance to emancipate himself anew, by dint of a better compromise with authority. The psychoanalytic encounter restages the old drama through 'transference'.

Transference and countertransference might be regarded as the 'reader theory' of psychoanalysis. In the non-clinical sense these phenomena are present to some degree in all our relationships: transference is a mode of investing persons and objects with positive and negative qualities, according to our early memories of significant experience of familial figures and the expectations founded thereon. 'Countertransference' defined in this mundane sense manifests itself in the 'knots' which result from the unending chain of mutual misreadings:

> Since Jack is afraid
> that Jill will think that
> Jack is afraid
> Jack pretends that Jack is not afraid of Jill
> so that Jill will be more afraid of Jack.
>
> (Laing 1974)

This process is unconscious: at its worst it leads to a futile reaction and counterreaction, but at its best it may lead to the shifting of old agreements and the making of new ones that better satisfy desire.

The managing of these phenomena in the clinical situation is directed towards helping this process where it has got stuck. The 'free association' of the patient, her saying whatever comes to mind (see the beginnings of this technique in Freud, II, p. 63), gradually reveals that which determines her. Freud distinguishes between two kinds of transference (for a detailed account see Laplanche and Pontalis 1973, on whom this discussion in part relies; see also Wollheim 1971, pp. 152–4). In the first instance transference was for Freud the displacement of feelings from one idea to another (see the section on dreams below). In the analytic situation intense feeling, or 'affect', is transferred to the analyst (the dreams the patient brings may have been dreamt 'for' him), and becomes organized around a group of hostile and loving wishes. The patient's wishes and demands are devices of resistance, the attempt to win the analyst by undermining his authority, so that the repressed wish may at last be granted. The interpretation of the resistance – the words and actions which block off access to the unconscious – is thus the key technique of psychoanalysis. The mechanism of transferring past experience onto the figure of the analyst is set in motion just when the repressed wish is in danger of emerging. Psychoanalytic reader-theory, as will be seen, looks for such points of resistance in both readers and texts, as manifestations of the compulsion to repeat.

The second kind of transference develops in the course of the treatment. Freud calls it the 'transference neurosis'. The nearer the analyst gets to the repressed complex which induced the illness the more the patient's behaviour becomes pure repetition and divorced from present reality. He is in the grip of the 'repetition compulsion', the uncontrolled return of the repressed. Freud's fascination with art is partly due to his admiration of the artist for the ability to control the return of the repressed, as his discussions of art show (see particularly his essay on 'The uncanny' in Part III).

Freud's view of countertransference was cautious: he saw it as the analyst's uncontrolled response to the patient's transference, an inappropriate reaction to be taken care of in the training-analysis. Laplanche and Pontalis define it as 'the whole of the analyst's unconscious reactions to the individual analysand – especially to the analyst's own transference' (1973, p. 92). For some analysts the psychoanalytic encounter becomes the mutual playing out of the subjectivities of analyst and analysand: there is transference and countertransference on both sides (see André Green in Part II, who works out a parallel relationship for writer and reader). For others, such as Jacques Lacan, transference and countertransference can only be negotiated via the spoken word: resistance that is played out between two bodies will only close up the unconscious. Speech, on the other hand, will open it up, for here resistance is directed against the father's law, the order of language, which implicates both analyst and analysand in something beyond a dual relation (Lacan 1977b, pp. 123–34). It is the narration of the analysand, rather than his behaviour, which will therefore enact the reality of the unconscious, which for Lacan is in the very structure of language (for a literary demonstration of narration as transference, see Shoshana Felman in Part III).

The most general implication of all this for a theory of reading is as follows: if the patient's 'text', his presentation of experience, can cause a disturbance in the analyst which allows for a new interpretation, this turns upside down the notion that the reader is the analyst and the text the patient, which has so infuriated opponents of psychoanalytic criticism. Readers do not only work on texts, but texts work on readers, and this involves a complex double dialectic of two bodies inscribed in language.

The value of Freud's opening up of the 'royal road' to the unconscious is that it led to the realization of the universality of this endless conflict and adjustment that bodies must perforce engage in if they are to effect any kind of social compromise, if they are to speak at all.

1.2 The dream and the strategies of desire

Dreams have a privileged place in Freud's metapsychology: 'the interpretation of dreams is the royal road to a knowledge of unconscious activities of the mind' (V, p. 608). As a result of investigating them, in himself and his patients, he found himself more and more engaged with conflict and the overlapping of interpretations. Dreams, *par excellence*, reveal themselves to be boundary phenomena, in that they occur where intentions are in opposition, where bodily desires have to come to terms with society.

Whichever of the three models of the psyche is drawn upon, what takes place at the frontiers of the divisions is of prime importance. For the 'dynamic' model one can ask how the primary process affects the secondary process; for the 'economic', how the reality and pleasure principles are evidenced in psychic conflict; for the two 'topographical' models, how the unconscious interacts with the preconscious and conscious, or how id and superego each invade the realm of the ego. Undecidability at the boundaries is likely whenever the restraining power is at its weakest, not only under times of unusual stress, but at the most normal ones, that of sleep.

In the condition of sleep the force of repression, according to Freud, is relaxed, because there is no immediate likelihood of unconscious impulse being carried through into dangerous action. Constraint is still operative in that the incursions of what is repressed are deflected from action, that is, from awakening the sleeper. This is why Freud calls dreams 'the GUARDIANS of sleep and not its disturbers' (IV, p. 233). This view has since been challenged as an empirical hypothesis by the fact that dreams have been shown to be regularly occurring events during a distinct state of sleep, with the implication that dreaming is something given which may be capitalized upon by unconscious impulses, not something which is *causally dependent* on being a dual creation of impulse and repressing force (for a thorough review see Jones 1978). However, the duality, and moreover the ambiguity, of dreams remains. It is Freud's vigorous exploration of the workings of these ambiguities that is of special relevance for the language of the arts, and for the activities of reading, writing and criticism. All the arts deal in illusion and Freud's exploration of the ruses and stratagems of the psyche is of immediate relevance to aesthetic experience, at the level of both the medium (the sounds and colours of the dream) and its interpretation.

A summary of Freud's account of the genesis and nature of dreams must precede a description of these workings, because they cannot be adequately assessed without acknowledging their causes in desire. According to Freud, the energizing force of dreams springs from an unconscious impulse seeking fulfilment, a desire not fulfilled in waking life. Unable to find expression in action, the impulse gathers to itself material both from recent experience, such as the effects of present bodily need plus the recollections of the previous day (the 'day's residues'), and from distant memories involving infantile sexual wishes. An unconscious wish meets up with a preconscious thought and strives for an illusory satisfaction. But the 'censorship', the force of repression, at the frontier between unconscious and preconscious will not allow these powerfully charged memories to reach representation in their original form. Instead, under the influence of this censorship, the material is transformed into a series of images, that is the dream. Hence Freud's dictum: 'A dream is a (disguised) fulfilment of a (suppressed or repressed) wish' (IV, p. 160). The disguise may be total as regards the judgement of the dreamer, or it may be insufficient. In either case, the repressed material has both reacted to and evaded censorship by this encoding into a not immediately recognizable form. Hence Freud calls the dream a 'compromise' between the demands of impulse and the intensity of the repressing force. The more intense the force of repression, the more obscure the encodings: the distortions of the material present in the dream are thus traceable to the power of the censorship.

The apparent irrationality of the dream is not only traceable to the resistance to censorship of the unconscious material. That material is already in a form to which the word 'rational' cannot be applied. It is subject to the flow of the primary process, that activity of unconscious desire, whereby an impulse seeks the repetition of achieved satisfaction by finding again the perception that accompanied it: more is included in the perception than the conscious mind can recognize. Hence this perceptual sorting is not some pre-given recognition but a perceptual 'identifying' of sensory patterns, complexes of colour, shape and sound across time, that do not necessarily correspond to what the repressing force, involved in the secondary process, takes as identical. Linkages made in the (unconscious) primary process are already absurd from the point of view of the conscious mind, and these have a profound effect upon the dream. It is therefore difficult to understand precisely the distinction, if it is indeed viable, between the irrational connections pre-existing in the primary process and the 'distortions' insisted on by the censorship. The mechanisms involved seem to serve at one and the same time a subversive purpose (primary process functioning) and a defensive purpose (the censorship of the dream-work). As Freud said, 'in any case the censorship profits from it' (XV, p. 173; quoted by Laplanche and Pontalis 1973, p. 83). When a patient reports a dream later, the rationality of daytime experiences gives the censoring force another opportunity, in that it can impose on the apparent absurdity of the dream-sequence a narrative sense and coherence, what Freud calls 'secondary revision'. This further distortion-towards-coherence represents another clue from the mode of the actual censoring as to what is being repressed. It would be a mistake, however, to view the question as being an exclusive distinction between the subversions of the primary process (its determination to have its wishes fulfilled) and the distortions of the secondary process (its determination to prevent those wishes from being realized). It is much more a matter of the two forces in some way interacting simultaneously, though Freud himself did not reach this theoretical position, in that he kept primary process and secondary process separate. It is precisely this lacuna in Freud which led to the polarization between id-psychology and ego-psychology and the consequent opposing literary-critical positions.

Nevertheless, Freud's discussion of the individual mechanisms of the dream-work show him to be operating with a concept of ambiguity. It is significant, and has been remarked upon before (see for instance, Lacan 1988b, p. 268, and Jones 1978, pp. 11–13, who make this point for and against Freud respectively), that in *The Interpretation of Dreams* Freud is nowhere engaged in tracking down the repressed infantile wish. What Freud is interested in is not the same old primal wish, but the forms taken by the language of desire, that which he calls the 'dream-work'.

The dream-work transforms the 'latent' content of the dream, the 'forbidden' dream-thoughts, into the 'manifest' dream-stories – what the dreamer remembers. Latent content goes piece by piece into the dream-stories via a string of associations. It is the reverse process from that traversed by the analyst, who requires the patient to retrace the chain of associations in order to decode the dream. The operations of the dream-work, its subversions and distortions, take four forms: condensation (*Verdichtung*), displacement (*Verschiebung*), considerations of representability (*Rücksicht auf Darstellbarkeit*), and secondary revision (*sekundäre Bearbeitung*). These mechanisms are of crucial interest to literary critics of all persuasions, though, as has been indicated already and as will become increasingly apparent throughout this book, the ideological perspective brought to bear upon these workings will vary considerably; a detailed description is therefore called for.

According to Freud, 'the first achievement of the dream-work is *condensation*. By that we understand the fact that the manifest dream has a smaller content than the latent one, and is thus an abbreviated translation of it' (XV, p. 18). But this is far from being a simple process of the mere omission of elements. Composite figures and structures are formed so that as little as possible is left out. Hence the concept of 'overdetermination', whereby several latent wishes converge on one manifest item, or the reverse, where one wish is represented a number of times in the same dream-sequence. The result in each case is a superimposition of elements. This ambiguity is most clearly demonstrable in the way condensation treats words or names. A thing with one name may be associated in a dream with an event with a similar name, even though neither *word* occurred in the dream. Freud relates a case, where someone dreamt that '*his uncle gave him a kiss in an automobile. He went on at once to give me the interpretation, which I myself would never have guessed: namely that it meant 'auto-erotism'* (V, pp. 408–9). The co-presence of the car and the kiss matches the linking of the two parts of the term 'auto-erotism' (inducing sexual pleasure in one's own body). Condensation is also one of the essential features of the joke since, as the above example shows, it produces an ambiguous word in which two thoughts come together. In his book on jokes Freud quotes a saying that old people tend to fall into their 'anecdotage' (VIII, pp. 21–2). Here condensation creates a neologism: the phonetic sequence /dout/ is the element where two meanings coincide – anec*dote* and *dot*age. Instead of saying that old people bore us with their endless stories in their old age, the two ideas are condensed into one sound-unit.

Rational associations with words can be disrupted even more markedly. It is in the nature of the primary process that the distinction between word-as-symbol and word-as-actual-sound can sometimes be wholly ignored. Words, which as sounds have an auditory form, are things in their own right, and associations can be made between the word-as-thing and the thing for which it stands. This is what happens in the case of the schizophrenic, where something in his experience has attracted a chain of associations onto a noise, and the actual word/thing distinction disappears altogether; the world gets sorted out according to private symbols instead of public ones. It is because absurdities of this kind occur in the dreams of normal persons that Freud was able to demonstrate that the unconscious has its own mode of operation.

The second activity of the dream-work is *displacement*, which, according to Freud, 'might equally be described [in Nietzsche's phrase] as "a transvaluation of psychical values"' (V, p. 655). This transvaluation is achieved by the elements in the manifest dream replacing elements in the latent dream-thoughts via a chain of associations for the purpose of disguise; this results in the intensity of an idea becoming detached from it and passing to other ideas, which in themselves are of little value. There is also the consequence that the manifest dream has a different centre from the dream-thoughts and does not reflect their relative importance: indeed they need not appear in the dream at all. Freud regards displacement as 'the most powerful instrument of the dream-censorship' (XV, p. 233). Displacement too has an affinity with the mechanisms of the joke in that a switch of context affords a play on words whereby the dream-work achieves its forced and often far-fetched linkages. One such example is cited by Freud and concerns a patient caught up in a series of dreams, in which her father, whom she recently lost, reappears. In this particular dream the father said: 'It's a quarter past eleven, it's half past eleven, it's quarter to twelve.' To this she made associations that her father set great store on punctuality, but this did not explain the source of the dream. Another chain of associations, apparently unconnected with the dream, led to a remark which occurred in a conversation she had heard the previous day: 'The *Urmensch* [primal man] survives in all of us.' This had provided her with the pretext to bring her dead father back to life, for she had turned him into an *Uhrmensch* [clockman] by making him proclaim the regular passing of the quarter hours (XV, pp. 234–5). The displacement here consists of a shift of association between the authoritarian father who insisted on punctuality and the clock to which he repeatedly made reference. What was associated with the father is shifted onto the telling of the quarters, in itself a trivial event. This example also illustrates the occurrence of condensation and displacement together, for not only is there a displacement from father to the recurrence of the quarters, but there is a pun between *Ur-* (primal) and *Uhr-* (clock). A number of displacements onto one element of itself produces condensation and facilitates overdetermination. Displacement and condensation are thus not exclusive and there is no limit to the modes of their occurrence.

Freud's examples in his explanations of condensation and displacement make no distinction between the associative links that depend on likeness (similarity) and those that depend on proximity (contiguity). When a professor's name, 'Gärtner' (gardener) reminds Freud of a botanical monograph, word-likeness is involved; when a laboratory reminds him of a colleague who works there, the association is of A being found with B, one of contiguity. Both these associations come into his discussion of condensation. Under displacement similar linkages operate: climbing stairs is metaphorically linked with 'going up in the world' socially; a girl born in May and married in May associates herself with may-beetles, a plague which once appeared in that month. It is only after Freud that similarity and contiguity have been singled out as the two fundamental poles of language (Jakobson and Halle 1956, pp. 76–82) and subsequently equated to the rhetorical figures of metaphor and metonymy, by confining condensation to metaphoric shifts of association (based on similarity) and displacement to metonymic ones (based on contiguity). All these tropes are based on one thing being a reminder of another, on one's memories. No limits can be laid down beforehand to dictate to the memory whether it should provide similarities or contiguities or both: that two entities are found together is no bar to their being in some way significantly alike and that two are alike is no bar to their being significant in their proximity. Freud realized the inextricability in practice of similarity and contiguity; Jakobson's theoretical distinction helps to clarify what happens when memories produce tropes. It implies no contradiction of Freud, being merely an analysis of the varieties of troping.

Both condensation and displacement can produce visual and auditory images for abstract thoughts, thus contributing to the actual process of representation in dreams. *Considerations of representability*, the way the dream-thoughts achieve representation in the dream via images, is the third activity of the dream-work. Freud stressed the affinity of this process to what already obtains in language. Just as words are created by appeal to sensory items, so latent material becomes imaged by them. The German for 'adultery' is *Ehebruch*, literally 'breach of marriage': 'you will forgive the dream-work for replacing an element so hard to put into pictures . . . by another breach – a broken leg [*Beinbruch*]' (XV, p. 176). The representation is a strange language, however, in that it is divested of logical and syntactical relations. It is nearer to a rebus, a series of ideograms or pictographs, in which the syntactical connections are left to be made by the dreamer (IV, pp. 227–8). The dream has its own order of relations, which can be deduced from the visual elements that actually appear. Contradictions can coexist in an image, for one image can stand for the opposite poles of conflict. Freud cites the phenomenon found by philologists that there are a number of words which are used equally for opposite meanings (Latin *sacer* meaning both 'sacred' and 'profane'). One thing that is the cause of another might appear in a close temporal sequence but without the causal relation being demonstrated. A chronological succession of events might be turned into an image containing them all in spatial proximity. All these transformations of rational linkages are accompanied by regression to infantile modes of thought and feeling.

Representations also make use of symbols that are independent of the individual dreamer, deriving from a variety of cultural sources: they either already have a fixed conventional meaning or else they are 'typical symbols' that recur in the reports of a large number of patients. In the first case, some feature of a familiar legend may make its appearance; in the second, there is a common identification of the male sexual organ with upright objects, and of the mother's body with horizontal ones or with enclosures of all kinds. The interpretation of such 'typical symbols' has led to what has become known as 'vulgar Freudian symbolism': a given and rigid code in which all images have a specific bodily association. Freud, while under the influence of Wilhelm Stekel, did accord a greater place to the conventional symbol, but in the course of his clinical practice he rejected such a mechanical approach, asserting that the interpretation of any symbol, however public, has to be mediated by the context in which it is found: 'as with Chinese script, the correct interpretation should be arrived at on each occasion from the context' (V, p. 353). Freud was thus no vulgar Freudian, even though as analyst he could not ignore the stock-in-trade of familiar symbols that are present in the culture.

The analyst is not the first interpreter of the dream: in narrating a dream the dreamer already acts as his own biased interpreter. *Secondary revision* is logically the last distorting activity of the dream-work. It can occur in the course of the dream, in that the censorship may already be singling out and emphasizing certain elements of the dream, operating 'simultaneously in a conducive and selective sense upon the mass of material present in the dream-thoughts' (V, p. 499). But secondary revision or 'elaboration' (*Bearbeitung*), as Freud also called it, is most obviously at work when the dream is presented in the form of a verbal account. The conscious mind prefers to put the irrational dream-sequence into recognizable and familiar logical order, involving a further distortion of the 'distortion' already achieved by the three mechanisms discussed above. This final revision is in the form of a gestalt-switch in that the dream-sequence is not altered, but the sorting of it is. The 'intelligible pattern' which the conscious mind wants to impose on the visual material can ignore or falsify what is patently there, in the manner of a reader who is so engaged in the text that he ignores the misprints (ibid.). What was visible to the mind's eye in the dream remains unchanged, but the conscious perspective produces a re-vision of it. The material is ignored in the determination to arrive at an acceptable rational narrative: the readymade formulations of the dream are abandoned, and new ones are made of the very same material. One might illustrate this with an example from Afferbeck Lauder's *Let Stalk Strine*, the comic guide to Australian pronunciation, taking the phrase 'Baked Necks'. The first clue, the actual letters as spelled out, suggest that a curious Australian cooked meat is being offered – perhaps an exotic 'prepared neck-end of lamb'. This clue is subverted in the context by the rival second clues that follow: 'A popular breakfast dish. Others include emma necks; scremblex; and fright shops' (Lauder 1965, p. 14). This is a fair analogy for the process of secondary revision: a first interpretation of a visual experience (the letters) was 'revised' by its being placed in a new context. In the patient/dreamer's account the censorship in its conflict with the primary process overlooks in its secondary revision obvious contextual clues. Secondary revision shows that it is a danger for all systematic thinking to ignore elements that do not fit into a desired pattern. Reading shares this danger with the reporting of a dream. Boundaries shift with contextual placings of the visual material of the dream or of any symbolic medium, including what we call art: the rivalry of interpretations both within subjects (conscious versus unconscious) and between subjects (teller versus hearer) remains a common characteristic of dream and art, in whatever other respects they may differ.

1.3 Art and the strategies of desire

Although Freud's essays on art and literature are admired for their elegant exposition, they have not, until fairly recently, received much serious critical attention. This is because in the past these writings have been invoked reductively, quoted selectively against his aesthetic argument as a whole. He relates art to the dream, along a path that leads 'from the investigation of dreams to the analysis of works of imagination and ultimately to the analysis of their creators – writers and artists themselves'

(XIV, p. 36). He relates the artist to the neurotic, this being his most notorious statement:

> An artist is once more in rudiments an introvert, not far removed from neurosis. He is oppressed by excessively powerful instinctual needs. He desires to win honour, power, love, wealth, fame and the love of women; but he lacks the means of achieving these satisfactions (XVI, p. 376).

Finally, the object of the whole enterprise is the fulfilment of an infantile wish: 'In the exercising of an art it [psychoanalysis] sees once again an activity intended to allay ungratified wishes – in the first place in the creative artist himself and subsequently in his audience or spectators' (XIII, p. 187). Id-psychological criticism is founded on these reductions: the content of the wish is paramount and as a consequence a direct relation between the artist and the work is presupposed and usually made the centre of the inquiry.

The key question around which these issues circle, 'from what sources that strange being, the creative writer, draws his material, and how he manages to make such an impression on us and arouse in us emotions of which, perhaps, we had not even thought ourselves capable' (IX, p. 143), has not stirred many minds outside psychoanalytic circles. The question is confined to motivation: it asks about the nature of the subject and not about the value of the object. It would therefore seem to testify to the inferiority of the psychological approach to aesthetics as compared to the philosophical. In the past this kind of argument has been influential (see Langer 1942, pp. 207–8), but more recently Paul Ricoeur (1970) and Richard Wollheim (1973) have argued for the relevance and modesty of Freud's investigations into aesthetics. Freud does not profess to deal with the question of aesthetic criteria: 'Before the problem of the creative artist analysis must, alas, lay down its arms' (XXI, p. 177). Throughout his work he never departs from this view.

In 'Creative writers and day-dreaming' (1908) Freud frankly admits that psychoanalysis cannot say how the artist achieves his 'innermost secret'. Ricoeur takes this essay as a prototype to argue that these writings on art are fragmentary in a highly systematic way. First, Freud proceeds by a series of analogies. Far from being reductive, these analogies make up the organizing principle of Freud's essays on art. By a series of displacements he works from the child at play, to the writer's fantasy-world, to the novelist's hero, bringing together dream and fiction in their joint function of fulfilling a wish (Ricoeur 1970, pp. 165–6). But Freud, as Ricoeur points out, also distinguishes daydream from artistic creation, by including the role of play, which goes beyond hallucinatory wish-fulfilment, and by stressing that the daydream makes use of the relation of fantasy to time, by taking 'an occasion in the present to construct, on the pattern of the past, a picture of the future' (IX, p. 148). Second, Freud has something to say about how the pleasure the artist gives us (from 'what we are inclined to take to be his personal daydreams' (p. 153)) is connected with the dynamics of the work of art, and this Ricoeur sees as the systematic aim of the Freudian aesthetic. Variously interpreted, there is no doubt that this theory has been an all-pervasive influence within psychoanalytic applied criticism. Dreams and art are not merely linked because they fulfil wishes, but because both have to make use of strategies in order to overcome the resistance of consciousness: 'work' is done by the dreamer and the artist to transform their primitive desires into culturally acceptable meanings. In order to undermine our resistance, the artist masks his egoistic daydream and at the same time lures us with the

> purely formal – that is, aesthetic – yield of pleasure which he offers us in the presentation of his phantasies. We give the name of *incentive bonus*, or *fore-pleasure*, to a yield of pleasure such as this, which is offered to us so as to make possible the release of still greater pleasure arising from deeper psychical sources (p. 155).

For this Freud has continued to come under fire, not only from aestheticians and literary critics, but also from the proponents of ego-psychology, who wish to argue that aesthetic form has to do with the ego's attempt to maintain and extend its boundaries over the id. Freud is damned out of his own mouth: 'In "Creative Writers and Day-Dreaming", Freud reduced form and beauty to resistance and defence . . . Form sugar-coats an offensive content, bribing critical powers with aesthetic pleasure (analogous to sexual forepleasure)' (Rose 1980, p. 7). While this school must be given credit for its attempts to relate form and content, it makes art, as will be seen, into an altogether fervent and solemn affair. It ignores the connection between the technique of the work of art and the effect of pleasure it produces, which Freud here adumbrates, albeit in a reductive fashion. For a full elaboration of his theory one needs to look at Freud's work on the technique of jokes, where the connection between the fore-pleasure generated (by the word-play) and the deeper instinctual pleasure released is brought out (Ricoeur 1970, pp. 167–8). The saving of the repression, the needless expenditure which gives rise to laughter, can only occur by means of the linguistic devices the 'joke-work' employs in order to divert the attention of those involved in the joke (Wollheim 1973, pp. 216–17).

Freud does not stop at asking where the artist gets his material and how he achieves his effects; he is also interested in the devices whereby the wish gets through. In an essay entitled 'Freud and the understanding of art', Richard Wollheim (1973) examines what part these devices play in Freud's view of art. He argues that Freud was fully aware of the difference between treating art as biographical evidence and treating it as an aesthetic object. The essay entitled 'Leonardo da Vinci and a memory of his childhood' is first and foremost an attempt at psychobiography, whereby Freud wishes to trace the continuing effects of sexuality as experienced in childhood on the adult life of a great man. In the course of tracing his subject's complex history Freud purports to explain why Leonardo turned from art to science and why even his homosexuality was present merely in an idealized form. Freud's study is rooted somewhat tenuously in a supposed 'childhood memory' of Leonardo's, a 'vulture' that opens the infant's mouth with its tail (and which turns out to be a mistranslation of the word *nibio*, meaning kite). He relates these biographical findings (which do not depend on the species of bird in any significant way) to certain of Leonardo's paintings, the *Mona Lisa* and the *Madonna and Child with St Anne*. As Wollheim stresses (1973, p. 207), Freud does not derive his biographical evidence from the paintings: he finds contextual information embedded within them which he decodes with the help of the findings already established. As regards the *Mona Lisa*, Freud argues that the smile condenses two images of Leonardo's first mother, one signifying tenderness and reserve, the other sensuality and seduction. As regards the other picture, both natural mother and equally loved stepmother are present and linked in a pyramidal structure; here the enigmatic smile can be read on both faces, doubly condensed in dreamlike fusion. The focus is thus on processes whereby a conflict of meanings can be discerned within the work itself: in psychoanalytic terms a wish, to yield to the tenderness of the mother, is confronted by a defence, the danger of yielding to this wish. In artistic terms there is an ambiguous element the viewer cannot account for, what has been called 'the daemonic magic of this smile' (XI, p. 108).

Dreams and fantasies require a frame of reference, the associations the dreamer/patient is expected to bring to them, that make salient their ambiguity for the analyst. The work of art has already itself provided that ambiguity. In his study of Jensen's story *Gradiva* Freud feels justified in investigating 'the class of dreams that have never been dreamt at all – dreams created by imaginative writers and ascribed to invented characters in the course of a story' (IX, p. 7). He finds all the associative elements in the story itself; his interpretation in no way depends on the intention of the author, conscious or otherwise. This is not to deny that Freud was primarily interested in the several ways in which the story corroborated his theories: indeed he treats it as an allegory of psychoanalysis, with patient as hero, analyst as heroine, and analytic setting as archaeological building-site. The clinical object of Freud's study may be summarized as four-fold; the fourth point brings together psychoanalytic and aesthetic ambiguity.

First, Freud plays on the obvious analogy between archaeology and psychoanalytical investigation, a favoured image to which he returns again and again. In *Gradiva*, the hero, Norbert Hanold, is an archaeologist who is investigating the buried remains of a city, Pompeii, and also, unknowingly, his "buried" childhood'.

Second, the story illustrates for Freud what he regards as one of the cornerstones of his theory, the return of the repressed: 'There is, in fact, no better analogy for repression, by which something in the mind is at once made inaccessible and preserved, than burial of the sort to which Pompeii fell a victim and from which it could emerge once more through the work of the spade' (p. 40). In the story the hero is wholly absorbed in his studies and has turned away from life and its pleasures. As Freud puts it, the emotions he is unable to give to women of flesh and blood he gives to women of marble and bronze. His fantasies come to centre upon a Roman relief and grow into a full-scale delusion. The sculpture is of a girl stepping out in an idiosyncratic way, whom he therefore names Gradiva, 'the walking one'. After searching for her in vain in his native city, Vienna, he has an anxiety-dream in which he sees her in Pompeii, where he had assigned her in his fantasy, as she lies down and is buried by a fall of rubble. Like the hero of Thomas Mann's *Death in Venice*, Hanold is now driven by 'an inner restlessness and dissatisfaction' to seek an uncertain destination until he finally 'finds himself' in Pompeii (p. 13). There he is disgusted by the presence of couples all about him and soon his thoughts and feelings drift from the moderate carnality of mating couples to the gross animality of copulating houseflies. When he sees his Gradiva in flesh and blood he knows at last what drove him to Pompeii. Subsequently it becomes clear that Hanold's fantasy is not a hallucination, but derives from the repressed memories of his childhood, 'a kind of forgetting which is distinguished by the difficulty with which the memory is awakened even by a powerful external summons, as though some internal resistance were struggling against its revival' (p. 34). What Freud is interested in is not the mere fact of the return of the repressed, but in 'the highly remarkable manner of that return' (p. 35). The instrument used to repress the unconscious, the name Gradiva, becomes the very means by which the repression is subverted. The unconscious fulfils the wish by means of a trick: 'Gradiva' turns out to be the translation into Latin of the repressed surname of Hanold's childhood love, Zoe Bertgang, meaning 'one who steps along brightly'.

Third, Freud wishes to show (and this is what first draws him to this story) that dreams have a meaning and can be interpreted. Though they cannot foretell the future, as antiquity would have it, they do have intentional significance; when the dream-text is finally revealed it represents the wishes of the dreamer as fulfilled. The creative writer, Freud says with one of his favourite gestures, knows better than the scientist. Dreams are not mere somatic stimuli, but have sense and purpose: they are 'the physiological delusions of normal people', giving access to the unconscious (pp. 62–3). But can literary dreams be analysed, when there is no dreamer to supply the associations for each piece of the manifest dream? Freud says this can be done by dint of 'borrowing' from his *Interpretation of Dreams*.

One of the principles he laid down is that some element in the dream is a piece of reality. Taking Hanold's first dream, in which Hanold is in Pompeii at the same time as Gradiva, Freud transcribes this circumstance as signifying 'the girl he was looking for was living in a town and contemporaneously with him' (p. 58). This is true inasmuch as it applies to Zoe Bertgang, the real elements being 'in a town contemporaneously with him'. But it is a displacement by way of a double reversal, because in the dream Hanold is living at the same time and in the same place as the historical Gradiva, whereas in 'reality' (the story's empirical world), she is living in *his* time and place, the Vienna of his day. It is this displacement which enabled the repressed wish to get through. According to Freud's dream theory there is a current wish which attaches itself to a wish to do with the past. In this case, the admissible wish of the archaeologist, 'to have been present as an eye-witness at the catastrophe in the year 79 AD', attached itself to the inadmissible wish of the would-be lover, 'to be there when the girl he loved lay down to sleep' (p. 93).

Fourth, Freud notes the overlap of psychoanalytic and artistic ambiguity in the course of the story's unfolding. The author of the story leaves the reader in suspense as regards the level of its reality, whether the Gradiva Hanold finds in Pompeii is a revenant or a hallucination. Freud points out that the reader's knowledge of the situation is in advance of the hero's and that this is part of the author's conscious strategy: 'Anyone who reads *Gradiva* must be struck by the frequency with which the author puts ambiguous remarks into the mouths of his two principal characters' (p. 84). The Gradiva in the streets of Pompeii is Hanold's old childhood friend Zoe and she understands what is going on. Both Zoe and Hanold share the symbolism which structures the story, the analogies between childhood and Pompeii, repression and burial. Zoe can therefore maintain her Gradiva role and yet at the same time try slowly to free Hanold from his delusion. Like a good analyst she works towards her goal indirectly, cultivating the ambiguities of the situation. What happens is that Gradiva Zoe sees two meanings where Hanold sees only one. Freud gives a number of examples, one when she says to her 'patient': 'I feel as though we had shared a meal like this once before, two thousand years ago; can't you remember?' (p. 85). Freud calls this handling of a double language 'a triumph of ingenuity and wit', but carried away by the psychoanalytic parallel of heroine-cum-analyst he seems to wish to assign the credit to the character rather than the author. This is because in the first instance he wishes to press home the analogy to psychoanalytic procedures: 'This striking preference for ambiguous speeches . . . is nothing other than a counterpart to the twofold determination of symptoms, in so far as speeches are themselves symptoms and, like them, arise from the compromises between the conscious and the unconscious' (ibid.). Freud sees a relationship between the symptomatic character of speech (all words as compromise-formations even when not obvious Freudian slips) and the writer's skill in the strategic use of language. The author achieves his effects by means of ambiguity: he speaks to the reader through Zoe, thus sharing his superior knowledge. Two meanings go to the reader, where only one goes to the hero. In his analysis of the story Freud shows that the strategies of desire are partly performed by the text. Here the author is not the one who is being analysed (although Freud did write to Jensen, and despite getting no lead, indulged in some lively speculation). However, he discusses the workings of the text only from the analyst's point of view, whether as himself, the author, or Zoe in her role as analyst; he does not here pursue any analogy between 'patient' and reader.

In the essay 'Psychopathic characters on the stage' (orig. publ. 1905/6) the spotlight is more on the audience. One question which occupies Freud in this highly condensed essay is how the audience's understanding of the repressed material will affect their response. If too much gets through, resistance will come into force and the spectator will not allow himself to be drawn in. The dramatist will fail to purge the spectator of his emotions and thus, according to Freud, not open up a possible source of pleasure. It is once again a question of strategy. In 'Creative writers and day-dreaming', the reader was to be 'lured' away from the writer's personal unconscious by the work's formal properties. In the present essay the spectator is to be drawn into the character's psychopathology by means of having his attention 'diverted'. The focus has thereby shifted from the author's need to that of the reader.

Freud's argument takes a somewhat roundabout route. The spectator wishes to identify with the hero, to have an illusion of greatness, but he does not want to undergo any real suffering. 'Accordingly', says Freud, 'his enjoyment is based on an illusion.' There speaks Freud the positivist, the same Freud who assumes that the child at play is like the creative writer in separating his world 'sharply' from reality (IX, p. 144; on this point see also Trilling 1964b, p. 44). This seems only to stress the negative aspect of illusion, not the positive one developed by Freud's later followers (see Part II). Freud does come round to the pertinent question as to how this illusion, that is 'only a game' (VII, p. 306), is to be maintained, but he never answers it straightforwardly. He approaches the problem of audience response by making a distinction between the theatre of the Ancients and the Moderns.

Greek tragedy essentially involves conflict with an authority, be it a struggle against divinity (religious drama), against the state (social drama), or against another individual (psychological drama); in all these examples two conscious impulses are in opposition. But, Freud argues, when instead of psychological drama we have psychopathological drama, 'the source of the suffering in which we take part and from which we are meant to derive pleasure is no longer a conflict between two almost equally conscious impulses but between a conscious impulse and a repressed one' (VII, p. 308). The neurotic spectator will react to the lifting of repression with a mixture of enjoyment (on account of the energy saved in not having to hold down the repression) and resistance (on account of any anxiety that may be caused). The dramatist, says Freud, must proceed with care to attune the *non*-neurotic spectator, whose gain is not so obvious; he must draw him in 'with his attention averted', lower his resistance, so that he does not know exactly where his emotions are leading him: 'After all, the conflict in *Hamlet* is so effectively concealed that it was left to me to unearth it' (pp. 309–10).

At the beginning of the essay Freud argues that in drama in general the spectator can identify with the hero without suffering: he can have the glory without paying the price. He knows his enjoyment is based on illusion and hence he does not mind plunging in. With 'psychopathological drama' there is the problem of coming up against resistance. Rebellion against an inner authority is a painful process. Even so, there might be a yield of 'masochistic satisfaction' in identifying with the hero's defeat (p. 306; Freud is here touching on his later economy of the drives as it appears in *Beyond the Pleasure Principle*). Hence a different strategy is required to draw in the spectator who does not consciously wish to be the person on the stage, one which takes account of an unconscious satisfaction. The first case, illusion, and the second case, 'diversion of attention', together are a joint strategy, applicable to all drama. The opening of Freud's essay is in keeping with the wish-fulfilment theory of 'Creative writers and day-dreaming', in that it stresses the play aspect, now in the light of the spectator's willingness to enter the illusion created by the playwright and the actor, who 'enable' him to play. At the end of the essay, however, the 'dramatist's skill' is presented as creating a surrogate neurosis. There is aesthetic pleasure in both, in providing the unconscious with a release, but in the former, play partakes of a collusion that is publicly validated, while in the latter the collusion is private. A new kind of space is thus created, a neurotic space. In his essay 'Theatricum analyticum', Philippe Lacoue-Labarthe points out that this has wide implications for a theory of the theatre, in that it marks a break with Aristotle's poetics of the drama. What takes place can no longer be taken as a representation of reality, the mere imitation of an action, but is to be seen as the production of reality 'outside representation' (Lacoue-Labarthe 1977, p. 25). Theatre, in Jean-François Lyotard's words, is 'de-realized space' (see 'Beyond representation', preface to the French translation of Anton Ehrenzweig's *The Hidden Order of Art* (Paris: 1974), cited by Lacoue-Labarthe; Ehrenzweig's theory of the creative unconscious is discussed in Part II).

'Psychopathic characters' has something of the richness of Freud's essay 'The uncanny', where he also stresses the power of the writer to control the return of the repressed and demonstrates, albeit unconsciously, how it is done: in foregrounding the uncanny effects in E. T. A. Hoffmann's *Der Sandmann*, via an argument for the Oedipus complex, he succeeds in 'diverting attention' from the uncanny effects of the repetition-compulsion as figured in the essay as a whole (see p. 128ff.). In these writings Freud discusses theory and practice together: he is interested in the work's devices and the pleasurable effect thereby achieved. Unfortunately id-psychology dropped this two-fold concern and took for granted that the ultimate task of the psychoanalytic critic was the recovery of a latent and true meaning, and that this meaning would inevitably be directly connected with the way the author was caught up in his or her private fantasy. Since, however, the scrupulous critics were interested in the way this fantasy was *figured* in the text, their readings, however predictable in terms of themes, already, before Trilling, linked psychoanalytic processes with rhetoric.

It must be said, however, that Freud's notion of collusion between writer and reader assumes that there is always a challenge from a neurotic infantile wish, never a wish that could be corrective of the repressive system, against that system. The ambiguities always work one way only, allowing spurious satisfaction, returning the repressed whence it came. This is indeed, as will be seen, the burden of D. H. Lawrence's objection, and, from an anything but radical position, that of the ego-psychologists and archetypal critics. Freud's theory, though it recognizes the subversive force of the unconscious, here neglects the possibility that on some occasions it may overcome the censor and produce an aggressive correction. As will be seen in Part III, his theory of the joke does something to make up for this omission.

2
Classical Freudian Criticism: Id-Psychology

Instinct-psychology (or id-psychology, as it came to be called) centres on the role of the sexual instincts as the determining force of an individual's life. In Freud's early topography of the mind, the dualistic one, the conscious and preconscious are engaged in conflict with the unconscious – or, to put the contrast in terms of instinct – the ego-instincts, concerned with self-preservation and the need to relate to others, are in conflict with the sexual instincts as the dynamic core of the energies in the unconscious (the term 'id' had not yet been adopted by Freud). The unconscious is thought of as close to the bodily sources of the pressure of need, from which libido derives, with its power to invade and transform experience, particularly in dream and fantasy. Its ability to mask itself thus enables it to appear in disguised form in activities wherein the sexual origin is apparently unrecognizable and only to be decoded with difficulty, even though the feeling they give rise to loses none of its intensity by such disguise.

The aesthetics of id-psychology are grounded in the notion that the work of art is the secret embodiment of its creator's unconscious desire. Classical applied psychoanalytic criticism related the work back to the author's psyche, which it explored via the analysis of the earliest childhood experiences gleaned from what is known of his or her life, the analysis of his or her characters and 'typical symbols' (vulgar Freudianism). Despite its obvious shortcomings, in that it neglects the art-aspect of the work, such an approach can be very illuminating for the way it works with figures of repetition. Its less scrupulous exponents, those who translate without due regard for context (a cigar, as Freud said, is sometimes just a cigar), have given it a bad name, but often it is dismissed out of hand from hearsay on account of the polemics of other critics. What follows below are three examples of classical applied psychoanalytic criticism where the practitioners each pay close attention to context. If one is disposed to give them credit for this close examination of the text one must acknowledge the peculiarities of the mode in which it comes. All treat the work as symptomatic in that its effect is dependent on an uncontrolled return of the repressed, thus privileging the unconscious of the author over his conscious mastery.

2.1   Psychoanalysis of the author: Bonaparte on Poe

The study of an artist's life to explain his works, or the study of his works to explain his mind, was already an established mode in the latter half of the nineteenth century, when pre-Freudian psychology made various attempts to relate genius to madness. Cesare Lombroso, an Italian professor of legal medicine, argued that creative genius was a by-product of psychosis, in that the advance of this condition can turn someone with an average mind into a genius (Lombroso 1891). This provoked a controversy as to who was sick, the creative genius (whose state of health does not in any case reflect on his work) or the society which chose to assign this status to decadents such as Wagner, Nietzsche and Baudelaire. The artistic products of the accused were investigated and brought in as proof of their decadence and as evidence of their lack of genius: 'Degenerates are not always criminals, prostitutes, anarchists, and pronounced lunatics; they are often authors and artists' (Nordau 1895, p. vii). What was at stake was thus not just the status of the artist, but what the criteria for morality were to be: 'Books and works of art exercise a powerful suggestion on the masses' (ibid.).

This is the background to what came to be called 'pathography': a study of the artist not for the sake of the work or even the man, but for the purpose of classifying a particular pathology. Studies of this type appeared in a periodical called *Imago* (published in Vienna, Leipzig and Zürich), from 1912 to 1937 the chief organ for the publication of writings dealing with the relation of psychoanalysis and the arts and all aspects of culture (see Fischer 1980 for examples). Freud was ambivalent in his attitude to pathographical studies, even though he designated his Leonardo essay as such (Freud 1953, XI, p. 130). He claimed he was working within the definition of the term, but then criticized others of his circle who were unable to match his commitment to the cause. Rather than being bent on validating a particular pathology he wished to throw light on the psychoanalytic process as such. This shift of concern seems to be reflected in the now more commonly used term 'psychobiography'.

Marie Bonaparte's full-length study of Edgar Allan Poe (Bonaparte 1949; orig. publ. 1933) is the classic example of psychobiography, although she called it *étude psychanalytique*. Freud's preface to it shows not only his approval but also his awareness of the delicate ground 'investigations of this kind' were treading on:

> In this volume my friend and pupil, Marie Bonaparte, has directed the light of psycho-analysis upon the life and work of a great writer of a pathological type. Thanks to her interpretative efforts, we can now understand how much of the characteristics of his work were determined by their author's special nature; but we also learn that this was itself the precipitate of powerful emotional ties and painful experiences in his early youth. Investigations of this kind are not intended to explain an author's genius, but they show what motive forces aroused it and what material was offered to him by destiny. There is a particular fascination in studying the laws of the human mind as exemplified in outstanding individuals (XXII, p. 254).

Bonaparte begins her study with Poe's life-story, which she gives in considerable detail, drawing her material from the best available scholarly sources of the time. A brief synopsis can do no more than outline the parallels she wants to make between the man and his work. Poe was born in 1809. His father disappeared when he was 18 months old; his pretty and childlike mother died of consumption about a year later. He was brought up by foster-parents, and he was neither legally adopted nor later left any money by his foster-father. He married his cousin Virginia when he was twenty-six and she was thirteen and already sickening; she died of consumption some ten years after their marriage. Poe died at the age of forty, after a life of poverty, debts, drink, drugs and depression, having completed a considerable mass of essays, poems and stories. Bonaparte goes to work on the stories, subjecting them to a minute scrutiny, and relating the events and figures (persons) in Poe's life to the events and 'figures' (in its rhetorical sense) of the text. Her basic contention is that Poe was a necrophiliac, someone for whom corpses have an erotic attraction (necrophilia being a pathological extension of the part played by normal mourning, when the mourner for a time refuses to accept the event). Bonaparte argues that Poe, through a fixation on his mother, was condemned to an eternal fidelity. He remains physically faithful to her, his first love, by marrying an ailing cousin and thus sparing himself the need to consummate the marriage. So now at last comes the point: as a psychoanalytic critic what does she do with this material? She declares the principle of her enterprise at the outset:

> Works of art or literature profoundly reveal their creator's psychology and, as Freud has shown, their construction resembles that of our dreams. The same mechanisms which, in dreams and nightmares, govern the manner in which our strongest, though most carefully concealed desires are elaborated, desires which often are the most repugnant to consciousness, also govern the elaborations of a work of art (Bonaparte 1949, p. 209).

Marie Bonaparte takes the characters in Poe's stories as imagos, that is as internalized images which are the result of past experience. She takes them as father-, mother- and sister-figures which have made their way from Poe's unconscious into his tales. The women particularly, consumptive and ethereal figures, she sees as prototypes, and hence she labels the second section of her book 'Tales of the mother'. In her analyses of these tales she wishes to show how the repressed feeling is transferred, via a displacement (dream-theory) onto fictional figures and objects. Thus a building too can do duty, the famous house of Usher, for instance, or the sea, the earth's depths and the stars. This is what is implied by Freud's notion of symbolism. The whole world can be absorbed narcissistically, the sexual drives can attach themselves to anything the senses perceive. In each tale, according to Bonaparte, Poe is reliving Elizabeth Poe's last agony and death. The third section of her book is entitled 'Tales of the father', in which male figures become the return of the repressed, the father who comes back to avenge Poe's imaginary parricide and incest.

For psychoanalysis Poe's work is thus an example *par excellence* of the compulsion to repeat – in Bonaparte's reading the repetition of a content in accordance with her interpretation of Freud's early instinct theory; in Lacan's reading (see Part III) the repetition of a structure in accordance with his interpretation of Freud's later instinct theory. Since the central tenet of Freud's theory of dream-formation was that dreams are wish-fulfilments, the compulsion to repeat raised a problem for him when it came to anxiety dreams, such as he found with those suffering from war neuroses, where the dreamer returned over and over again to the memory of his traumatic experience. Freud came to think of anxiety dreams in general as attempts to fulfil wishes accompanied by the performance again of the ego's initial repression of the dangerously challenging upsurge from the id, as if to renew and strengthen the resistance to that wish (XXII, pp. 27–30). Poe's fiction, according to Bonaparte, embodies the wish to become reunited with his dead mother; since this must needs be a censored wish we should not be surprised that Poe's tales hardly read like wish-fulfilments.

In carrying out her task Bonaparte avails herself of Freud's theory of dream-interpretation. She takes Poe's tales as the manifest part of the dream and believes that, by finding associations from persons and incidents in Poe's life, she is recovering the latent part. The problem is not so much in what she does (which is very interesting), but in what she claims: that this is where the true meaning is to be found. '[It] is as though Poe himself were to declare *"Because* I am still fixated on my mother, I cannot love another woman"' (Bonaparte 1949, p. 655). Freud warned against such a view:

> Now that analysts at least have become reconciled to replacing the manifest dream by the meaning revealed by its interpretation, many of them have become guilty of falling into another confusion which they cling to with equal obstinacy. They seek to find the essence of dreams in their latent content and in so doing they overlook the distinction between the latent dream-thoughts and the dream-work. At bottom, dreams are nothing other than a particular *form* of thinking (V, p. 506n.; see also p. 580).

In her operations on the text Bonaparte goes beyond her reductive statements. The fourth section of her book is devoted to an explanation of the mechanisms of the dream-work, of which she has made use throughout. The nearest she gets to literary criticism is in her analyses of the configurations within the text. A brief example can be extracted from her reading of *The Black Cat*. She places this tale in the second section of her book, 'Tales of the mother', under the sub-title of 'Tales of the murdered mother'. The psychoanalytic theme here is the part the woman plays in the arousing of castration-anxiety. There are two cats in the story. The first one is an all-black cat, which the narrator loved greatly. One night he returns home drunk, and fancying that the cat is avoiding him, he seizes it roughly, only to get bitten. In a fit of rage he gouges out one of its eyes, whereupon the mutilated creature fills him with such horror that he finally hangs it. Not as finally as he thinks, for there appears a second cat, which according to Poe has 'a large, although indefinite splotch of white, covering nearly the whole region of the breast'. Since it already has a missing eye it too inspires horror in the narrator, becoming a victim of his hatred, and the cause of his downfall.

In the course of her interpretation Bonaparte makes use of the activities of the dream-work, particularly the mechanisms of condensation and displacement. She sees the ambivalent emotions which Poe (according to her biographical findings) feels for his mother displaced onto the cats. The first cat represents the mother seen as all bad (figured as all-black in contrast to the second cat), avoiding him and thus arousing memories of unfulfilled needs. The second cat, on the other hand, momentarily arouses memories of fulfilled needs, for its white splotch, she argues, represents milk both by its colour and its position. Moreover, she points out, the second cat is found in a tavern, where one drinks, and it is sitting on top of a barrel of gin. Here one might see an example of condensation since two images to do with drinking are condensed into one scene. What provokes the fate of both cats, however, is the missing eye, because it is through this mutilation that each cat inspires such horror: this is another displacement in that fear of castration is displaced onto the disappearance of the eye (Bonaparte 1949, pp. 472–3).

In her analysis Bonaparte seeks to understand the psychology of the author by unravelling the meaning which a vast number of objects in Poe's own life have acquired in a chain of addition and substitution. To this extent her reading corresponds to the sign-system of the dream. She shows how a manifest meaning is subverted by a latent meaning or meanings via an associative link. The link is in the form of a trope, metaphorical (white is *like* milk) or metonymic (milk is *found with* breast). The meaning was changed as a result of the irruption of a wish; there is thus a link here between the role of desire in dreams and the figuration and structuring of the text.

There are two levels of objection to this. The first is one of complete sceptical negation of such decodings. This, of course, implies a wholesale rejection of the findings of psychoanalysis, and thus a rejection of such configurations outside this text, both in other texts and in life, which invite this kind of reading, and a rejection of the possibility that, if Poe's tales were an anonymous *oeuvre*, such readings could be adduced. The second level of objection concedes that a neurosis appears in the text, but maintains that dramatically it belongs to the narrator. This is the argument of the orthodox critic:

Poe's narrators should not be construed as his mouthpieces; instead they should be regarded as expressing, in 'charged' language indicative of their internal disturbances, their own peculiarly nightmarish visions. Poe, I contend, is conscious of the abnormalities of his narrators and does not condone their intellectual ruses through which they strive, only too earnestly, to justify themselves (Gargano 1967, p. 171).

This is merely the converse of Bonaparte's position. The one is trying to assign the figures of desire exclusively to the unconscious of the author, the other is trying to assign them to a neurotic narrator under the detached control of an authorial consciousness. One is making the dream encapsulate art, the other is making art encapsulate the dream. Bonaparte disregards the public aspect of Poe's utterance and classifies it as belonging to 'that conscious, logical and aesthetic *façade* which we call creative writing' (Bonaparte 1949, p. 663, my italics), behind which the true unconscious is at work. The orthodox critic disregards the private aspect of Poe's utterance in believing the unconscious can be safely confined within the boundaries of a character.

Can one separate Bonaparte's reductive principle from the results of her application of it, the effects she displays in the text? Although her argument from biography is gratuitous because one cannot estimate how true or false it is, this need not mean that her criticism is worthless, given that there is an undeniable typicality in the symbolism she reveals. Her aim was the vindication of psychoanalysis, yet her reading of Poe does not depend on the truth of the psychobiographical method. She took for her frame of reference the author's life, but it is the stories which get her going. She calls them 'transference stories', since, in accordance with her reading of Freud and Poe, they are subject to 'repetition compulsion which dominates our instinctual life, and impels us always to seek the same emotions in the same forms, whatever the object' (pp. 221–2). Like many others she has herself succumbed to the 'Poe-etic effect' (see Felman 1980, pp. 119–25, for an analysis of critical reaction to Poe in terms of transference phenomena) but the rigour of her approach, its very reductiveness, makes her analysis of the tales into a compelling fantasy, rather like a strange poem in its own right, as much her own as Edgar Allan Poe's. She ignores what is commonly regarded as literary in refusing to remain at the level of public symbolization, yet her reading partakes of literary criticism because she is a gifted reader with an eye for picture-puzzles, a gift she shares with Poe. Paradoxically, she has shown him to be a master of ambivalence, and, above all, a provoker of fantasy, but she gives all the credit to his unconscious, whereas her unconscious too is actively involved. Though she believed herself to be the analyst of the text, she was as much an analysand as her patient. It is not only the author who is in transference to his medium, who has unconsciously invested it with his fantasies; her reading is equally subjective. This throws new light on the supposed reductiveness of psychoanalytic interpretation: the very reductiveness, instead of achieving the objectivity of which it was in search, reveals, in the intensity of its concentration, a subjective response given public articulation. The analysis she pursues of Poe contributes to an interpretation of the stories.

2.2   Psychoanalysis of the character: Freud and Jones on *Hamlet*

The psychoanalysis of literary characters has not fallen into as deep a disrepute as the psychoanalysis of the author. It is still a flourishing industry, even if under the sophisticated guise of post-Freudian developments in psychoanalytic theory. That is to say, although the id-psychological model, with its emphasis on the sexual instincts trying to find representation in images and symbols, has been abandoned, other models, based on Freud's second topography and focusing on pre-oedipal conflict, have taken its place. This means that the terms of the equation have changed but the assumptions and attendant problems have not. I quote as an example from a recent psychoanalytic interpretation, entitled 'Melville's lost self: *Bartleby*': 'I believe that Bartleby's arrival at the office and his subsequent breakdown into negativity is a mimetic representation of a need to find a nurturant space where he can regress toward the healing of a "basic fault" in the self' (Bollas 1976, p. 226). Although this clinical formulation is like a red rag to a bull to literary critics I am not citing it for that purpose; the essay is a clinical study of the classical kind which openly declares itself and which has considerable explanatory force in terms of unconscious character-motivation. It is after the pattern of Freud's method in his analysis of Hoffmann's story *Der Sandmann* (XVII, pp. 227–33), in the course of which Freud argues that the central character is suffering from a castration complex. The point I wish to make is that the limitations of psychoanalytic character-analysis are analogous to the limitations of literary character-analysis. This problem is nicely illustrated by an assertion, couched in contrary terms, by the co-author of another recent book on applied psychoanalytic criticism:

Fictional characters are representations of life and, as such, can only be understood if we assume they are real. And this assumption allows us to find unconscious motivation[s] by the same procedure that the traditional critic uses to assign conscious ones (Kaplan and Kloss 1973, p. 4).

Here too, it is a question of 'mimetic representation'. Neither Bonaparte nor Lawrence (see the next section of this chapter) works on the assumption of a one-to-one equation between fictional characters and flesh-and-blood persons: Bonaparte worked with condensed and displaced figures, and Lawrence with literary stereotypes. There are now new literary developments in psychoanalytic character-analysis, where the oedipal model is shown to work as a triangular structuring force, breaking up dyadic relationships, in the context of a history wider than the subject's personal one. But these follow on from the theories of structuralism and post-structuralism. What we are now looking at in this section is no more literary than psychobiography, though to literary critics it may seem more palatable than Bonaparte's work.

In his *Interpretation of Dreams* (IV–V, pp. 336–68) Freud provides another clinical study of a literary character, later made famous by his disciple, Ernest Jones, who devoted a book to the same subject (Jones 1949). Freud, following on from an analysis of Sophocles' *Oedipus Rex*, from which he derived his founding complex, turns his attention to Shakespeare's *Hamlet*. As often, the indignation of readers who react to his apparent reductiveness ignores the subtlety of his reading. Freud begins by commenting on the different socio-historical worlds inhabited by King Oedipus and Hamlet: whereas in the first play the fantasy of the child is treated as a fulfilled wish, in the second it is repressed and is known only through its effects. For Freud these effects take the form of the difficulties that Hamlet has in carrying out the act of retribution on Claudius, the usurper. This, Freud argues, cannot merely be because as an intellectual and/or neurotic he is incapable of action, since on two other occasions in the play he is able to act quite ruthlessly. It is rather the case that Claudius is acting out Hamlet's own repressed wishes and is thus a living reproach to him: 'Hamlet is able to do anything – except take vengeance on the man who did away with his father and took that father's place with his mother, the man who shows him the repressed wishes of his childhood realized' (p. 367). Freud speculates (as Jones subsequently does) that the death of Shakespeare's own father, which preceded the writing of *Hamlet*, triggered the dynamics of the play. Freud adds: 'But just as all neurotic symptoms, and, for that matter, dreams, are capable of being 'over-interpreted' and indeed need to be, if they are to be fully understood, so all genuinely creative writings are the product of more than a

single motive and more than a single impulse in the poet's mind, and are
open to more than a single interpretation' (p. 368).

This elegant fragment of an analysis was elaborated by Jones, who
stresses the clinical aspect and makes it more of a case-study. For Jones,
Hamlet is in the grip of a psycho-neurosis, driven by an unconscious
conflict, reactivated by a new rival, Claudius, coming onto the old scene
(the son's jealousy of the father): 'It is his moral duty, to which his father
exhorts him, to put an end to the incestuous activities of his mother (by
killing Claudius), but his unconscious does not want to put an end to
them' (Jones 1949, pp. 90–1). It is also Jones who first emphasizes the
mother's contribution to the conflict: Gertrude is a sensual woman and
immoderately fond of her son. Hamlet chooses a woman, Ophelia, who in
her piety and obedience is least like the Queen, enabling Hamlet to act
out a kind of inner rebellion, which he later denies by projecting an excessive sensuality and wantonness on Ophelia.

It is true that in a sense Jones puts a literary character on the analytic
couch, which might seem a 'fundamental error' since 'unlike a real analysand, he cannot lie down on the couch and free-associate about his
dreams or recapitulate the traumas of his infancy' (Ellmann 1994, p. 3).
But let us take each part of the equation, literary text/analytic text, in turn.
From the viewpoint of the literary text, there is no harm in doing a fictive
analysis on a fictive character. After all, if in a play we hear that someone
has a mother, we do not stop with some dictionary definition of 'mother'
if we want to learn about the depths and subtleties of the mother–child
relation. From the viewpoint of the analytic text, the assumption is that
somehow the analysand is in a position to verify the analyst's interpretation
in an unambiguous way, instead of there being a dialectical interchange,
where the utterance of both parties is material for further interpretation.
Both literary and analytic texts (those of authors and critics, of analysts
and analysands) have to prove themselves repeatedly and must expect to
be treated with suspicion.

2.3 Psychoanalysis of culture:
Lawrence on American literature

D. H. Lawrence does not fit neatly into id-psychological criticism, for he
opposes his notion of the unconscious to a distorted view of the Freudian
unconscious. His misreading of Freudian concepts and the 'post-mortem
effects' he displays in the texts (the unconscious coming through) must
therefore be taken together, if his relevance to classical psychoanalytic

criticism is to be made clear. His writing falls into the category of applied psychoanalysis in so far as its object is to recover the true latent meaning of the work; but unlike the classical psychoanalytic critic he is not interested in the individual psychology or pathology of the authors he investigates. Lawrence's own commitment shows through, to defend the body considered to be the source of all energy and integrity from the oppression of prurient and sadistic puritanism, culturally imposed. Hence he is a psychoanalytic critic of a special kind, for he is launching a critique of psychoanalysis while adopting its essential concern with the placing of the body in culture.

Studies in Classic American Literature (Lawrence 1977) first appeared in 1923. The earlier versions of these essays, all but two of which had appeared in periodicals from 1919 onwards, were collected and reprinted in 1962 under the title *The Symbolic Meaning* (Lawrence 1962); they are more stable than the *Studies* in argument, though less powerful in effect. Lawrence has undertaken a double mission: he wants to investigate the American canon of the nineteenth century in order to reveal the return of the repressed in the puritan consciousness as a whole, 'the dangerous *negative* religious passion of repression, this passion which so easily becomes a lust, a deep lust for vindictive power over the life-issue' (1962, p. 25). At the same time he wishes to 'save' the text from the author: 'Never trust the artist. Trust the tale' (1977, p. 8). In Lawrence's reckoning the author has no control over the return of the repressed. Here he rejoins Bonaparte in asserting that the true meaning of the text resides in its latent content, but he departs from her again because for him 'two blankly opposing morals' are involved: the latent true one of the tale, and the manifest false one of the artist.

What is most interesting about Lawrence's criticism from the psychoanalytic point of view is not just the famous polemic, but that he shows, as Freud does in *Gradiva*, that the very instrument of repression, here the puritan conscience, can become the vehicle by which the repressed desire returns. Lawrence's campaign involves an attack on three related duplicities: first, that of the Pilgrim Fathers, who came (ostensibly) in search of liberty, 'they seemed to seek, not liberty, but a gloomy and tyrannical sense of power. They wanted to have power over all immediate life' (1962, p. 25); second, that of the artist, who produced myths to celebrate the occasion, 'the old American artists were hopeless liars. But they were artists in spite of themselves' (1977, p. 8); and third, that of the reader who (unlike Lawrence) accepted these myths ingenuously, 'we like to think of the old-fashioned American classics as children's books' (1977, p. 7).

In order to understand the thrust of Lawrence's endeavour one has to take account of his assessment of Freudian psychology. Reference will here be made to two extended essays making up one book (Lawrence 1961a and b; orig. publ. 1923), *Fantasia of the Unconscious* and *Psychoanalysis of the Unconscious*. Like so many others of his time, Lawrence regarded Freud as a pan-sexualist, as one 'who makes sex accountable for everything' (1961a, p. 13). He could not or would not understand Freud's concept of polymorphous sexuality, being himself totally committed to the pure heterosexual genital act. For him 'the act of coition is the essential clue to sex' (p. 12). He thanks Freud only for very small mercies: 'The orthodox religious world says faugh! to sex. Whereupon we thank Freud for giving them tit for tat' (*sic*, p. 13). He will have nothing to do with the Freudian unconscious, describing it as 'the cellar in which the mind keeps its own bastard spawn' (1961b, p. 204). In particular he rejects what he calls the 'incest-craving' of the psyche, which he argues is a conspiracy of culture, 'the mind, that is, transfers the idea of incest into the affective-passional psyche, and keeps it there as a repressed motive' (p. 203). In this respect Lawrence is here oddly in accord with Deleuze and Guattari (see Part IV, pp. 145–54), however different the rest of his premises. Lawrence equates the unconscious with a life force, albeit with a special qualification: it is not to be thought of as general but as unique in each individual organism. He believes in a self from the moment of conception; the fulfilling of the unique self is the goal of its life. He will have no truck with any kind of determinism: 'We refuse any *Cause*, whether it be Sex or Libido or Élan Vital' (1961a, p. 13).

Given this view of the unconscious, as 'by its very nature unanalysable, undefinable, inconceivable' (1961b, p. 211), it is hardly surprising that Lawrence sees the Freudian enterprise as a second Fall; the will to know the unknowable becomes a mission of doom. What is the point, he argues, of revealing the unconscious only to prohibit what you find there? He sees in the American conquest of the native an allegorical parallel. The white settlers came to America to find freedom, only to impose their own rigorous laws on the other consciousness, to master it, without making any attempt to absorb the 'otherness' of the new place and its native inhabitants. Their will to know, like the will to know sex, resulted in the wilful repression of all that is joyous and intuitive, what Lawrence calls the mind's attempt to conquer the 'blood' (1977, pp. 91–2). For Lawrence the political repression imposed on the native is like the personal repression imposed on the blood. Though this notion of 'the blood', within its pantheist context, needs to be sharply distinguished from the Freudian notion of the instinctual drives, the essential analogy between Lawrence and Freud holds, in so far as there is a natural force trying to get through and a harsh civilizing force trying to stop it. Hence Lawrence can be seen as an id-psychological critic *avant la lettre*, holding a similar brief to that held by Freud in *Civilization and its Discontents* (1930).

In his *Studies* Lawrence believes he is revealing the latent myths of his writers; he approves of some myths and disapproves of others. The myths of which he approves are those which acknowledge and play out the conflict between the old and the new consciousness, without subjecting the process to an obsessive scrutiny: 'What true myth concerns itself with is not the disintegration product. True myth concerns itself centrally with the onward adventure of the integral soul' (Lawrence 1977, p. 69). Into the category of 'true myth' go Cooper, Melville and Whitman, who all get qualified approval. Into the category of 'false myth' go Hawthorne and Poe, who get qualified disapproval. Since both types of myth are taken as latent within the work, we have here to distinguish between a true myth (integrity) and a false myth ('disintegration product'). This distinction brings in a moral judgement on Lawrence's part, levelled indiscriminately against the author and his characters. He makes no sharp division between the two, but shares out the moral–psychological failures between them. In one sense he therefore disregards the autonomy of the author as the centre of the work, but he does so only in order to reinstate him as the privileged source of a particular type of language, that of 'art-speech', imaginative writing, in his view the repository of truth.

It is the creators of false myths (the 'disintegration product') whose works are particularly prone to the return of the repressed. Outwardly they subscribe to the victory of mind over matter, but inwardly they cannot leave the matter alone. In Poe's work Lawrence sees the murderous impulse to destroy that which cannot be mentally possessed and mastered. The heroines of *Ligeia* and *The Fall of the House of Usher*, who have been betrayed by their lovers' spiritual obsessions rise up from the grave to get their revenge for having been cheated of life. The sensual rises against the spiritual: 'To try to *know* any living being is to try to suck the life out of that being . . . you know your woman darkly, in the blood. To try to *know* her mentally is to try to kill her' (p. 76). For Lawrence, Poe is the prime example of one who probes the objects of his love, including himself, to the point of disintegration, 'reducing his self as a scientist reduces a salt in a crucible' (p. 70).

Hawthorne's works similarly reveal for Lawrence the secret triumph of the sensual over the spiritual and he traces this theme directly through from Poe to Hawthorne. He sees Hester Prynne, heroine of *The Scarlet*

Letter, as 'the KNOWING Ligeia risen diabolic from the grave. . . . This time it is Mr Dimmesdale who dies' (pp. 95–6). That is, in this case Lawrence sees the male as victim of the repressive process, though he does not return from the dead: what returns are the displaced and perverted forms of desire as intimately related to the repressing force. Hester is compelled by the community to wear the letter A (for adulteress) on her bodice, 'stitched with gold thread, glittering upon the bosom. The proudest insignia' (p. 94). She thereby, according to Lawrence, secretly exults in her fall and is able to go on expressing her voluptuousness, flaunting her sin and her child, while her erstwhile lover, the young puritan minister Arthur Dimmesdale, whose sin is not known by the community, 'has a good time all by himself torturing his body, whipping it, piercing it with thorns, macerating himself' (p. 96). In order to attain its ends, the denied impulse avails itself of the very means that repressed it. This is also the thrust of Freud's analysis of *Gradiva*: 'in and behind the repressing force, what is repressed proves itself victor in the end'. Freud cites 'the typical case of repression in the lives of saints and penitents' and illustrates it by reference to an etching which shows Sin emerging in the very spot where the monk looked for refuge, on the cross itself, where the image of the crucified saviour is displaced by the image of a voluptuous naked woman in the same pose (IX, p. 35).

A similar configuration appears in *The Scarlet Letter* when its Christian hero, accompanied by the beautiful Hester, exposes himself as a sinner to the assembled crowd in the market-place, baring his chest in order to reveal to their horrified gaze the letter A branded thereon:

> 'People of New England!' cried he, with a voice that rose over them, high, solemn, and majestic, – yet had always a tremor through it, and sometimes a shriek, struggling up out of the fathomless depth of remorse and woe, – 'ye, that have loved me! – ye, that have deemed me holy! – behold me here, the one sinner of the world! At last! – at last I stand upon the spot where, seven years since, I should have stood; here, with this woman, whose arm, more than the little strength wherewith I have crept hitherward, sustains me, at this dreadful moment, from grovelling down upon my face! Lo, the scarlet letter which Hester wears! Ye have all shuddered at it! Wherever her walk hath been, – wherever, so miserably burdened, she may have hoped to find repose, – it hath cast a lurid gleam of awe and horrible repugnance round about her. But there stood one in the midst of you, at whose brand of sin and infamy ye have not shuddered!' (Hawthorne 1978, p. 180)

He who was regarded as holy is suddenly revealed as the greatest sinner, and the mode in which he reveals himself is also that which betrays his passion, a branded A appearing in conjunction with the beautiful woman beside him.

Lawrence attributes effects of this kind to the 'duplicity' of the author; that is to say, like Bonaparte he thinks the author has no control over the return of the repressed. The effects of its return in 'the tale', however, have enabled Lawrence to catch the author out in the act. But in the act of what? The 'post-mortem effects' of Lawrence's own texts are intimately connected with those he displays in his authors. He is a puritan turned on his head, attacking puritanism for its refusal to countenance the pure sexual act in all its plenitude. In his eyes both Freud and the Puritan Fathers are the knowers: his central attack is on that knowledge which invades and inhibits feeling. The 'post-mortem effects' in Lawrence's texts are those of a puritan son engaged with the knowing, incestuous Puritan Fathers. What returns in his texts is the hatred of the father, the 'duplicity' of the author/father, who '*knew* disagreeable things in his inner soul' and 'was careful to send them out in disguise' (Lawrence 1977, p. 89; my italics).

The value of Lawrence's reading is bound up with the effect the text has had upon him. With the help of his reductive formula Lawrence is able to show the way guilt feelings are figured across a number of texts at a particular moment in history. Where Bonaparte extracts a fantasy that is completely private, he detects a myth which is publicly shared, even though the ground of this myth is the Protestant family.

3
Post-Freudian Criticism:
Ego-Psychology

Ego-psychological approaches to art strongly oppose the notion that the mainspring of art is a neurotic infantile wish. The endeavour is rather to show that the pleasure of artistic activity derives from a controlled play with infantile material, in the course of which this material is transformed into something publicly shareable. The difference from Freud's theory lies in the view that what is pleasurable is not the fulfilment of an infantile wish, as he believed, but the mere fact of bringing the primary process into play at the ego's behest. To understand what this theory involves in terms of a psychoanalytic contribution, the relationship of the three elements of Freud's second topography needs to be clarified.

In his first topography Freud thought of the ego as entirely equivalent to the conscious and the preconscious; the instinctual energies were confined to the unconscious. In the second topography, elaborated in *The Ego and the Id*, he wants to see the ego as developed out of the instinctual energies, 'from bodily sensations' (Freud 1953, XIX, p. 26, n. 1), and therefore he does not draw a logical boundary between the ego and the unconscious. Similarly, the third element in this topography, the superego, also has an unconscious component. The advantage of the second topography is that the deciphering of the unconscious is not now simply a matter of rigid interpretation, but must take into account the interplay between unconscious and conscious. There is no longer just a force trying to get through and another force preventing it. To begin with, the ego is now seen as in part constructed from the instinctual energies: it connives with them as much as it controls them. In addition, these energies, which Freud now calls the 'id', are also operative in the superego, particularly in their destructive form, directing aggression upon the ego. It is therefore clear that the conscious/unconscious boundary cannot be maintained so simplistically, because the ego must be performing some kind of mediating function, which involves both (pp. 54–7).

Id-psychology, which focused on the instinctual drives, led to a type of psychoanalytic criticism which privileged the private fantasy. Ego-psychology, on the other hand, stresses the managing of this fantasy, and this leads to a type of psychoanalytic criticism which emphasizes the maintenance of identity. The ego-psychologists could derive support from Freud's statement in *The Ego and the Id*, that 'psychoanalysis is an instrument to enable the ego to achieve a progressive conquest of the id' (p. 56), and it is in this sense that they interpret Freud's dictum, 'Wo Es war, soll Ich werden' (translated in the *Standard Edition* as 'where id was, there ego shall be' (XXII, p. 80)). But what is thereby ignored is the context in which the ego is spoken of as being in the service of the id. The ego is a 'frontier-creature' (XIX, p. 56), endeavouring to facilitate the traffic and trade as much from the external world to the id as from the id to the external world. A dialectical reading of Freud, such as the French Freudians have made, will interpret the 'Ich' as becoming and developing within the id rather than as an 'ego' dislodging it. This allows for negotiations between inner demands and external prohibitions without forcing the 'Ich' to be wholly at the mercy of either. The ego-psychologist reads 'Ich' as 'ego', regarding it as a given identity, strengthened by socialization. He therefore wants all the traffic to be in one direction, namely from the ego as a publicly adjusted identity, towards the id, as having to accept the limitations so imposed.

3.1   Aesthetic ambiguity: Kris

One of the earliest ego-psychologists was Ernst Kris, a practising psycho-analyst in America and a former member of Freud's circle in Vienna. His influential book, *Psychoanalytic Explorations in Art* (Kris 1964; orig. publ. 1952), marked a first turning-point in psychoanalytic aesthetics, though Kris acknowledges and makes use of William Empson's contributions in *Seven Types of Ambiguity* (1930), and of Lionel Trilling's essays, 'Art and neurosis' and 'Freud and literature' (Trilling 1964a and b; orig. publ. 1945 and 1947). Kris proposes a theory of creativity in which the emphasis is shifted from the subversive operations of the id to the managing capacities of the ego. Though he retains the analogy of art to dream, this no longer rests on the notion of an unconscious wish that wants to find expression, but depends on the way the unconscious wishes are modified by the preconscious operations of the ego. It should be remembered that the preconscious is everything that is freely and safely recoverable by the ego.

To be consistent and sufficiently secure as a basis for criticism, Kris's view had to be grounded in a psychoanalytic theory which gave pre-eminence to the ego. He therefore had to find some theoretical justification for claiming that the workings of the unconscious can safely be brought within the control of consciousness. Lionel Trilling makes the same point when he claims that, although there is an undoubted similarity between the mechanisms of art and those of the dream, 'the work of art *leads us back to the outer reality by taking account of it*' (1964b, p. 45). Kris sets out to give psychoanalytical backing for this taming of the unconscious, and so he must find in its theory something that can perform the task.

In *The Ego and the Id* Freud speaks of a 'displaceable energy, neutral in itself', which can be added to an impulse and change its quality, say from love to hate. 'The only question is where it comes from, what it belongs to, and what it signifies' (XIX, p. 44). He calls it 'desexualized', but by this he merely means it is not specific to the libido or the aggressive instinct. It can be regarded as an intensifying agent in that whatever it is added to becomes more powerful, but in itself it belongs with no particular impulse. Kris (1964) and another ego-psychologist Hartmann (1964; orig. publ. 1955) take up this notion, calling it 'neutralized' energy. It is important for Kris's aesthetic theory that this neutralized energy can be directed by the ego, enabling it to manage the impulses and fantasies that emerge from the id.

Kris is now able to argue that there is no one-way influence of the primary process in the unconscious upon the secondary process, but he does this by virtually positing a one-way influence in the other direction, in having the secondary process acting upon the primary via the 'neutralized energy'. He maintains that in 'aesthetic ambiguity' the ego is in control and produces a 'multiplicity' of meaning (Kris 1964, pp. 245–59). He makes a new equation between art and dream: the ambiguity found in art, particularly poetry, is like the overdetermination Freud found in the dream-work.

In his chapter entitled 'Aesthetic ambiguity' (written in conjunction with Abraham Kaplan), Kris discusses the different types of ambiguity and states his position with regard to Empson's work. He wishes to relate ambiguity not only to poetry, as Empson does, but more generally to a 'theory of the poetic process' (p. 243). On the one hand he wishes to abolish any rigid distinctions between poetry and prose and between the scientific and the poetic; on the other hand he wants to argue that this need not threaten the standards of interpretation implicit in Empson's own practice and explicit in Empson's concern that the reader may construct the 'wrong poem'. In connection with his seventh type of ambiguity, condensation, Empson speaks of those who 'have enough detachment not to mind what their sources of satisfaction turn out to be' and 'whose defences are strong enough for them to understand them' (Empson 1930, pp. 247 and 248). Both Kris and Empson want to secure the work of art from the unbound energies of the primary process. The problem is how to avoid 'reading into the poem meanings not present to others' (Kris 1964, p. 260). What Kris comes up with is still by and large a traditional view of reader competence, involving: (1) 'standards of correspondence', that is knowledge of the communal symbols on which the reader draws; (2) 'standards of intent', that is knowledge of the artist's sources and intentions; (3) 'standards of coherence', that is the structural unity of the poem (pp. 260–1).

It is clear that what Kris proposes is a relatively safe concept of ambiguity, a plenitude of meanings made up of associations within culture. Any latent ambiguities are safely under the control of the ego: 'creativeness is a relaxation ("regression") of ego functions . . . the regression in the case of the ego is purposive and controlled' (p. 253). This is the great slogan of ego-psychology, to which this chapter has been leading. The types of ambiguity Kris lists arise from richness of connotation. In them the competing ('disjunctive') or overlapping ('additive') meanings are all directly interpretable by a public code: 'The word "cat" may be taken to refer to a tabby or a tiger: for the layman these alternatives are disjunctive; a zoologist would construe them as additive' (p. 247). Such 'construings' – a logician's term in itself – show how far Kris is from examining the strategies of the unconscious. At the other end of the pendulum's swing, Marie Bonaparte is at least nearer to an understanding of the possible manoeuvres of the unconscious in taking the cats in Poe's story *The Black Cat* as displacements for a fantasy and in discussing this fantasy in terms of Poe's ambivalent feelings for his mother. Though reductive, Bonaparte's account admits the subversive nature of desire in language and allows for the possibility that multiple meanings might be created within a work without any reference to any publicly agreed code.

Kris is similarly conservative in his discussion of laughter. He takes for granted that any laughter, because it 'spreads' (that is it is often infectious), becomes a 'social act' (p. 220). This is ambiguous with a vengeance: the 'social act' is just as likely to be one of the undermining of a group unity, aiming at the rejection of social constraints. Indeed, this is implicit in Freud's theory of the joke, seen in particular in his analysis of the obscene joke as a prototype (see Part III). In Kris's case the emphasis is on the ego's control of the instinctual drives: of the rhythmic shaking of the body in laughter he says that an 'archaic pleasure in movement is reactivated and is socially permissible' (p. 225). In the chapter 'Ego-development and the comic' he says that the adult's enjoyment of wit can be 'justified before the superego' (p. 207) and that it is a pleasure that has grown from the child's delight in playing with words. Similarly, Ernst Gombrich calls on Freud's joke theory for a view of play as innocent experimentation (1983, p. 138), arguing that the artist's 'social game', his playing with given historical forms and conventions, involves a combination of preconscious and unconscious activity (for a different reading of Freud's joke theory see Part III, pp. 124–8). In both these arguments it is questionable whether sufficient place is given to laughter and play as corrective of social convention.

Ego-psychology has left its mark on psychoanalytic criticism and started it off on another trend. Through its focus on preconscious processes ego-psychology makes an analogy between the movement of psychic energies under the control of the ego and the play of language within a cultural context. This has placed the emphasis on formal devices of art, namely the varieties of ambiguity, rather than on content. It has therefore helped to make psychoanalysis literary and respectable, but at the expense of purging literature of its bodily parts, as Goethe's angels decontaminated Faust before allowing him to proceed on his way to heaven.

3.2 The dynamics of response: Lesser and Holland

Ego-psychological criticism began by allying itself with Empson and the New Criticism, proclaiming the autonomy of the text. It sought meanings not in the individual psyche, in private fantasy, but in the public encodings of the private, in what was mutually shareable. A reader only counted in this schema in so far as he was thoroughly institutionalized as regards 'standards' of 'correspondence', of 'intent', and of 'coherence' (see last section). The concept of the reader has since been subjected to a more searching analysis. It is a matter of considerable controversy: 'Is he the "Actual Reader" (Van Dijk, Jauss), the "Superreader" (Riffaterre), the "Informed Reader" (Fish), the "Ideal Reader" (Culler), the "Model Reader" (Eco), the "Implied Reader" (Booth, Iser, Chatman, Perry), or the "Encoded Reader" (Brooke-Rose)?' (Rimmon-Kenan 1983, p. 118). The theorists who now follow have directed attention to yet another species, to what might be called the Personally Desiring and Aspiring Reader, though in the case of ego-psychology the second element takes over.

Unlike id-psychological criticism, which was almost exclusively author-centred, ego-psychological criticism begins the process of analysing the response of the reader. There is a move from the wish-fulfilling fantasy of the author to the shared wish-fulfilling fantasy of reader and author, as adumbrated by Freud in 'Creative writers and day-dreaming' and 'Psychopathic characters on the stage'. Author and reader are in collusion: the formal properties of the work disguise the fantasy, allowing the reader a yield of 'fore-pleasure' through his also being able temporarily to circumvent his own repression. In *Fiction and the Unconscious* (1957) Simon O. Lesser moves from the dynamic theory of Freud, of pleasure principle versus reality principle, to the structural theory of *The Ego and the Id*. He argues that form in fiction works in three ways: as an id function it gives pleasure, as a superego function it relieves guilt and anxiety, and as an ego function it facilitates perception, the 'single objective' being 'the communication of the expressive content in a way which provides a maximum amount of pleasure and minimizes guilt and anxiety' (p. 125). Form is here brought into play not in order to do just that – play – which it could hardly do if it were committed to the 'communication of an expressive content', but to reinforce powerful institutional pressures. The dynamics of the work are no longer seen in terms of strategies employed to facilitate the production of pleasure for both author and reader, but as a normative device whereby harmony and balance are maintained. Freud is here turned on his head, because where he saw fiction as an outlet for unconscious wishes, for Lesser 'fiction provides an outlet for idealistic and contemplative tendencies thwarted in our daily experience' (p. 82). The work is now a consolation for the guilt felt at the pleasure of the body having interfered with the higher pursuits of the mind, instead of vice versa. The cleansing operation of the body of the text undertaken by Kris is herewith extended to the body of the reader, himself a Faust on his way to heaven.

Lesser's interpretative procedures amply bear out his belief in the harmonizing text. In his discussion of Hawthorne's story 'The Birthmark' he argues that the hero's obsessive wish to rid his wife of this mark and make her perfect 'represents no more than an extension of a tendency present to some degree in nearly everyone,' that 'at the same time as we recoil we can identify with Aymler and through him act out some of our secret desires' (pp. 95 and 96). Since the story concludes with the wife's death, the reader, according to Lesser, is forced to recognize the impossibility of Aymler's demands. This leads Lesser into banalities in no way dependent on the help of psychoanalytic theory: 'Fiction endeavours to gratify as many of our longings as possible, but the very effort to teach us

how they can be reconciled with one another and with reality compels it
to take cognizance of the ineluctable limits of the human situation' (p. 98).
A certain kind of reader is here presupposed, one implied by the text, but
this reader is entirely passive, his task consisting of the constructing of
'analogizing fantasies' (compare with Jung – see next section) which are
to be salutarily dismissed. In this presupposition Lesser is conflating an
epistemological and philosophical issue with a moral issue within the historical process: of his dictum 'Form allays anxiety' Lesser tries to make
out that this is a general aesthetic principle, whereas the fact is that in
some historical situations an emphasis on conformity, and in others a
challenge to conformity, may be found desirable. The very same work might
thus be read from a conservative or a radical point of view, depending on
the context. To try to claim that either of these positions is given is to take
up a political position, though this is unrecognized in Lesser's argument.

Lesser's *Fiction and the Unconscious* naturalized psychoanalytic criticism in America, rendering it a respectable mode. His style, however,
made it more of a sermon than a theory, and thus required a more systematic framework. This has been supplied by Norman N. Holland, initially
in his book *The Dynamics of Literary Response* (1968), and later in a
series of revisions. It is worth while considering Holland's position at
some length because it begs a number of important questions regarding
readers and reading.

The early Holland is not far from the orthodox Freudian view as
expounded in 'Creative writers and day-dreaming'. His extension of it
is that the source of pleasure we get from literature is derived from
the *transformation* of the unconscious wishes and fears into culturally
acceptable meanings. The text becomes a scene of collusion between
author and reader round a 'core-fantasy' shared by both. Holland provides a
'dictionary of fantasy', following the Freudian phases of infantile development, one or other of which, he claims, determines the way the fantasy is
embodied in the text. In accordance with ego-psychology he sees form
as having a defensive and adaptive function, by means of which the
unconscious wishes get past the censor. He wants to provide a model for
the way fantasies move from the level of unconscious to that of conscious
meanings, and hopes to found an objective assessment upon it, arriving at
an aesthetics of response.

Thus, for example, he claims to detect a core-fantasy in the most recalcitrant of passages. Take, for example, his discussion of the 'Tomorrow,
and tomorrow, and tomorrow' speech in *Macbeth*, which, as he points
out, has been criticized for the mixing of its metaphors:

To-morrow, and to-morrow, and to-morrow,
Creeps in this petty pace from day to day,
To the last syllable of recorded time;
And all our yesterdays have lighted fools
The way to dusty death. Out, out, brief candle!
Life's but a walking shadow; a poor player,
That struts and frets his hour upon the stage,
And then is heard no more; it is a tale
Told by an idiot, full of sound and fury,
Signifying nothing.
                                                    (V v 18–27)

Holland believes that the power of this speech resides in the evocation of
a primal scene, that incident one mythical night when the child fancied it
witnessed its parents in sexual encounter and thereby suffered the greatest trauma in denial of the mother and successful rivalry with the father.
The 'tomorrows' and 'yesterdays' creeping past are marking the fateful
nights between; the 'sound' and 'fury' are the unnameable things heard;
the 'brief candle' that must 'out, out' is inevitably the plainest of phallic
symbols. The childish wish to express the oedipal hatred is the declaration
that the sounds and strutting of the father upon the stage of life 'is a tale/
Told by an idiot, full of sound and fury,/Signifying nothing' (V v 25–7).
One might feel uneasy about the *ad hoc* quality of these attributions;
then again one might concede that with Macbeth at the end of his tether
such regression to infantile modes of thought is credible. The question is
to what extent does the fantasy contribute to the metaphorical power of
these lines, when the latent images of familial relationships ('strutting'
actors/fathers) are also closely bonded with the manifest meaning, a king
whose symbols of power have ceased to command respect?

   Holland's later position is an attempt to shift the focus from text to
reader; he concludes that 'poems do not . . . have fantasies or transform
them towards themes – people do' (1975a, p. 110). He has given up
viewing the text as a fixed entity producing calculable effects upon
readers ('text-active' theory). Nor does he opt for an interaction between
reader and text on the lines of a determinate cause allowing indeterminate
effects ('biactive' theory), such as an objective 'meaning' giving rise to
varying 'significance' in individual readers (Hirsch 1976). A text, according to Holland, cannot be defined apart from readings of it ('transactive'
theory). For the transactive process he employs the analogy of a feedback
loop, both of which metaphors imply that there are two elements in play,

'feedback' suggesting the continuous alteration of a cause by its effect, 'transaction' suggesting a process of negotiation.

In his most recent statement he translates his literary theory into a general one, whereby 'a hypothesis or "schema"' is seen as operating on raw sense data and is continually corrected by feedback (Holland 1997, p. 2) Each of us is forever testing out these hypotheses and correcting them in this way: 'we are either satisfied or dissatisfied with how our hypothesis works' – if we are dissatisfied, we look for more data and try again, and thus 'actively construe reality' (ibid.). The idea of someone proceeding with viable but corrigible notions of things and persons around them always includes him- or herself, and this becomes the central focus of Holland's inquiry.

Holland defines the responses of the reader as a search for reassurance, a warding-off of anxiety. This security is achieved by the projection of a safe fantasy into the work. As the reader 'transacts' with the work, he elicits modes of adaptation and defence which are effective for him alone, since they will be those which arise from his own identity theme. Here Holland bases his ideas on a revision of ego-psychology proposed by Heinz Lichtenstein (1961, 1965), who, while he rejects the notion of a self as given from birth, believes in a basic 'organizing activity' (1965, pp. 121ff.) which allows a 'primary identity' to emerge through the infant's interaction with the nurturing mother, this identity remaining basically invariant throughout life. From this Holland argues that the infant, born into the world with a 'general style', establishes an unchanging personal identity through its relation with the mother, which it will bring to bear on all its transactions, later including those with a text, assimilating idio-syncratically to itself and thereby strengthening and enriching character. Neither Lichtenstein nor Holland inquire into the social determination of the mother–child unit presumed to have such a formative influence upon this permanent identity. The transaction is described by Holland in four stages: the reader's initial approach to the text ('expectation'), his being selective in what he takes in (mode of 'defence'), his projection of wish-fulfilments (characteristic 'fantasy'), and his translation of them into themes ('transformation'). He coins the word DEFT, an acronym, for this process of identity maintenance. How deft are these transactions of the reader as attempts to put theory into practice?

Holland experiments both with transactions of his own and those of others, noting the relation between their free associations to a text and their personalities as revealed in free-association tests (Holland 1975b). He makes his own transactions the focus of his criticism in his essay, 'Re-covering "The Purloined Letter"' (1980), taking the part of both reader and analyst, exploring the history and the features of his personal acquaintance with the text from a first reading at an early age. He bases the reading transaction on the psychoanalytic phenomenon of transference, which he believes in its general sense to be inescapable ('Why, this is transference, nor am I out of it', Holland 1982). The novelty of Holland's model of reading-as-transference is that the text is the *analyst*, triggering off responses in the reader/analysand, although when Holland becomes the reader/analysand he is at the same time conducting a self-analysis, examining his responses as a reader. He is both patient in transference and analyst in countertransference, examining his responses to his patient/self. His identity-theme perforce must operate in its idiosyncratic way upon the text, just as the patient performs a transference of his familial patterning upon the analyst. (Compare this consoling view of the text as ego-psychological analyst with Lacan's much less consoling view of the text as analyst enigmatically 'encouraging renunciation' (see below, p. 109).

The oddity of Holland's 'transaction' is that he leaves out in theory what he takes account of in practice, the influence of the text on the reader. The text as object cannot theoretically disappear into a feedback loop entirely maintained by a single reader, for this ignores the social nature of language. As part of its interaction a literary text comes with a most indissoluble tie forever knit with other texts, which contribute to its existence and without which it could not even be read. The writer as much as the reader is in transference with that intersubjective existent, the text, and neither alone can define what is pleasure, what functions are to be brought into play and how tenaciously.

His practice, however, presents a paradox through its own exemplifications. His recent comments regarding the 'active construing of reality' (see above) raise the question of the part played by other members of the community. Although he maintains that some hypotheses will be shared and others will not, he does not proceed to the obvious conclusion that a need to communicate to others will issue from *difference*. With the emergence of difference comes the pressure to employ a persuasive rhetoric, to speak with the purpose of redirecting another's desire. Feedback does not merely occur between the external world and the individual, it works between individuals. The construing of identity is not a solo performance, for identity itself, both at ego and 'non-ego' levels (Holland 1993, p. 5), is responsible for the directing of action in concert with others; the 'theme and variations' of identity development are played out among others. Many criticisms levelled at Holland reflect the absence of this aspect of intersubjectivity in his theory, for example, his neglect of historical and ideological factors (Bennett 1995, pp. 43–4). In practice one finds Holland busy about interpersonal negotiation in the very matter of literary criticism (Holland 1978) in a way which makes a distinct contribution to university pedagogy. His students and colleagues do provide that essential feedback to each other, but this dimension is not given the central place it should have in the theory. Both literary and critical texts are acts of communication. There is a common 'theme and variations' (the symbolic and its disruptions) and it is *under the constraint of this* that subjects have to play out their own theme and variations.

4
Archetypal Criticism: Jung and the Collective Unconscious

The only critic so far considered who has taken into account the historical dimension is Lawrence. His aim was not to define the effects of supra-cultural symbols in literature as a whole (the proper field of myth criticism), but rather to make clear the distortions produced by a specific culture upon the psyches of the individual authors within it. Archetypal criticism, on the other hand, pleads for the existence of universal symbols, specific neither to the individual nor to his immediate cultural setting. This insist-ence on universality is what marks the distinction from Freud's 'typical symbols' which were to be interpreted within a specific cultural context.

Like Freud, Carl Gustav Jung (1875–1961) saw the mind as a centre of conflicting forces, beginning in childhood and following a developmental course throughout an individual's life. His theory of the human personal-ity is built on the concept of a self as the true centre of the psyche which, for Jung, comprises 'the totality of all psychic processes, conscious as well as unconscious' (Jacobi 1968, p. 5). In 1913 Jung coined the term 'analytical psychology' to distinguish his new psychological science from Freud's movement out of which he saw it as having evolved (Samuels et al. 1986, p. 76; for a lucid extended discussion of Jung's analytical psychology, see Ellenberger 1970, pp. 657–748). He rejected Freud's theory of libido as energy underlying the transformation of the sexual instincts, postulating instead a concept of libido as 'an energy-value which is able to communicate itself to any field of activity whatsoever' (*Symbols of Transformation*, 1976, p. 137). For Jung this meant that a flux of undifferentiated energy gets channelled into certain privileged symbols, detached from the workings of language.

The core concept of Jung's system, individuation, is generally described as being both process and ultimate goal. It is to be sharply distinguished from Freud's libidinal stages by being viewed as a series of transformations, starting with the infant's emergence from a collective unconscious (whose immediate representatives are the family) and pushing to its becoming an individuated (separate) self. Jung sees the self in the course of its life experience (but particularly in middle life) struggling, on the one hand, with archaic images of omnipotent selfhood, and, on the other hand, with the demand made by social norms. He regarded the dreams and fantasies brought by his patients (mainly suffering from schizophrenia) not only as issuing from their unconscious instinctual wishes, but also as creations derived from a common store of 'primordial images' perceived across cultures, 'the inherited possibilities of human imagination as it was from time immemorial', to be found in every individual: 'The fact of this inheritance explains the truly amazing phenomenon that certain motifs from myths and legends repeat themselves the world over in identical forms . . . I have called these images or motifs "archetypes"' (Jung 1972a, p. 65).

These primordial or archetypal images, issuing from a 'collective unconscious', collective 'because it is detached from anything personal and is common to all men' (ibid., p. 66), manifest themselves in bizarre and extravagant fantasies which threaten to dissolve the boundaries between self and world. Jung has categorized this panoply of privileged symbols which makes up the totality of the psyche and demands a hearing at appropriate moments in a person's life. Some symbols emerge from the personal unconscious, some from the collective one; some reside in both. They take the form of an inner set of characters, one of the most interesting being the 'shadow', which is probably the nearest, although in a different system, to the Freudian 'id'. The shadow cannot be denied or discounted (i.e., repressed in the Freudian sense), since it is the psyche's innermost substance, seen as integral to rather than conflicting with the individuation process. Other archetypes are 'anima' and 'animus' (feminine and masculine aspects of the psyche; 'puer' and 'senex' (both positive and negative aspects of youth and old age); 'trickster' (a clown figure, connected with the shadow, capable of providing clues to alternative meanings); 'magna mater' and 'wise old man' (both 'mana personalities', figures invested with an aura), which can occur contra-sexually as projections onto significant others, such as the analyst. All these figures can come up both in the analytic encounter or in myths and fairy tales (see next section).

Although Jung is to be sharply distinguished from Freud in having evolved a theory of reconciliation rather than one of conflict, his notion of individuation, when seen clinically, is likely to be as painful a version of separation as the less exalted one of Freudian castration. What is

interesting in Jung is his empirical discovery of a set of collective fantasies within particular forms of mental illness which psychoanalysis was
hitherto somewhat reluctant to treat. His psychological treatment is an
attempt to move from these imaginary effects (his patients' projections,
the images which overcame them) to symbolic ones (the integration of
these effects into a symbolic system meaningful for the patient). However, the problem of whether his archetypes are 'innate' or socially transmitted founders without a theory of language. Jung would resist such a
theory at all costs, for, as will be seen, he will make a categorical distinction between the language of poetry and the language of science. Hence,
the kind of interpretation that takes place in the analytic encounter focuses
on how symbols mean via the sequences in which 'primordial images'
occur, rather than on how language means, via condensation and displacement. It makes the assumption that images depict something, an inherent
meaning, and that there is another meaning on top of what they depict
according to the way the analyst and patient relate them. By a process
Jung calls 'amplification', the material is subjected to a comparison with
analogous symbolic structures from myths, legends and fairy tales. This
has given rise to a certain type of criticism which relies on what might
be termed 'vulgar' Jungian symbolism in order to trace a sequence of
archetypal figures in individual works. The aim of these interpretative
efforts, psychological and literary, is the establishment of harmony in the
psyche, unity in the work.

In his lecture 'On the relation of analytical psychology to poetry' Jung
asserts that psychology can only concern itself with the creative process.
Like Freud, he does not wish to pronounce on art's 'innermost essence':
'The question of what art is in itself can never be answered by the psychologist, but must be approached from the side of aesthetics' (1972b,
p. 65). What does this mean? It is not as humble as it sounds, for it rules
out the proposition that insights can be derived from science, and makes
assumptions about the nature of aesthetics. On the one hand, it denies that
science might contribute something relevant about social responses to
colour and form; on the other hand, there is no mention here, as there is
elsewhere (Jung 1978, p. 82) that the imagination might have a place
in science. Kekulé arrived at his theory of the molecular structure of
benzene as a result of seeing a mental image of a ring, a (Jungian) snake
biting its tail. The relationship between science and art is problematic but
it is not one of simple exclusion, as Jung here claims: 'Art by its very
nature is not a science, and science by its very nature is not art; both these
spheres of the mind have something in reserve that is peculiar to them and
can be explained only in its own terms' (1972b, p. 66).

The philosopher of science Gaston Bachelard draws on archetypal images precisely in order to challenge the mind's preconceptions regarding a supposed distinction between the familiar objects of the life-world and the special objects of science. He considers that an 'epistemological obstacle' arises from too rigid a separation of imagination and science: the mind ignores whatever endangers an existing organization of thought. It is the very overcoming of this obstacle that allows the advance of new insights (Bachelard 1938). Yet, with Jung, Bachelard claims that the images which facilitate this advance are not personal. For example, the reveries that come from a contemplation of fire are evidence of a pure, even non-sexual, desire for knowledge, undoing the old metaphors by the 'most elaborate transformations' (Bachelard 1968, p. 111). He is also with Jung, whom he cites repeatedly, in seeing a sublimated (desexualized) libido as the energy behind such insights (p. 30). The 'primitive instincts' remain at a deeper level; the impulse towards a disinterested knowledge takes place in an 'intermediate zone' (p. 12), where intuition and scientific rigour can interact, without collapsing into either guideless subjectivity or rigid objectivity. Bachelard conducts a phenomenological inquiry into the communicability of poetic images (1969, 1971), whereby he removes them from the sphere of the personal unconscious.

Jung above all wants to save the work of art from the psychoanalyst's clinical scrutiny, from the equation of art and neurosis. He does this by exalting the creative process as such, as distinct from exalting the 'poet as person' (Jung 1972b, p. 74). In this one might see the beginnings of the dethronement of the author from a central position. The effects of this are limited, however, because Jung replaces one idealization, a personal one, with another, a supra-personal one, in that the poet becomes the mouthpiece for a universal language of symbolism: 'The unborn work in the psyche of the artist is a force of nature that achieves its end either with tyrannical might or with the subtle cunning of nature herself quite regardless of the personal fate of the man who is its vehicle' (p. 75). To this creative process he gives the name of 'autonomous complex' because it is split off from consciousness. He sees this complex as a central force in the mind, manifesting itself through the archetypes of the collective unconscious. For Jung the collective unconscious is the pure source of art, muddied somewhat by the 'tributaries' from the personal unconscious. The more muddied it is the more it becomes a symptom rather than a symbol. We respond to art the way we do because of the psychological effect of the reactivation of the archetype in us. He slides over the problem of the transmission of archetypes, with the dubious explanation that a *potentiality* for them is anatomically transmitted.

Need we therefore deny Jungian thought and analysis any kind of validity? I do not think so. Somewhere within all this are two perceptions: 1. that there is no human being without the communal symbolic, hence the insistence on the collective aspect of the unconscious; 2. that communication proceeds by individual correction of how the symbolic is applied to the world. From Jung's point of view this correction arises not from the individual *per se* but from the collective unconscious: that is to say, something social within the individual ('supra-personal', as Jung would have it), the archetypes, is given personal expression which corrects the existing and rigidified social. The problem is that Jung idealizes both the self and the social by attributing to them a numinous origin. But cultural topoi that have lasted for centuries lose none of their force by not being accorded divine power.

4.1   Archetypal symbols: theory

Although there is, therefore, a theoretical vacuum behind Jung's grandiose claims, the impulse they have given to the search for the recurrence of symbols has been fruitful for literary criticism, going beyond the reductiveness of vulgar Jungian criticism.

Objectivity in criticism is one of the declared aims of Northrop Frye. He sees in archetypal criticism a possibility for the scientific understanding of texts according to a classificatory system of modes, symbols, myths and genres. The strength of his approach is that his categories can be seen as exemplifying historically established patterns across texts, although he wants to take this patterning as evidence of value-free objectivity, arising from a common desire to make form. The order of words that we find in literature is structured by archetypes spread out over a series of 'pregeneric' elements, four narrative categories which he calls *mythoi*. These transcendent genres, the romantic (summer), the tragic (autumn), the ironic or satiric (winter), and the comic (spring), are to be seen as 'four aspects of a central unifying myth' (*Anatomy of Criticism*, 1957, p. 192). Conflict supplies the basis (archetypal theme) of romance, catastrophe of tragedy, confusion and anarchy of irony and satire, and rebirth of comedy. Each of these aspects has a succession of phases. In the case of romance the quest-myth is central: Frye singles out four stages, which correspond to his *mythoi*, namely, conflict, death, the disappearance of the hero, and the reappearance and recognition of the hero. He sees these as the 'mythopoeic counterpart' of Jung's individuation process where 'the heroic quest has the general shape of a descent into darkness and peril followed by a renewal of life' (Frye 1978, p. 122). For Frye the task of poetry is 'to illustrate the fulfilment of desire' and also 'to define the obstacles to it' (1957, p. 106). Art must project 'the goals of human work' so that desire may be satisfied (p. 115). Frye envisages an apocalyptic end for this desire, an 'anagogic', mystically exalting phase, finding in literature key works, such as *The Tempest*, which self-reflectively concern themselves with poetry's own striving to apply words to the whole of nature via its imaginative projections (pp. 117–19). Though such an ideal completion remains forever unrealizable it represents the final wished-for union of desire and nature, taking on a symbolic form in which nature becomes the body itself of a divine poetic creator. Art here comes to reflect a nature which is harmonious through and through.

Unlike Jung, Frye does not want to see the archetypes as psychic determinants, seeing this as a slide towards subjectivity. Maud Bodkin, on the other hand, in her book *Archetypal Patterns in Poetry*, prefers to found archetypes upon 'emotional tendencies', configurations of which she sees persisting over time as subjective realities 'in the minds of those who are stirred by the theme' (Bodkin 1934, p. 4). The reader is linked to the writer by these common patterns (p. 8), a biological and social inheritance (p. 25). Bodkin regards the very appearance of archetypes as self-justifying, unlike Frye, who is interested in revealing a conceptual framework without explicitly saying that it guarantees aesthetic value. She sees the reader drawn into a communal experience and proposes a reading practice whereby he or she is told to dwell upon the poem, 'wander with it, muse, reflect and prophesy and dream upon it' (p. 29), an analogous process to Jung's 'amplification'. This might be looked upon as a step towards reader-response criticism: the reader has access to the power of fantasy in the form of archetypal patterns.

Frye and Bodkin are together in stressing the communicability of such symbols. Frye maintains that there is no private symbolism, 'the "onlie begetter" of Shakespeare's sonnets . . . was not Shakespeare himself . . . but Shakespeare's subject' (1957, p. 98). Here he accords with Jung: 'It is not Goethe that creates *Faust*, but *Faust* that creates Goethe' (Jung 1972b, p. 103). Frye is with Jung in so far as Jung's emphasis on the communal aspect of the creative process and on the work of art undermines the favoured view of the artist as an original genius and instead makes him a medium for the transmission of archetypal myths and images. The poet 'is at best a midwife, or more accurately still, the womb of mother nature herself: her privates he, so to speak' (1957, p. 98). Frye's mode of criticism leads to an understanding of recurring verbal structures in literary works, creating the possibility of a systematic reading, as distinct from a criticism which applies a set of psychic categories in order to identify recurring themes.

A major theoretical weakness is to turn what are undeniable historical recurrences, contingent patterns detectable within cultures, into some given absolute realities, autonomous and all-pervading. Tempting as it may be to feel that such recurrence removes arbitrariness from the symbol, Frye is on unsure ground when he makes convenient links between natural successions such as the seasons and the cultural meanings assigned to them into 'literary universals'. Repetitions in nature, such as the rising and setting of the sun, can hardly be taken as evidence of a unity found in nature, one it is poetry's task to imitate. It is dubious to assert on these grounds that there is a universal core, that 'some symbols are images common to all men', for instance, food and drink, the quest, light and darkness, sexual fulfilment (Frye 1957, p. 118). Bachelard, who makes similar claims for the symbolism of the four elements (1971, pp. 176ff.), asserts that 'imagination is the true source of psychic production' (1968, p. 110), but nowhere gives an analysis of what this central concept of imagination is.

In making the archetypes rise neither from the individual nor from an immediate historical culture, archetypal criticism has made the concept float free of all human genesis. Frye addresses himself to the problematic relationship of desire and culture. First, desire is idealized as a demiurge which informs the human patterns of labour upon nature but is in turn aseptically untouched by them. Frye does not want to reduce it to the 'simple response to need' of the animal (1957, p. 105), nor will he accept any definition with respect to particular intentions. When he defines it as 'the energy that leads human society to develop its own form', desire is still being kept separate from human society. Second, what desire produces is idealized. This is a kind of paradoxical corollary of the above, for the archetypes that Frye catalogues as corresponding to four natural 'recurrences', for example, the romance, with its unchanging dramatis personæ, are also idealized, transcending history. Where, for instance, does Frye consider the relation of the epic hero of the quest to the feudal/ tribal warrior? Neither Jung nor he questions the expectations of social role which produce this kind of hero. If the influence of social forms upon desire remains out of the inquiry, the influence of desire upon those forms will remain equally mystifying, especially if rigidified into universal and objectively accessible symbols. There is, finally, no dialectical relation between desire and the forms in which it appears.

These criticisms aside, Frye has made use of symbolic structures as they exist within western culture, and, at a deeper level, to contingent recurrences of fantasy. His system provides a ready analytic tool by which a critic can make an approach to fantasy in literature. Even though his classification lacks the underpinning of a more fundamental theory, this does not mean that the fantasies do not have the image-structures he detects, only that they cannot be given the status of some numinous derivation from 'forces of nature'.

4.2 Magical archetypes: practice

One of the most prolific exponents of archetypal criticism is the Jungian analyst and critic Marie-Louise von Franz. She has written extensively on the application of Jung's thought to myth and the fairy tale. For her these magical genres illustrate *par excellence* the workings of the collective unconscious. Her analyses rise above a simplistic application because in her treatment of *Problems of the Feminine in Fairy Tales* (1972), for instance, she is able to discuss with some subtlety how women suffer through accepting the man's anima projections (mother, seductress, angelic figure). Women who fall in love with man's anima fantasy become 'anima women' and will mirror what the man demands. It is interesting that Franz asserts that 'on a primitive level, the image of the real woman and the image of the anima of man is more or less the same thing' (1972, p. 3), thus resonating with a celebrated formulation of womanliness as masquerade (Riviere 1929).

In discussing one of the many versions of 'The Sleeping Beauty', or 'Briar Rose', as the Grimm Brothers' title translates, she points out an interesting anomaly. The core of the story is the curse put on an infant princess by an angry godmother who was not invited to the christening feast; the curse is subsequently softened from death to a sleep lasting a hundred years by another godmother. When the princess is fifteen years old, the spell becomes operative as she pricks her finger on a spindle, whereupon she and the whole palace fall into a profound sleep. After many years she is redeemed by a young prince who manages to penetrate through the near-impenetrable hedge which has grown around castle and court, at which point the spell is lifted and he wins the princess. This basic tale has acquired a number of variations in different countries since it was discovered by the Grimms. The number of godmothers at the feast varies, and so does the reason why one is left out; there are also other complications and trials. Franz raises the question of whether the hero is to be regarded as an ego, with the obvious corollary that the princess is his anima, but she does not rush into an answer. She makes the point that the figures in fairy tales are archetypal figures from which subjectivity has been subtracted and which require amplification by the reader, or the dreamer in the case of a dream. What is collective and what is individual is a matter of interpretation. She picks out certain archetypal motifs in the story: the birth of the child followed a period of sterility until a supernatural figure (a frog) appeared in order to grant their wish for a child; the daughter-goddess disappears – sometimes persecuted by her mother – which suggests the evolving of new forms of femininity. There is also the motif of the forgotten godmother/goddess/god: 'If a god or goddess has been neglected, it means that a specific natural psychological way of behaving has been omitted' (1972, p. 25). One can see here how Jungians have split from Freud, for whom there is nothing natural in human sexuality. Franz sees in this fairy story an awakening of sexuality, but in an archetypal mode. The frog's gift of the child is an offer of new possibilities, enabling the unconscious to feed into the conscious; 'nevertheless we must expect, and can see from the story, that payment will be exacted; the demands of the dark world will probably still come up, as they do in the baptism' (ibid., p. 32). Fairy tales, as Franz's Jungian and by no means reductive readings amply demonstrate, deal with figures of the unconscious, linked to traditional rituals and customs. There is an air of magical realism about these tales, and it is to the genre thus designated (whose self-consciousness they lack) that I now turn for another fruitful application of Jungian psychology to literature.

Magical realism has a long history, stretching notoriously from the *Decameron* to D. M. Thomas's *The White Hotel*. In its postmodern form it has perhaps become something of a Latin-American speciality, being best known through distinguished popular authors such as Gabriel Garcia Márquez and Jorge Luis Borges. But for all its cultural differences and particularities it is strong in its intertextual operations, alluding to other texts both diachronically – through history, and synchronically – at certain moments of history (for an illuminating and up-to-date survey of the field, see Zamora and Faris 1995). Magical Realist fiction is particularly receptive to psychoanalytic inquiry because it explores and transgresses boundaries while at the same time playing with the fusion of a variety of worlds, staging both transformations and dissolutions, a constant challenge to representation. It has been argued that it is more receptive to a Jungian approach than a Freudian one because of its propensity for relating the magical elements to collective rather than individual experience, *The White Hotel* being a case in point (Faris 1995, in Zamora and Faris, op. cit.).

For a brief example I shall make use of a Jungian reading of a postmodern text. The essay in question is entitled 'Magical Archetypes:

Midlife Miracles in *The Satanic Verses*' (Walker 1995, in Zamora and Faris, op. cit.). Steven F. Walker sees Salman Rushdie's infamous text as an allegorical account of a Jungian midlife crisis, enacted dialectically by the two main characters, both of whom he sees as an example of the *puer aeternus* archetype (eternal youth), from which one of them, Saladin Chamcha, succeeds in freeing himself by integrating his shadow, while the other, Gibreel Farishta, succumbs to his shadow archetype (in its persecutory aspect). Saladin's acceptance of his shadow is doubly figured: first, in his struggle to reject the white western side of his character; and, second, in achieving a love for his father, who had maltreated him in the past. At the core of the text is a need to reject an English colonial father and to become reconciled with an Indian father.

In arguing that Jung 'prefers personification to abstraction' Walker reveals the metaphorical nature of analyses of this kind. Once these categories of figures have been applied, they do indeed provide the reader with a grasp of the tensions within the text. However, there is a disregard of the text's articulation of its verbal elements. Jungian literary criticism does not go by the letter and hence the problem of the relation of identification and language is never raised.

PART II

5
Object-Relations Theory:
Self and Other

Where ego-psychology was concerned with the psychic mechanisms which mediate the relationship between the ego and the id, and the consequences this has for the individual work and the individual reader, object-relations aesthetics is interested in the psychic processes which mediate the relationship between self and world, and the consequences this has for the formal aspects of art. This concern widens out into an investigation of what psychoanalysis might have to contribute to understanding what goes on between the artist and his medium, the critic and his art-object. The focus thereby moves from what happens within the psyche to what happens between one psyche and another. I shall first examine the theory of Melanie Klein, and then give an account of its impact on art criticism. I shall go on to the theory of D. W. Winnicott, with an account of its consequences for an understanding of aesthetic illusion.

5.1 Fantasy and reality: Klein

In the work of Melanie Klein (1882–1960) the instincts of the body and the tensions and conflicts they give rise to again become a central concern. Although in her theory she takes a great deal for granted, she cannot be accused of ignoring the birthpangs of a self in a human body subjected to the mouldings of experience. In this respect Klein's work marks a return to Freud and offsets the impact of ego-psychology. Klein allows the unconscious its due place in the interaction of the infant's (Latin: *in-fans*, 'non-speaker') body with the external world, which it has at first no means of distinguishing. It is this interaction that establishes 'object-relations', the structurings 'projected' outwards and 'introjected' inwards which form the pattern of a self's dealings with the world, including other people. Projection is a process whereby states of feeling and unconscious wishes are expelled from the self and attributed to another person or thing. Introjection is a process whereby qualities that belong to an external object are absorbed and unconsciously regarded as belonging to the self. The infant thus tries to create an ideal object by getting rid of all bad impulses from itself and taking in all it perceives as good from the object.

The critics to be considered in this section make use of particular features of Klein's theory, especially those concerning what she calls 'part-objects', an aspect of this process of projection and introjection. Their aesthetic theories will be the better understood if Klein's concept of a development in the child from an inadequate perception of things and persons to a viable one is explained in some detail.

The term 'object' is not to be taken only in its usual sense of a thing, but is extended to persons, though without any pejorative implication. Objects, for the child, are not at first clearly delimited and secure in their separateness as they are for the adult. The reality of the external world has to be worked for, beginning with 'part-objects'. These are what an adult would perceive as parts of other things or persons but which the child invests with powerful fantasies both pleasing and frightening. In particular, the child will in fantasy invest a part of something with the characteristics of a person, the result being that it will waver between love and hate towards this 'part-object'. At the core of Klein's theory is an awareness that good and bad can alternate and coexist within a single concept, an insight that has much wider implications than those for child development, since the same ambivalence could be claimed to infect all our attempts to apprehend the world in terms of self-favouring images. The relevance to art is immediate, for it too is concerned with waverings between acceptance and rejection, satisfaction and denial.

In the course of her work with very young children Melanie Klein observed how their feelings for reality were structured by certain fantasies to do with the child's relation to the mother's body. The fantasies played out were often of a sadistic and destructive nature, concerned with an experience of the mother's body as a container full of dangerous and threatening objects. Why was this so? Following Freud, Klein affirms the dualism of death instincts and life instincts from the very beginning of life (see Part III, p. 129, for a definition; for a full examination of this controversial issue within Freud's metapsychology see Laplanche 1976). In this respect Klein remains within the bounds of an id-psychology, but she departs from Freud in asserting that a rudimentary ego is present from the beginning, capable of certain defensive strategies designed to protect a pre-symbolic, pre-linguistic self, whose theoretical status is far from clear, since it seems to have a primitive notion of its own sex.

Klein believes that this rudimentary ego becomes exposed to the destructiveness of instinctual aggressive urges. The anxiety produced within the organism causes the primitive ego to split. The infant defends itself by means of projection, expelling the bad, and introjection, absorbing the good: the breast, its primary object, is experienced as a 'good object' and a 'bad object' in turn. According to Klein, the infant can adopt one of two 'positions'. She uses the word 'position' rather than 'phase' in order to emphasize the fact that the infant can move from one to the other and back again, a possibility that remains throughout life. These positions need defining here, because, as will be seen, in the view of Kleinian critics they are relevant to the relation of the artist to his medium and the audience to the work of art. In the first of these two positions, the 'paranoid–schizoid', the infant lives in fear of the 'bad' breast as an imaginary persecutor punishing it for its aggressive attacks. This is accompanied by an idealization of the 'good' breast in which the infant mentally abolishes the 'bad' breast and sees the 'good' breast as never failing to yield satisfaction to its demands. When the infant learns to perceive the mother as a person, it is possible for it to take up the 'depressive' position. Because it fears that it has caused the mother injury, it is filled with guilt and regret. It thus comes to have the urge to 'make reparation'. For followers of Klein the depressive position plays a crucial part in the creative process.

Klein introduces the notions of envy and gratitude arising from the fantasy that the breast keeps for itself the gratification denied to the child, giving rise to a primary envy of all that the breast possesses and leading to the defence of 'projective identification', the locating in another body of an aspect of the self felt to be particularly critical or threatening, perhaps in order thereby to control it more easily, but often with the result that it becomes persecutory from the outside instead of from the inside. In the Kleinian view there is a constant psychic struggle, never finally resolved, between the sadistic destructiveness of the schizoid–paranoid position and the remorseful creativity arising from the fear that the object may now be irretrievably damaged.

The movement from one position to another hinges upon the ability to invest fantasy with symbol, and in Klein's clinical practice one can find examples of how this is to be done. To escape from being at the mercy of fantasy, some measure of symbolic control has to be achieved. A key article 'The importance of symbol formation in the development of the ego' (1977; orig. publ. 1937) shows how Klein views the beginning of symbol formation and illustrates the central place she assigns to fantasy in the course of development. (The article is discussed in Lacan 1988a, pp. 68–70, 81–8 for its relevance to his 'mirror-stage'.)

> The first time Dick came to me, as I said before, he manifested no sort of affect when his nurse handed him over to me. When I showed him the toys I had put ready, he looked at them without the faintest interest. I took a big train and put it beside a smaller one and called them 'Daddy-train' and 'Dick-train'. Thereupon he picked up the train I called 'Dick' and made it roll to the window and said 'Station'. I explained: 'The station is mummy; Dick is going into mummy.' He left the train, ran into the space between the outer and the inner doors of the room, shut himself in, saying 'dark' several times. I explained to him: 'It is dark inside mummy. Dick is inside dark mummy'. . . .
>   During the third hour, however, he also, for the first time, looked at the toys with interest, in which an aggressive tendency was evident. He pointed to a little coal-cart and said: 'Cut.' I gave him a pair of scissors, and he tried to scratch the little pieces of black wood which represented coal, but he could not hold the scissors. Acting on a glance he gave me, I cut pieces of wood out of the cart, whereupon he threw the damaged cart and its contents into the drawer and said, 'Gone.' I told him that this meant that Dick was cutting faeces out of his mother. He ran into the space between the doors and scratched on the doors a little with his nails, thus showing that he identified the space with the cart and both with the mother's body, which he was attacking. He immediately ran back from the space between the doors, found the cupboard and crept into it (Klein 1977, pp. 225–6).

This four-year-old psychotic boy is unable to relate to real objects in a useful way because he takes them all to be embodiments of his dread. Klein's theoretical explanation is that the boy's anxiety is so great that he cannot made an adequate symbolic 'equation'. In normal development there is a sufficient quantity of anxiety (not an excess), leading the child to transfer from the original organs of interest, the parents' organs, to other objects, which it identifies with them, a process which causes it to move on as they come in turn to provoke anxiety. The brute interpretation which Klein offers the child, that the station is the mother's body which he wishes to penetrate if only the father were not in rivalry with him, encourages the boy to structure his rudimentary fantasy into an early oedipal sub-system. 'So what did Melanie Klein actually do?' asks Lacan. 'Nothing other than to bring in verbalization. She symbolized an effective relationship, that of one named being with another' (1988, p. 85).

Lacan recognizes what is at issue. Whether her interpretations were correct or not does not matter so much as that two people together got an overlap of reference, a linguistic rapport. The two fantasies, hers and the boy's, were about the child's relationship with the symbolic: the dark space between the two doors into which he ran is not so much the mother's body but the undifferentiated space whence he came, his flight into darkness figuring his rejection of the distinctions that language demands. Klein may force her interpretations on him, but, even though the child may not grasp the oedipal structure, nevertheless enough of what she says coincides with the child's fantasy so that he gains a foothold in language. Here Helen Keller's first use of a word comes to mind: it is often assumed that it was her matching her recognition of water to the word 'water' which marked her first moment of speech, but it is rather the fact of another person's being able to co-ordinate with her in referring to something hitherto mutually undifferentiated that began it. By the same token, Klein manages to play the reference game by putting labels onto fantasies (hers and the child's), thus enabling the child to use a word for the first time, when up until then he had only mocked at language, parodying and distorting his mother's words.

Klein's aims are first and foremost therapeutic: the alleviation of anxiety situations to prevent them becoming fixation points for psychosis. She shows the necessity of symbol formation in both the schizoid–paranoid and depressive position, without in either case giving an account of the relationship of symbol to language. The effect of the mother's fantasies on the child is never theorized and hence Klein's attribution to the child of a very early knowledge of its parents' sexual organs is not given any principled foundation: the interaction between the child's fantasies and a prior structure of desire, that of the mother and her history, has been developed by the Lacanian child analyst, Maud Mannoni (1970, 1973). Unlike Klein, Mannoni does take account of the effect of the mother's unconscious on the child, which brings back into the argument the social dimension it has lacked.

Through structuring their fantasies in play Klein enabled her young patients to gain access to the unconscious and establish a relation between the self and the object world. What both her theory and her practice amply demonstrate is that fantasy is a precondition of any engagement with reality. Unfortunately this radical insight, which could lead to a better understanding of the ambiguous perception of objects (implicit in Freud's 'The uncanny'; see Part III), has been neglected by those of her followers who have developed the aesthetic implications of her theory, moving mainly in the direction of ego-psychology.

5.2   Object-relations and aesthetics

Freud saw art as a privileged means of attaining instinctual pleasure. In order to achieve this end without suffering fear or guilt the censor had to be caught unawares: the successful strategies of the artist in getting an audience to share the pleasure was what Freud called the artist's 'innermost secret' (Freud, IX, p. 153). Object-relations aesthetics starts out from a different premise: art is seen as a privileged means of relating to an object. Far from deriving any 'innocent' pleasure from this encounter, artist and audience are deeply implicated in a process of attrition and contrition. For Kleinians aesthetic pleasure resides in the creating and perceiving of an object whose integrity has been fought for (see Segal 1977; orig. publ. 1955). Guilt is assuaged rather than circumvented.

The prototype for the aesthetic interaction both as regards the artist to his medium and the audience to the art-object is the (unconsciously) felt encounter between infant and mother. The medium of the artist becomes the mother's body; the separating out of the bodily self from the primal object is the central mode of experience. The creative act repeats the experience of separating from the mother. It can take place in the context of either of the two Kleinian positions, the schizoid–paranoid or the depressive, according to whether the artist is experiencing his objects as fragmented or integrated. Although Kleinians regard the depressive position as providing 'the mise-en-scène for aesthetic creation' (Stokes 1978, p. 222), the artist will invest his medium with the fantasy appropriate to his continuing stage in desire. The schizoid–paranoid position is one swing of an oscillation between identification with the breast and separation from it, which initiates, according to Klein, all objectifications. The theory can therefore claim to account for two types of aesthetic experience, one which one might see as harmonizing, the other as rebellious. In either case, however, the emphasis is on the conservative pole of the experience:

> Art of whatever kind bears witness to intact objects even when the subject-matter is disintegration. Whatever the form of transcript the original conservation or restoration is of the mother's body (Stokes 1978, III, p. 326).

Insofar as a good pictorial space . . . is inherent in any painting, one
could say that it represents the minimum content of art, an enriching
experience of envelopment and unconscious integration . . . the work
of art acts as a containing 'womb' which receives fragmented projections of the artist's self (Ehrenzweig 1970, p. 185).

In both cases the unconscious is seen as investing the *form* of the art-
object through the interaction of artist and medium. 'The image in form'
and 'the hidden order of art' are key concepts respectively of Adrian
Stokes (1902–72), painter and art critic/historian, and Anton Ehrenzweig
(1909–66), lecturer in art education and writer on aesthetics, both of
whom have developed the implications of object-relations for the theory
and criticism of art. The starting-point of each is the relation of an individual's bodily experience to those cultural objects we value for their
aesthetic appeal, though the direction taken is somewhat different.

Ehrenzweig sees this relation as a problem concerning the perception
of all objects. He raises the issue of how objects come to be selected
for perception in the first place, because he sees it as crucial for an artist,
and for the creative individual in general, to be able to return to a state of
primal sensing. He was initially interested in opposing gestalt psychology
for its postulation of a firm and stable structure in perception: he maintains that such structure has to be learnt, that in the beginning perception
is uncertain in its ranging over a field of view, and that, however reliable
mature perception may be, early sensing is fluid and unstable. Vestiges
of it are still accessible to us in dreams, in mental imagery, and in the
hypnagogic visions that occur in the twilight state between dream and
waking (1970, pp. 100–1). He argues that gestalt psychology makes
too ready an assumption that simple organizations, the so-called 'good
gestalts', are inevitably selected from the beginning, and, by a fortunate
coincidence, happen to correspond to the external objects of most use to
the developing child. As Ehrenzweig points out, the objects it selects are
hardly immune to libidinal interest (pp. 26–34).

According to Ehrenzweig, the ego can throughout life get rid of existing categorizations through a process he calls 'dedifferentiation', whereby
it 'scatters and represses surface imagery' (p. 34); that is to say, it will
dispose of the mundane sortings of experience which fail to satisfy the
id. A change of repression is involved in the form of a new mediation
between id and superego. Ehrenzweig argues that when the ego has been
the servant of the superego for too long the ego collapses, or 'decom-
poses', as he puts it, and falls back on the id for sustenance, getting new
sensory evidence, new material for image-making (pp. 230–1, 283–5).

He maintains that the decomposing of the ego is not necessarily a regression, that 'far from being autonomous of the id, the ego's perception is constantly at the disposal of unconscious symbolic needs', but without being at the id's command (p. 274). He thereby explicitly opposes Ernst Kris, who does not give the unconscious a sufficiently constructive role in the creative process, thinking of it as essentially primitive and as striving towards regression to earlier fantasies (see Part I). Ehrenzweig postulates a developing unconscious which turns 'disruptive' effects into 'constructive' ones (p. 273). He has a concept of 'unconscious scanning' (pp. 46ff.), whereby the ego and id together sort from an undifferentiated field of experience. It is a process analogous to proof-reading, where rational expectations have to be suspended if the break in the figure is to be perceived.

Ehrenzweig postulates a developing productive id which can alter perception for the public good. Creativity results from an interplay between conscious ordering and unconscious scanning which can forever reorganize the old images. The true order is thus not at the level of the ego *per se*: that is why he entitles his book *The Hidden Order of Art*. He argues that there is in all art a tension between conscious surface gestalt, a kind of secondary revision, and a hidden sub-structure, the part played by the primary process. In modern art, however, there is an open conflict between the two. In some cases there is an 'extreme dissociation of the surface and depth functioning', as for example in action painting, yet this kind of art too is not exempt from a hidden order which 'redeems' its 'near-schizoid' character (pp. 81–2). However, this presents a challenge to the viewer, who is implicated, for his own good it seems: 'A modicum of surface fragmentation is always needed in order to bring into action the usually starved low-level sensibilities' (p. 80). He too has to join in the scanning process, learning to proof-read with an open mind, so as to detect the new gestalt, the hidden sub-structure, and be relieved of his anxiety. One might here make an analogy in reverse with a reader confronted by what Roland Barthes calls a 'writerly' text (Barthes 1975): where Barthes turns a 'readerly' text (a classic by Balzac) into a 'writerly' one by breaking it up into fragments, Ehrenzweig turns 'writerly' texts into 'readerly' ones by finding a hidden order.

So how does he do it? Ehrenzweig sees the artist as having to go through an initial psychotic phase, in that the essential process of dedifferentiation involves the destruction of links with reality. But whereas the schizophrenic's inability to tolerate the 'ambiguity' of dedifferentiation makes him resort to self-destructive splitting in order to be omnipotent, to be in as many places as possible, the creative individual must get beyond this fixation point. Otherwise he will, like the sorcerer's apprentice in Goethe's poem, hack the broom to bits with each bit becoming a new broom continuing the destruction, while he fails to gain magic control (Ehrenzweig 1970, p. 132). This first phase, the projecting of fragments, corresponds to Melanie Klein's schizoid–paranoid phase. For the second phase, however, Ehrenzweig departs from Klein. Instead of the depressive phase (which he reserves for a final phase which may or may not come about) he postulates a 'manic–oceanic' phase, where 'creative man prepares, as it were, in his work a receiving "womb", the image of a benevolent mother figure, to contain and integrate the fragmented material' (p. 204). This state is not to be regarded as regressive, but as the re-experience of a primal state which enables the artist to integrate the fragments within the flux of experience, on an 'unconscious undifferentiated level': 'James Joyce's splinter language is of this kind. His fantastic word conglomerates are not just violent compressions of language splinters, but establish counterpoints of dreamlike fantasies that run on below the surface and link word clusters into an unending hypnotic stream' (p. 132). Thus the most 'writerly' of texts is turned into a 'readerly' one. Joyce can, of course, be read either way; the comparison is made to let each position provide a context for the other.

For Ehrenzweig every artist is initially a schizophrenic (not a neurotic as in Freud) before the chaotic fragments of his material have been assimilated in the unconscious, but he has no satisfactory explanation of how this comes about. He has a tendency to speak of the unconscious as providing a new 'coherence' of itself, as if a true order, already established within the primary process, can be drawn into alliance with the ego's systems and refurbish them. The 'depth coherence' of 'oceanic envelopment', which gives Cubist painting 'a hypnotic, almost mystic quality' draws us into 'the manic womb of rebirth' (pp. 135–41); the schizophrenic mysteriously lacks this 'depth coherence' and is logically therefore 'incoherent'. Since it is this very coherence for which an explanation is called for as the *sine qua non* of creative achievement, we are here stuck, as with Jung's archetypes (though Ehrenzweig favours Sir James Frazer's account of 'poemagogic' images (pp. 194ff.)), with another non-explanation. However, despite his concern to stress the redemptive pole of sensuous experience, Ehrenzweig does acknowledge the central relevance of the material of bodily perception, whereas aestheticians, from Plato onwards, have usually been suspicious of it.

The manic–oceanic blissful encounter that Ehrenzweig stages between artist and medium, spectator and art-object, is repeated in reverse form in the experience of the Barthesian reader/writer seeking ecstasy in *The*

Pleasure of the Text (Barthes 1976). For in both there is involved a celebration of the senses ('drifting occurs whenever I do not respect the whole' (Barthes 1976, p. 18)). Where Ehrenzweig's artist gathers up his fragments within the 'containing womb' of his projected vision, Barthes is making the text of pleasure serve as a 'fetish object' (p. 27), splitting it into parts ready for the exchange consumption of perverse fantasies. What for Ehrenzweig is a yielding to priority, a return to authority, is for Barthes a transgression, the archaic desire of one 'who plays with his mother's body' (p. 37), dismembers the text, perversely enjoys schizoid sensations without any attendant persecutory effects. The model of the artist/spectator 'sucked and enveloped . . . inside the picture plane' (Ehrenzweig 1970, p. 133) mystically partaking of a new identity has its radical counterpart in the *jouissance* of the Barthesian reader/writer pursuing unabashed his polymorphous–perverse non-identity within the fragmented body of the (mother) text. It is true, however, that Barthes' theory allows for a double reading, a 'contradictory interplay of (cultural) pleasure and (non-cultural) bliss' (Barthes 1976, p. 62). And with a different emphasis this is also true for Ehrenzweig.

For Kleinians the two essential poles are the schizoid–paranoid and the depressive phase, but for Ehrenzweig, as already mentioned, the depressive phase is not so central. It is not the origin of creativity (that is the attempt to regain the whole mother), but the result of the non-realization of the vision, when the unconscious linkages do not translate themselves into surface coherence. Unity and coherence still obtain, however, in the 'hidden order'. In Ehrenzweig's view the truth of art is to be found in a coherent 'substructure' which redeems the fragmentation of the surface gestalt.

Where Ehrenzweig was concerned with the unconscious exploration of bodily experience as such, Adrian Stokes is concerned with the sensations aroused when the body – and the self within it – relates to the object-world, either in contemplation of what is separate and self-sufficient or in an attempt to merge with and absorb what is before it. This applies equally to the relation between artist and medium and to the relation between spectator and art-object. Stokes wishes to stress that the imagery of this double experience resides in the form of the created object, wherein an expressiveness may be detected, though not as readily as in subject-matter as such. Form itself is representational and what it represents is the mode in which the unconscious fantasy of the artist/viewer invests the medium/art-object according to which of the two orthodox Kleinian positions is the prevailing one, the schizoid–paranoid (which Stokes sees in its merging rather than in its splitting moment) or the depressive:

Our relationships to all objects seem to me to be describable in the terms of two extreme forms, the one a very strong identification with the object, whether projective or introjective, whereby a barrier between self and not-self is undone, the other a commerce with a self-sufficient and independent object at arm's length. . . . the work of art is *par excellence* a self-sufficient object as well as a configuration that we absorb or to which we lend ourselves as manipulators (Stokes 1978, III, pp. 151–2).

There is in Stokes a quite specific ethical commitment: the quality of the artist's/viewer's aesthetic experience and its lasting value, as regards both the creation of art and the criticism of it (one assumes), depend on the degree to which the 'otherness' of the medium/object has been allowed for.

In his early writings Stokes discusses how in the Renaissance the medium used seems to respond to the artist's fantasy, depending on whether he is carving or modelling (1978, I, pp. 29–80 and 181–259; orig. publ. 1932 and 1934). In his later writings he uses the same terms, but no longer in their specific technical sense: carving and modelling now define the two most general ways in which the artist might relate to his medium, extending to the visual arts. The 'carving' mode respects the integrity and separateness of the medium, symbolizing the whole object and the integrated ego; the 'modelling' mode functions in reverse, in that the individual forms are more sharply distinguished, epitomizing the part-object relation and the unintegrated ego, enveloping the spectator (1978, I, pp. 237–9).

A virtuoso performance of Stokes's actual criticism can be found in 'Stones of Rimini' when he discusses the Tempio Malatestiano reliefs. He develops the spectator's attention to the details of the contrasts in the marble between the swirls of wave-drapery and the firm outlines of limb and mountain, not neglecting to hint at the power of sexual challenge in those waves, inhabited by angry dolphins and fierce-jawed sea-monsters (1978, I, pp. 250–5). In all of this, however, he totally disregards the historical matrix for this energetic conflict which he sees as harmonizing and presumably integrated. In 'Form in art' he writes: 'we can always discover from aesthetic experience that sense of homogeneity or fusion combined, in differing proportions, with the sense of object-otherness' (1977, p. 407). By this he means that the sense of unity with the object is balanced by an acknowledgement of its uniqueness.

But the confident matching of the disjunction of these two modes of creating and viewing with an analogous opposition of forms, carving and modelling, is by no means given: to assume so is to ignore the social context of this sensuous object called the work of art. Although Stokes specifically asserts that all works of art 'must reflect typical concatenations of experience, of endeavour, in the milieu in which the artist and the public live', thus allowing for changes in style (1978, III, p. 230), he wants at the same time to hold to a given attachment to these modes as sensuous forms. He thereby neglects the social and historical ground from which these forms issue and fails to explicate how certain thoughts, feelings and expectations attach themselves to them. Take the love of stone as evidence of a value placed on the sensuous and subjective side of the aesthetic, that is to say the actual bodily experiences of colour, shape and texture, and Stokes can be credited with a correct emphasis upon form. But in failing to show how its significance is dependent on context, he is working with an idealized, a-historical (though not, of course, an unhistorical) creator and viewer.

The flaws of the object-relations theories of aesthetic response come out all the more markedly when these theories are applied canonically, as in Peter Fuller's book, *Art and Psychoanalysis* (1980). He contents himself with validating his interpretations by freely quoting from a wide array of orthodox texts of the object-relations school, combining them to suit his purposes. This citing of authority (which includes two Marxist critics, Sebastiano Timpanaro and Arnold Hauser) has two consequences. One is that Fuller takes over the essential place of the biological (from Timpanaro's materialism) without pursuing the attendant problems. The other is that he gestures towards a historical explanation (Hauser's mention of the appeal of ruins and torsos as a Romantic symptom), yet leaves out the question why this should be so (Fuller 1980, p. 129). He argues that the constant appeal of the *Venus de Milo*, 'relatively speaking' (p. 126) is due to the fact that at one moment in history (the Greek moment) the figure is sensuously appreciated as whole and perfect (emphasis on the reparative aspect because of that perfection), and at another moment in history, the Romantic moment, it is sensuously appreciated as mutilated and imperfect (emphasis on both schizoid–paranoid and reparative aspect, because the mother, attacked in fantasy, has survived). While his development of the historical fortunes of the statue is very suggestive, there is a lack of an adequate account of its aesthetic appeal, such as Stokes provides in his discussion of the Tempio reliefs. Where Stokes and Ehrenzweig have offered extensions to the theory of the sensuous features of art, Fuller takes over the theoretical place already assigned to such features. He claims that since 1821 the reparative element has been dominant, the response of 'millions', but on the other hand that neurotic viewers might be impressed by the destructive aspects of the statue in that it arouses fantasies of mutilation of the mother, a response he considers to be pathological (pp. 121–2).

In this view, then, no positive value is being given to the schizoid–paranoid position, as is the case with Ehrenzweig, who argues for the value of 'dedifferentiation' as a way of reorganizing the id/ego/superego system (Ehrenzweig, op. cit.). More recently, it has been pointed out that 'it is central to Kleinian theory that the anxiety which leads to fixation and regression in both sexes also plays its part in precipitating the libido on its forward path' (Rose 1993. p. 167): the argument here is that the concept of negativity, a notion that is not mere nullity but something from which a dialectical advance can be made, has not been sufficiently extended in the work of Klein (ibid., p. 176).

There are now signs that this approach has began to translate itself into psychoanalytic criticism. It has recently been argued that Klein may be profitably used to interrogate ambivalence in the literary text. Instead of keeping the orthodox Kleinian legacy of focusing mainly on art as a vehicle of reparation that restores the damage inflicted on the loved object, there has been an attempt to trace the oscillations between the paranoid–schizoid position as the moment of aggression and destruction, and the depressive one as the moment of remorse and mourning. In line with the criticism of Leo Bersani (1986), Nicolette David (1995) sees this apparently redemptive view as totalizing and life-denying, betraying a moralistic stance. She draws on a number of literary texts to argue for a constant psychic struggle, never finally resolved, between the sadistic destructiveness and remorseful creativity arising out of the two Kleinian positions. To take an example, in Rilke's novel, *Die Aufzeichnungen des Malte Laurids Brigge*, David recognizes the clinical relevance of Rilke's poetic configurations, particularly as regards the Kleinian concept of projective identification. She alights on disturbing images of dismemberment which she sees as originating in fantasies of entering and plundering the contents of the mother's body, revealing repulsive residues of bodily substances therein and thus betraying the effects of the subject's sadism. This, then, is an example of finding negativity at work as meaning fragments itself in a severing of links.

What this kind of response to a text seems to hinge on, given the Kleinian concept of projective identification, is that the reader can choose whether she is prepared to 'contain' and process the disturbing fantasies or whether she prefers to take flight from the anxieties it arouses. At any rate there is here an attempt to institute a Kleinian reading practice not grounded simply in the idea of reparation.

5.3 Playing and reality: Winnicott

The character of the mother-and-child dyad and the particular patterns of development that it follows have been the concern of a paediatrician and psychoanalyst whose theory is of immediate relevance to art, and especially to the presence within it of illusion. D. W. Winnicott's (1896–1971) empirical discovery regarding a young child's use of a favoured soft object raised the question of the kind of interplay that was going on between inner and outer worlds, between fantasy and reality. Unlike Klein, Winnicott wanted to explore a space between inner psychical reality as investigated by Freud and his followers and outer reality as provided by the environment. Where Klein worked with the content of fantasy as revealed in the young child's play, Winnicott understands the role of fantasy as leading to illusion and a certain structure of play. He designates an 'intermediate area of experience', in which the child sorts out body parts from non-body parts and in doing so creates 'transitional' phenomena and objects (*Playing and Reality*, 1974; the key article came out in 1951). Winnicott observed how the child sucks and hugs a soft cloth or object; sucking and rolling it up makes it like the breast and the child ignores what is not the breast, what is different. It is able to suspend disbelief (for the object is not what it really wants) and make use of illusion in order to test out which parts of experience are under its control and which are not, in Winnicott's words what is 'me' and what is 'not-me'. The transitional object is partly the child's and partly the first 'not-me' possession. It is thus a form of defence against separation from the mother. It might be seen as a first step towards symbolization but it is not yet a symbol, it is rather an as-if object. What is important is not what the object stands for but what it enables the child to do, namely, to enter the field of illusion, moving from the subjective (as created by the child) to the objective (as found in the environment). The transitional object has the 'specific capacity to change the "given" into the "created"' (Pontalis 1981, p. 142). The capacity thus to *play* with illusion is what distinguishes this experience from the fixed delusion which may later turn a transitional object into that permanent security prop, the fetish (Greenacre 1970), both in the Freudian sense (it disguises the actuality of the lack) and in the Marxist sense (it functions as a commodity that manipulates human want).

Winnicott is ultimately concerned with the child's ability to use objects in a non-exploitative way, but this can only happen if the illusory play with the object will extend to the mother, who can initially allow the child to enjoy its 'ruthless relation' to her, allowing it to wear her out even while it is only fulfilling its playful needs (Winnicott 1958, p. 154). Her survival of the child's later not-so-playful aggressiveness will actually serve to teach it that the world is outside its omnipotent control but is also something shareable, 'which the subject can use and which can feed back other-than-me substance' (1974, p. 111). Although later 'a stage of concern' will set in, the child fearing that it has damaged the mother (1958, p. 206), Winnicott, unlike Klein with the 'depressive position', will not link this stage with creative capacity. On the contrary, for him the creative act is bound up rather with a certain ruthlessness and absence of guilt (1979, p. 26; see also Phillips 1988, pp. 112–13). For it is precisely 'the ongoing destruction in unconscious fantasy' (Winnicott 1974, p. 106) which constitutes a piece of new reality and a better understanding of desire. A parallel thought can be found in Goethe's *Faust*, where Mephisto's function as the devil is to play the part of the spirit who negates and destroys, and who, through that very negation and destruction, keeps the life-process moving. The ambivalence of the creative act is an insight which gives art a more subversive potential than that of reparation, for it implies that the symbolic needs constant re-adjusting and that this is a more radical and painful process than the conforming notion of reparation.

The child's ambivalent relation to its objects and Winnicott's praxis as outlined above speak for themselves in a well-known case-history. It might be said that whereas Klein's narratives partake of the Gothic, Winnicott's have an absurd Beckett-like quality. The heroine in the account that follows is a little girl called 'the Piggle', who is being treated for night-terrors and general disturbance following the birth of a sibling.

> PIGGLE: Now the Winnicott baby has all the toys. I'll go to Daddy.
> ME: You are afraid of the greedy Winnicott baby, the baby that was born out of the Piggle and that loves the Piggle and that wants to eat her.

She went to her father and tried to shut the door as she left. I heard the father working overtime in the waiting room trying to entertain her, because (of course) he did not know where he was in the game.

I told the father to come into the room now, and the Piggle came in with him. He sat in the blue chair. She knew what must be done. She got on his lap and said: 'I am shy.'

After a while she showed her father the Winnicott baby, this monster she had given birth to, and it was this that she was shy about. . . . Then she started a new and very deliberate chapter in the game. 'I'm a baby too,' she announced, as she came out head first onto the floor between her father's legs. . . . She went on being born from father's lap onto the floor, and she was the new baby and I had to be cross, being the Winnicott baby that came out of the inside and was born out of the Piggle – and I had to be very cross wanting to be the only baby. . . . There came a new development. She was now having a different way of being born out of the top of the father's head. [footnote: Being conceived of, i.e., born as an idea in the mind; wanted. D. W. W.] It was funny. I felt sorry for the father and I asked him if he could stand it. He replied: 'O.K., but I would like to take my coat off.' He was so hot. However, we were able to finish at this point, because the Piggle had got what she came for (Winnicott 1977, pp. 28–31).

In the scene above, as directed by Winnicott, the Piggle is trying to place herself with regard to the new (Winnicott) baby that she has created with the help of the therapist. (One might see her as testing out her use-value as against her exchange-value. Is she valued as a subject – as her self – or is she merely an object which has been produced for the satisfaction of superior agents?) Both the 'objects' she uses, the father/progenitor and the therapist/baby-sibling, are joining in as the child re-enacts her birth and separation from the mother and re-creates herself in play. The self is here itself a transitional object, testing out its reality, not in a private fantasy, as was the case with Klein, but in an intersubjective structure of play: 'the object, if it is to be used, must necessarily be real in the sense of being part of a shared reality, not a bundle of projections' (Winnicott 1974, p. 103). All the participants are aware that they are taking part in a serious game: the Piggle 'knew what must be done', starts 'a new and very deliberate chapter', and knows when to finish it; the father knows he has a part to play even before he knows what it is; the therapist is both amused and sorry for the father, but no whit less involved. There is a nice irony in the way that the father is being implicated in the transference by having to act out the birth for which he is responsible. There is a metaphoric shift from mother to father and a shift in time: the illusion is created that the father is the mother, a former time is now, and the Piggle is a new baby. As a result, the child is able to tolerate objects towards which she feels ambivalent instead of being at the mercy of them.

It is this intersubjective structure of play which aestheticians have taken up. There are, however, certain presuppositions underlying object-relations theory which need close examination precisely because they are inevitably and unnoticeably transferred into the aesthetic theories that base themselves upon it. The object, however it is viewed, whether as a transitional object or as a familiar object, is considered to be already singled out, separate, with clear boundaries. If the transitional object is to be taken as a paradigm of some sort for art and culture in general, this unexamined premise will, for all the emphasis on play, import into all forms of creativity and interpretation a prejudice for objects already assumed to be ready for human recognition. Play, however, is more radical than Winnicott allows, for it can involve the very boundaries of the object. The Surrealists, in particular, set out to exploit the instability of limits. Objects flow into and out of each other's edges, watches melt (Salvador Dali), birds blend with leaves or mountain peaks (Magritte). It is not only in Surrealist art that this is the case, for it may happen without the artist's intention: in Millais' *The Return of the Dove to the Ark* (1851), a dove can be seen as a breast, kissing as suckling. Although Winnicott allows for the overlapping of boundaries in clinical practice (for example in the famous 'squiggle game', see below, p. 90), the possibility of the object blending and flowing does not come into the theory, and this has repercussions for aesthetics and politics.

The concept of the transitional object has attracted the attention of critics and aestheticians precisely because it is analogous to the play of illusion in art. In illusion, as in the Millais picture, objects can overlap. Winnicott does not see that the unconscious has the power to invade these boundaries. He writes of 'the *paradox* involved in the use by the infant of what I have called the transitional object' and asks 'for it not to be resolved' (Winnicott 1974, p. xii). To use the figure of paradox as a metaphor is poetically attractive, pointing as it does to the contradictory nature of reality, but it is also a symptom of a certain theoretical blindness on Winnicott's part. As will be seen in later sections of this book, Freud has theorized this structure with the concept of the uncanny and Lacan with the neologism of 'extimacy', without resorting to the comforting notion of paradox. To rest on paradox is to assume the recognition of objects before they have been differentiated, a positivist habit. There is an inconsistency in his holding to the transitional object in an undefined space between 'inner and outer' and his calling its existence a paradox.

Transitional space, for all that it testifies to clinical inspiration, might better be theorized in terms of 'the creation of a common dream space, rather than relating to the concept of an object that is not quite the "me", but which is not yet the "not-me" either' (Widlöcher, in Clancier and Kalmanovitch 1987, p. 148): although the concept of transitional phenomena captures the elusiveness of the subject's move from the purely subjective to the almost objective, it is misleading to make them the foundation of intersubjectivity. Alfred Lorenzer and Peter Orban point to 'Winnicott's untenable separation between the self and the outer world *before* the formation of the transitional objects and transitional phenomena' (Lorenzer and Orban 1978, p. 749). They argue for the sequence to be reversed, that transitional objects be seen as steps in the development of a subjective structure. Winnicott, they suggest, is not clear about how the self arises from the undifferentiated experiences; he talks of 'an intermediate area of *experiencing* to which inner reality and external life both contribute' (Winnicott 1974, p. 230), whereas Lorenzer and Orban say the converse: 'the inner and outer do not *make up* this intermediate area: instead they *differentiate themselves out of it* . . . into transitional objects and phenomena' (Lorenzer and Orban 1978, pp. 474–5). It follows that such differentiation will be subjective and variable, that the boundaries of objects can be argued about. The ambiguous (permanently transitional) object is thus produced out of experience that is historically determined, not out of units assumed to pre-exist, such as a mother-and-child dyad.

The problem of accepting the mother-and-child dyad as a constant transfers itself to a certain use of D. W. Winnicott's theories to which he himself points. He extends the trust necessary between mother and child to that between individual and society. The play with transitional objects, which takes place in an intermediate area he calls 'potential space' (1974, p. 126), becomes by continuous development the creative use of cultural objects: 'Cultural experience begins with creative living first manifested in play' (p. 118). What is not clear is where this creativity with objects shifts into a general acceptance of them, as can be seen in what follows.

An attempt to use Winnicott for a theory of culture has been made by Richard Kuhns (1983), who endeavours to base a philosophy of art on psychoanalytic theory, taking the development of the ego as the critical principle. He contends that the ego achieves growth through fictional play with transitional objects, reaching a communal stage with 'cultural objects', performed through public 'enactments' (art, ritual, ceremony): 'Culture is a tradition of enactments' (1983, p. 53). Freud, he argues, ignored tradition from the ego point of view, concentrating on the art-objects as highly invested with narcissistic libido. Kuhns regards art as a highly invested cultural object, perhaps in the sense that Walter Benjamin (1982 [1936]) defined the art of the past as drawing the viewer within its orbit through its 'aura', the stored human associations which seem to emanate from it with the full authority of past cultural enactments (for a further discussion of this issue, see Wright 1989, pp. 76–8). The viewer's response to the artist's use of tradition (his countertransference to the artist's transference) will be a source of ego-strength. Culture is the domain of ego-functioning: cultural enactments are part of the maturational process and therefore have a profound influence on individuals within that culture in the stages of both primary and secondary socialization (both play and culture in a 'potential space'). Cultural objects are transitional objects because they are shared. Through them the relation between self and object (that is the object in a mundane sense) is mediated. What is not clear in this argument is how the child's transitional object turns into the existing object, or what the distinction is between a cultural object ('enacted') and an object in a mundane sense (p. 63). Kuhns' 'developmental approach' (see the title of his book) assumes a favoured trajectory for the transitional object, dividing art-objects from mundane objects, designating a play area where one can harmlessly pursue illusion in order to adapt creatively to a traditionally given order of existing objects, thereby confirming the status quo.

This assumption is particularly evident when he comes to propose a theory of tragedy (pp. 104–13). Kuhns claims that he is Aristotelian in his approach to tragedy. He links Aristotle's catharsis to Freud's concept of 'splitting', defined as the ambivalent taking up of two incompatible attitudes, owing to 'a conflict between the demand by the instinct and the prohibition by reality' (Kuhns 1983, p. 109, citing Freud 1940, XXIII, pp. 275–7). In tragedy, according to Kuhns, the conflict between the two and the impossibility of reconciling them is brought into focus; the mingling of pain and pleasure so produced effects the cathartic relief. This uncertain mingling makes the tragedy into a transitional object. As the child has conflicting experiences (fear and relief) with its transitional object, so too does a spectator with tragedy, and, just as the child proceeds to a mature and confident handling of reality via his play with the object, so the spectator is able to ameliorate the tensions between 'private sexual need and public political obligation' (Kuhns 1983, p. 109). The honorific word 'reality' is confined to the public political world; as applied to the inner, the unconscious, it is conspicuous by its continual absence. Objects viewed from the standpoint of private sexual need remain fictional; reality belongs with the public object. Kuhns thus contradicts his attempt to keep ambivalence in the argument: tragedy becomes tamed to an experience which will enable spectators to refashion unreal inner needs to the mould of the real public and political system.

5.4 Potential space and the field of illusion

The theory implicit in Winnicott's practice is actually better than the one he explicitly holds. The use of the 'squiggle game', where analyst and child take it in turn to draw a squiggle for the other to make into an object (Winnicott 1958, pp. 108–10), shows a pragmatic understanding of playing. Analyst and child play a game of rival interpretations of the random squiggle in front of them, making their own partial selections according to free associations. The semiotician Julia Kristeva and the French psychoanalyst and writer André Green have a better theoretical understanding than Winnicott of what is involved in the process.

For Kristeva play begins at the meeting-place of nature and culture, a play that is productive of all objects and persons, including that of mother and child. Her theory of play is relevant to art both in its explanation of the importance of signs and symbols and in its showing how bodily experience provides the material for that use. Both these aspects concern that which resides in the margins of language. Moreover, her examination of the pre-linguistic stage in the infant shows the importance of these margins for the use of language thereafter. Kristeva believes that something like play begins before the self comes into being. Nature asserts itself in the infant's body, before any self has made its appearance, as unorganized pressures of desire, constituting what she calls a *chora*, a 'receptacle' of as yet undirected experience, a space prior to the infant's entry into a sign-system (Kristeva 1980, pp. 281–6). These currents of experience have their own rhythms and patterns, but do not yet have any consistent relation to need. Through sudden linkages, produced by the gatherings and releases of tension – one might say, not unlike Wordsworth's 'chance collisions and quaint accidents' (*The Prelude*, Book I) – the infant comes to laugh. There is the fun of play in passing from 'fright' to 'peace' (Kristeva 1980, p. 285), when an illusion, the result of some chance concept-experiment, shows itself a joke: the father, say, was *not* throwing the infant away – only up, to be caught again in safety. Sometimes the infant has the joke turned against itself, as when the 'good-enough mother' (Winnicott's concept, cited somewhat ironically by Kristeva), allows it some disillusionment, helping it to free itself from over-dependence, 'scoring a point' on her own account, but easing the moment with laughter (p. 282). This is a complement to Klein: Kristeva's child chuckles its way into selfhood, Klein's, an anguished soul from birth, beats its own breast. In Kristeva's modification of Klein both these may be moments in the beginnings of the self; there can be a synthesis of thesis and antithesis.

These jokes and disillusionments prepare the way for the next stage: 'Winnicott's "potential space" elaborated by a "transitional object", perfects the necessary conditions for semiotic functioning and transition to language acquisition' (p. 286). Semiotic functioning depends upon the *chora*, the private experience of the bodily drives, which has a key part to play in the learning of language, in enabling the child to participate with some equality in the fun of meaning. The zest of experimentation, the *chora* disrupting the order, does not cease at some critical point at which language becomes mature and complete; the semiotic is as active as ever. The implications of this reading of Winnicott are more radical since Kristeva's theory goes beyond a developmental account. The potential space can now be a place from which to challenge the parents' language, to be a 'bad-enough' child (a concept notably absent in Winnicott) in that it can be subversive of the order of things. She has in fact suggested that Marxism, like some conservatisms, has been too much tied up in the Symbolic, failing 'thereby to understand the potentially revolutionary force of the avant-garde's exploitation of the semiotic' (Lechte 1990, p. 133).

André Green is also concerned to keep the interaction between persons, their intersubjectivity, in the forefront of theory, though he is closer to Winnicott's practice than to his theory. Drawing explicitly on object-relations theory and combining it with other Freudian theory, including that of Lacan, Green has extensively explored the correspondence between the analytic encounter and that of writer and reader, extending it to the parallel relationship of producing and consuming in all the arts. His focus is on there being two conscious and two unconscious minds at work in any such interaction. In the analytic situation both analyst and analysand are operating with hypotheses about self and other. A negotiation about them can go on, and it is one that affects and develops both, a double dialectic. The analyst and analysand elicit speech and gestures from each other which have not existed before, because they grow out of the relations between the two, the 'I' and the 'me' on both sides, the 'I' being the subjective play (like Winnicott's squiggle), the 'me' what the other side picks up (the modification): 'What the analysand communicates is an analogue, a double of the effect produced on his own bodily, affective, and intellectual experience by the patient's communication' (Green 1978a, p. 180). This takes place in a potential space in which the nature of the illusion is left unrealized for the time being.

Green sees that there is an ambiguity on both sides of the writer/reader communication which is analogous (though not homologous) with what goes on between analyst and patient. In each case two subjects are engaged in the mutual production of a transitional object, the analytic 'text' and the literary text, both an illusion of agreement. The literary text, unlike the patient, cannot be subjected to further cross-questioning, but there is material in the figures of the text that can be worked on like an analysand's associations. What alters, 'overflows', is the *re*-reading done by any interpreter (Green 1978b, p. 277), who brings to bear upon the text his lived experience, which is 'outside the sentence' (p. 281, Green quoting Barthes 1976). This experience is first and foremost affective: the analyst–interpreter seeks to interpret the emotions the text awakens in him. Green describes this encounter as 'trans-narcissistic', a concept which avoids the past id-psychological approach that fantasy alone is a pre-text for writing and reading. Fantasy has a *double* effect, because conscious and unconscious on both sides are involved, each with its own perspective. To the degree that the encounter fulfils a private wish it is narcissistic, but since this inevitably involves confronting another's unconscious, the wish is thereby modified, and this transcends the narcissism of the single subject.

In his book, *The Tragic Effect* (1979), Green extends his theory to account for the emotional effect of tragedy: the 'potential space' becomes tragic, a place for misrecognitions. Green discusses the affective drama of Artaud as a prototype of the modern theatre, for it is with the insights that modern drama offers that we can go back to tragedy proper. Artaud's insistence on the 'physicality of signs' makes us forcefully aware of the unconscious bodily aspect of utterance, bursts the bounds of ordinary speech and shocks the spectator out of all passivity, so that 'the intelligibility of the spectacle is no longer, as in the past, related to its emotional resonance' (Green 1979, pp. 9–10). This goes directly counter to the theory of Aristotle, who had no place for the uncontrolled unconscious. Nevertheless, Green contends, Aristotelian recognition (the passing from ignorance to knowledge, involving an emotional change) has not been banished from the stage: what has happened is a change in what is recognized. The post-Freud theatre is a 'theatre of desire, a theatre of the primary process'. It shows the characteristic processes of the unconscious as revealed by Freud. Green argues that the central unconscious concern is with the Oedipus complex, in particular its failures. It is the psychoanalytic critic's task not merely to proclaim the bad news, but to examine the process of veiling that hides the oedipal dynamic within the immediate structures of the play. Tragedy resides in the blindness of the protagonist who is as much involved with surface understandings as the 'naive' spectator. What is at stake is not just the blindness of a deceived consciousness but that of a consciousness out of touch with the unconscious. It is in this double view that the transitional nature of the play-object shows itself, in this case as a 'tragic effect': there are misrecognitions both by the characters within the play and by the spectator. Neither Hamlet nor the spectator knows, for instance, why Hamlet cannot get to the point of killing his uncle. The play-object is not what it appears to be.

Green sees the critic as one engaged in the play of the veiling/unveiling process. One of the three tragedies on which he practises his theory is *Othello*. Where Freud said that, until he examined *Hamlet*, no one knew the source of its fascination (VII, pp. 309–10), Green is virtually saying the same for *Othello*. He maintains that this play has always been considered not quite satisfactory, despite its obvious power to arouse strong emotion. Like Freud in his essay 'Psychopathic characters on the stage', Green holds that the spectator is able to get pleasure from drama (in particular tragedy), because his attention has been diverted:

> Between what Shakespeare presents to our senses and what he allows the unconscious to say there stands the difference that Freud aims to decipher. What must be restored is the thing that was offered on the stage, aimed to divert rather than to rivet the spectator's attention. What took place on the other scene must be the object of another reading, with the help of another type of link between its signifying elements, uttered according to another mode of scansion, marked by another punctuation, expressing a discourse that resists verbalization, being itself a veiling of a discourse, without which there would be neither tragedy, hero, spectacle nor spectator (Green 1979, p. 135).

The veiling is thus essential to all the constituents of the tragic experience, since action is at the mercy of drives of which the subject is unaware.

Green's general argument in the book is that aesthetic pleasure resides in the simultaneous arousal and control of the drives. Arousal is possible because of diversion of attention: there is fear, but the reason is not known. What controls the direction of the drive in *Othello* is not the cultural expectation of jealousy: a mundane assumption, that a man is jealous of a woman as object of desire, provides a screen, but the force is rather envy, that of the position of a subject in the social structure. The jealousy disguises the envy of a subject who is refusing castration. To refuse castration is not to accept the repression from the father, to cling to

a narcissistic view of one's power and freedom. Green wants to distinguish between that level of understanding which accepts Othello as a
warrior-hero subjected to a conventional challenge to his honour, reacting
with 'simple jealousy', and that level which detects both Othello and Iago
as governed by envy of the father, the power of the Venetian state. Both
are alienated, one by race, the other by rank, from the envied image of
Cassio, the favoured Venetian. The envy binds desire narcissistically to
the power-structure with the result that both aim at the death of Cassio
and project elsewhere, upon Desdemona and Emilia, (homo)sexual jealousy of Cassio which conceals their father-hatred. This is not *simply*
saying that Iago and Othello desire Cassio homosexually. It is attributing
the source of that desire to envy and explaining the jealousy with regard
to the women as, for both of them, a transformation of that envy. It is not
an analysis that looks for historical explanations for the centrality of that
concern in a play produced in the late Renaissance; Green, in fact, dis-
misses Iago's relations to Machiavelli with the remark that his function
(in being motivated like Othello, with an imperious castration complex)
'far exceeds that contemporary interest' (p. 121). What is significant for
Green is the castration complex in general, not the historical form it takes.
What he is investigating in the three tragedies of his choice is 'the other
side of the Oedipus complex' (p. 32), always present in some form, where
a firm identification with the 'right' parent (for a man the father, for a
woman the mother) is undermined by an identification with the parent of
the opposite sex.

The strength of Green's practice here is that it manages to account for
strong emotion in terms of a rhetoric in the text. According to his theory
there is a latent private fantasy (denial of castration) and a manifest public
one (the desire to possess a woman), which interact in a potential space, a
field of illusion, where two fantasies commingle in a desire for possession. Where previous critics linked the castration complex with a universal structure in the author's mind, Green neither brings in the author nor
analyses a single character as being subject to the complex, but shows
instead how the configuration of characters stages the castration complex
in terms of a set of contested power-relations. Pleasure resides in the
characters being put through anguish while the spectator can mingle pleasure and pain through a double identification: a conscious imaginative one
miming the jealousy-pattern, and an unconscious imaginary one miming
the narcissism-pattern.

In his criticism Green makes characters and past 'naive' readers into
analysands, reading falsely, while he, being both analysand and his own
analyst, reads correctly. This would seem to reflect a similar problem in

psychoanalysis itself in its assignment of intersubjective rights to the analysand in theory, while there remains the question of his being able to take them up in practice. Would he be, as in Winnicott's theory, already, as child, himself inscribed in 'potential space'? Green is an expert analyst, but he has, as with a formal session, brought his analysis to closure. For all the subtleties of his interpretation, to which no summary can do justice, the text has been frozen into a single stable ambiguity. What is missing is what is left out of any totalizing reading, not only a psychoanalytic one: an engagement with the text rather than with the characters. The text ought to be in potential space. He has not shown up any labour in the text as indicative of the conflict between the two meanings. He, for instance, underestimates Othello's desire to be a successful warrior and a victorious general to the point of omitting the clear evidence in the play that he was. Othello's doubting his fulfilment of the role is no disproof of his fulfilment of it. The rivalry in the illusion is of two real desires. This leaves open the question of the text as a whole (the rhetoric *of* the text as opposed to the rhetoric *in* the text), which would include within it this lower-level character-conflict, relating it to the text's own history – why, for instance, it has been valued as a 'good object' for so long.

In Winnicott's case the practice was better than the theory; in Green's case the theory has been better than the textual practice. He saw the intersubjective principle in Winnicott's practice, but he imported into his own critical practice a totalizing view. The task of praxis is to unveil the gap between theory and practice.

Green has brought together object-relations theory and French theory, linking fantasy, play and intersubjectivity. Negotiation of meanings takes place through illusion, where the double-match of conscious orderings and unconscious experience can be tested out for the degree to which they satisfy desire. The intentions of authors and readers are subject to this negotiation in the 'potential space' of reading/writing. Emotion is involved on both sides of the negotiation, and it is Green's strength that he acknowledges this in both theory and practice. The dialectic, however, may be prevented from advancing where it fails to allow for language reaching out to more than the analyst–analysand, author–reader duo. It is this aspect which Winnicott did not take into account and which is to be developed in the next section.

PART III

6
Structural Psychoanalysis: Psyche as Text

The psychoanalysis of Jacques Lacan (1901–81) could be said to found itself on the failure of language to match the body. Winnicott drew attention to play and illusion in the child's engagement with the world, but ignored the relation between the identifications of objects and the accession to language. Objects, even when viewed as 'transitional', are not necessarily permanent and unchanging. Nor are 'subjects', the term used by French theorists in order to avoid connotations of selfhood and personhood, for this would be to anticipate discussion of how selves come into being. Language has put its network upon the world: the part illusion plays in its workings as a result of the split between conscious and unconscious cannot be ignored. Lacan's Freudian revolution is the systematic claim that the unconscious is more than the source of primal instincts linked at random to ideas and images. Lacan rejects this randomness. Conscious and unconscious are asymmetrically co-present: the inner structure maps the outer conceptualizings. This mapping is above all governed by linguistic experience. However, in putting Lacan in this section, I am aligning him with the structuralist period since it was this period that was important in the emergence of a textual criticism. The later Lacan (from the mid-sixties onwards) moves the emphasis from the subject's alienation in language to its confrontation with that which is recalcitrantly both inside and outside language — the real (see particularly section 9.3).

6.1 Psychoanalysis and language: Lacan

Lacan begins with the infant in an amorphous state, with no boundaries to its experience of sense or of need, as a jumble he punningly calls 'l'hommelette' – *homme-lette*, 'little man'; *omelette*, 'shapeless mass' of egg (Lacan 1977b, p. 197). To mark the initial stages of separation Lacan returns to Freud's early concept of the ego in the latter's paper 'On narcissism' (Freud 1953, XIV), and to the key metaphor of narcissism, that of the mirror. For Lacan there is a mythical, and sometimes a literal, moment of a mirror-stage (Lacan 1977a, pp. 1–7), in which the infant makes an imaginary identification with its reflection in a mirror. Lacan explores and widens the implications of the narcissistic metaphor. The child looks in the mirror and is delighted by several qualities of its own image simultaneously. Whereas before it experienced itself as a shapeless mass, it now gains a sense of wholeness, an ideal completeness, and this all without effort. This gratifying experience of a mirror-image is a metaphorical parallel of an unbroken union between inner and outer, a perfect control that assures immediate satisfaction of desire. Lacan calls this pre-linguistic, pre-oedipal stage the realm of the 'Imaginary'. He takes the infant to be modelling itself upon the mother, since that is the first being with whom it has interaction. But this model is an illusion, since the mother is assumed, like the mirror-image that follows its every movement, to respond to every impulse, which is not the case. Hence the mirror-image is already 'a homologue for the Mother/Child symbolic relation' (p. 196).

What is imagined in particular is a primitive belief typical of this stage, a belief Lacan terms the 'Desire of the Mother' – a double genitive referring to both the mother's desire and the desire for the mother. First, the child imagines itself to be the desire of the mother in the sense that it is all that the mother desires ('desire' taken as a metonym for what is desired, much as we use 'wants' as a noun for what is wanted). The child wants to become all that would satisfy the mother's lack, in psychoanalytical terms becoming the 'phallus' for the mother, all that would complete her desire. The mother herself has suffered deprivation, by division from her own mother, and by denial of her own father, and can thus be drawn into a collusion with the child that it will assuage the lingering pain of those separations. Second, the 'Desire of the Mother' is the child's own desire for the mother, as that part of its experience which has been prompt to satisfy its needs. Hence it too is drawn into this fantasy of completion. Since repression is neither experienced nor acknowledged, there is, according to Lacan, no unconscious at this stage, except, of course, the mother's.

Both of these aspects of the 'Desire of the Mother' combine to keep the child's ego-concept in a profoundly illusory state. The absence of a gap for the child between a concept and its application is a proof of the concept's inadequacy; the ego-concept has never been tested in use. The gap appears with the initiation of the child into the order of language, what Lacan calls the 'Symbolic Order'. The structures of language are marked with societal imperatives – the Father's rules, laws and definitions, among which are those of 'child' and 'mother'. Society's injunction that desire must wait, that it must formulate in the constricting word whatever demand it may speak, is what effects the split between conscious and unconscious, the repression that is the tax exacted by the use of language.

Lacan makes appeal to the linguist Ferdinand de Saussure, who viewed the sign as split into two parts, a signifier and a signified. A signifier is typically a word-sound, recognized by being heard as different from others within an expected range. A signified is a concept, singled out from an originally undifferentiated continuum of thought. The link between them is entirely arbitrary, for any sound can be linked with any concept. Once bonded in use, however, the combination is secure, as firmly bonded together as the two sides of a single sheet of paper (Saussure 1977, p. 113; orig. publ. 1915). Saussure expresses the combination by the formula s/S where S stands for the signifier and s for the signified. Lacan begins his critique by throwing doubt upon the security of the combination. He gives an example where what appears to be the same signified, namely a door, can be marked with two different signifiers, 'Ladies' or 'Gentlemen'. This sly example brings out what critics within linguistics had already pointed to, namely that Saussure ignores the problem of reference, the process whereby parts of the world come to be referred to as things or persons. Illusion can enter the sign-system because the identification of the signified depends upon human judgements, which can, notoriously and justifiably, differ. The Saussurian security is here removed: a hidden gap opens up between signifier and signified, the bar no longer a bond, but a division.

For Lacan the most general effect of this division is the assigning of gender roles. He treats the fact of having a male or female body as irrelevant before the division: without language there is neither gender nor gender-oriented desire. Once inserted into language the subject becomes at once 'discordant' with it:

There is nothing in the unconscious which accords with the body. The unconscious is discordant. The unconscious is that which, by speaking, determines the subject as being, but as being to be crossed through with that metonymy by which I support desire, in so far as it is endlessly impossible to speak as such (Lacan 1975, in Mitchell and Rose 1982, p. 165).

Language places the subject in the chain of words which binds it to one gender or another, but the force of the unconscious can subvert that definition (see Part V, 10.1 for Lacan's account of sexual difference).

To indicate the dominance of the Father's signifier over the signified, Lacan inverts Saussure's formula, putting the signifier, S, on top, and the signified, s, under the bar: S/s. This also metaphorically suggests the place of unconscious desire as beneath the range of the conscious level of language, out of sight and unnoticed, yet able to shift unpredictably. In an endeavour to clarify this shifting 'under the bar' Lacan speaks of an interaction between the Imaginary and the Symbolic in their operations upon what he calls the Real. The Real for Lacan is the given field of brute existence over which the Imaginary and Symbolic range in their rival attempts to control: one can say that it is that to which all reference and action have relevance, but which can only be handled through signifying practices. This contested field he conceives as a Möbius strip (a band of flat paper with one twist in it, making two sides into one) where Imaginary and Symbolic ambiguously meet. The strip is like the Real; the ambiguity of the side(s) represents the conflict between Imaginary and Symbolic. This is the place where illusions occur, for example, where the ideal ego (the mirror-image) interacts with the Father's definition of the subject, as compared with the way the subject envisions itself in its relation to the mother. In a diagram (Lacan 1977a, p. 197; see also n. 18) he marks a cross-hatched area between two parts of a square: in this grey area the Imaginary sees a signifier one way, the Symbolic another, splitting conscious from unconscious.

This double view of the signifier produces effects of ambiguity. Words are turned in meaning, are 'troped' upon, most notably in metaphor and metonymy. Lacan borrows again from linguistics, this time from Roman Jakobson, who argued that these two tropes were the prime constituents of language (Jakobson and Halle 1956). For Lacan metaphor and metonymy are linguistic formulations of what Freud discerned in condensation and displacement, although the parallel is not exact (1977a; see pp. 23–4). Unconscious desire can mistake one appearance for another *similar to it* and be led to substitute one signifier for another; or it can shift from one thing to another *found with it*, discerned as being more significant for desire, so producing a metonym. Such metaphorical and metonymic effects are constantly at work in language without speakers being aware of it.

Lacan sees an identity between language-forms and the response to repression: the dictum 'the unconscious is structured like a language' is more than an analogy, for the unconscious is born to be no more than its linguistic birthmarks. The fact that every word indicates the absence of what it stands for intensifies the frustration of this child of language, the unconscious, since the absence of satisfaction has now to be accepted. Language imposes a chain of words along which the ego must move while the unconscious remains in search of the object it has lost.

Lacan likens the pattern of metaphor to what happens when the Father's Law, the 'Name-of-the-Father', replaces the 'Desire of the Mother'. He quotes a line from Victor Hugo's 'Booz Endormi' (1977a, p. 156):

> His sheaf was neither miserly nor spiteful.
> (Sa gerbe n'était point avare ni haineuse.)

The sheaf, metonymic itself for all the fertility and fruitfulness of harvest, stands as a metaphor for the potency and generosity of Boaz, the Old Testament patriarch, making clear his role as father and provider in that which grows tall, giving love to his wife and his people. The providing father, offering a delayed satisfaction, is on this account able to say 'No', to demand that delay, to exact that repression. The 'Name/No-of-the-Father' (Lacan's pun – *Le Nom-du-Père/Non-du-Père*) is thus substituted for the 'Desire of the Mother' (p. 200; on this parallel see Muller 1979, p. 44). Where the Desire of the Mother was a lure, the metaphor of the Father's word becomes a kind of trick, playing with an interanimation of the old desire with a promised, forever deferred satisfaction of that desire. The Saussurean bar takes on a temporal dimension: the object is not lost, but merely delayed – for how long in future time, he who is patient enough to learn to speak the Father's 'non' will discover. This implies an incessant referral of the subject from one signifier to the next: the absence of one can only be replaced by another, equally marked with absence. The phallus is transformed into the symbol of patriarchal law (Boaz's 'sheaf' made out to be never 'miserly' and 'spiteful'), whereas it is a signifier of loss, the result of the split caused in the subject upon entry to the Symbolic.

The Father's words, those definitions out of which the object-world is ready-made for the child, are thus fraught with illusion. This is a new development in Freudian theory: every single utterance, spoken or written, is invaded by the unconscious. Lacan's own style, frustrating for the reader, continually mimes this illusion by means of puns, innuendos and outrageous conceits. It is by no means clear whether the theory is thereby shown to be undermined or validated by his own practice in writing or speaking (on this point see also Bowie 1979, p. 149).

Although Lacan thus argues for every single utterance being invaded by the unconscious, the overriding impression is that the Imaginary and the Symbolic are by no means given equal status, that Lacan is disinclined to give the unconscious any power to correct the order which has created it. To say this, however, is to take insufficient account of the very problems posed by the theory, a theory which tries to split in the abstract what cannot be conceived as split in the concrete. In his late seminars Lacan tried to address himself to the problem of the relationship of his three orders. He became increasingly interested in the image of the Borromean knot (three rings, no two of which actually intersect, but are kept knotted together), which he saw as analogous to the relation of his three orders: if one ring is cut, all three fall apart. This gives no pre-eminence to any one of them, and makes any alteration, to say the least, unpredictable. One might here take Beckett's brief play, *Not I*, as an illustration of what happens when the rings fall apart. The central focus of *Not I* is a mouth, picked out by a faint light from the rest of the face, frantically voicing disjointed words and phrases. The Imaginary (the body's experience) is being severed from the Symbolic (the speech of the subject), producing not an illusion, but a delusion of a part-object (a mouth) in the Real, desperately searching out sensory experience:

> when suddenly . . . gradually . . . all went out . . . all that early April morning light . . . and she found herself in the . . . what . . . who? . . . no! . . . she . . . found herself in the dark . . . and if not exactly . . . insentient . . . for she could still hear the buzzing . . . so-called . . . in the ears . . . and a ray of light came and went . . . came and went . . . such as the moon might cast . . . drifting . . . in and out of cloud . . . but so dulled . . . feeling . . . feeling so dulled . . . she did not know . . . what position she was in . . . imagine! . . . what position she was in! . . . (Beckett 1973, p. 2)

Mouth is reliving the trauma of the primordial moment when the body senses its split from the Real. This experience can neither be included in the Imaginary, the realm of illusory wholeness, nor can it be part of the Symbolic, the domain which grants a conditional identity. The traumatic moment can thus return in psychosis as the experience of the 'fragmented body', unique for every subject, remainder and reminder of this fracture, appearing in art as images of grotesque dismemberment – Lacan cites Bosch (Lacan 1977a, p. 4). Language both reveals and conceals the fracture. For Lacan, narrative is the attempt to catch up retrospectively on this traumatic separation, to tell this happening again and again, to re-count it: the narrative of the subject caught in the net of signifiers, the story of 'The Purloined Letter', the story of the repetition compulsion.

6.2 Lacan, literature and the arts

What, then, are the implications and applications of Lacan's theory of
the subject for literature and the arts? Lacan's own example of critical
practice is not to be taken as exemplary. It is nevertheless essential to an
understanding of what is new in psychoanalytic criticism. Although his
treatment of Poe's story is not itself a form of deconstructive criticism as
variously understood by literary critics, it can be seen as playing a part
in sustaining such a criticism. Even when taken as a form of applied
psychoanalytic criticism (Derrida 1975), its emphasis on text-structure
takes it beyond the well-trodden domain. My first purpose is therefore to
explicate it as a form of textual criticism. My second purpose is to use
Lacan's 'Seminar on "The Purloined Letter" ' (1972; orig. publ. 1966)
as a point of departure for more general critical issues, namely its implications for the reading-process (the unconscious as a reader) and, analog-
ously, for the seeing-process (the unconscious as a viewer), and the
relevance the latter has for a criticism of the visual arts.

The traditional Freudian psychoanalytic approaches to literature examined so far have centred on the analysis of the personal psyche, whether
this was the author's, the character's, the reader's, or a combination of
these. The new psychoanalytic structural approach centres on the workings of the text as psyche, based on the theory that the unconscious is
structured like a language. As *Gradiva* was for Freud an allegory of the
return of the repressed, in the form of specific imagery, Poe's 'The Purloined Letter' is for Lacan a symbolic repetition of a structuring fantasy,
his linguistic version of the repetition compulsion. The story is seen as an
allegory of the supremacy of the signifier over the subjects it brings into
being, the way they are forever at the mercy of the repressive differences
exacted by the structure. The traumatic entry into language enforces
the repetition by the unconscious of its own creation. Lacan's reading
of the story concentrates on a repeated scene, only loosely connected with
the mundane events, yet inadvertently structuring their dramatic import.

Poe's tale concerns the double theft of an incriminating letter, initially
sent to an exalted personage Lacan calls 'the queen'. Caught unawares
by the entrance of the king, she leaves it lying innocently on the table.
Enter Minister D, who takes in the scene at a glance, steals the letter in
full view of the helpless queen and the unsuspecting king, and leaves
another in its place. The queen engages the prefect of police to recover
the letter. When, after a systematic search of the minister's apartment, he
fails to recover it, he calls in Dupin, an amateur detective. Dupin reckons
that the minister, like the queen, would leave the letter unconcealed as the

best way of hiding it: thus he finds it, dangling from the mantelpiece in a card-rack, and, arranging a distraction, he steals it, leaving another in its place.

I have explored more fully elsewhere the various analogies to the psychoanalytic process (Wright 1982); here I am only concerned with the bare structure of the repetition and the mode in which it is enacted. For Lacan the story is structured round two scenes, which he calls 'primal scene' and 'repetitive scene'. There is a change of locale and a repetition of a pattern involving three protagonists: scene 1 in the royal boudoir, with the king, the queen, and the minister; scene 2 in the minister's apartment, with the police, the minister, and Dupin. There is a parallel operation: the minister/Dupin takes the letter that the queen/minister leaves unguarded, while the king/police are oblivious. It is this repeated structure, rather than the theft itself, which interests Lacan:

> Thus three moments, structuring three glances, borne by three subjects, incarnated each time by different characters.
>
> The first is a glance that sees nothing: the King and the police.
>
> The second, a glance which sees that the first sees nothing and deludes itself as to the secrecy of what it hides: the Queen, then the Minister.
>
> The third sees that the first two glances leave what should be hidden exposed to whomever would seize it: the Minister, and finally Dupin.
>
> In order to grasp in its unity the intersubjective complex thus described, we would willingly seek a model in the technique legendarily attributed to the ostrich attempting to shield itself from danger; for that technique might ultimately be qualified as political, divided as it here is among three partners; the second believing itself invisible because the first has its head stuck in the ground, and all the while letting the third calmly pluck its rear (Lacan 1972, p. 44).

A glance, a look, are here open to illusory reinterpretation: the letter is precisely what is not seen (by some) and seen differently (by others). In each case the possessor of the letter is made to stand helplessly by while the theft takes place. Each time the letter is appropriated, the subject is captured by the signifier, for which the real letter stands: a love-letter whose content is never revealed, a metaphor for desire, and a pun on the common metonym (letter for letter). 'Falling in possession of the letter – admirable ambiguity of language' (p. 60) is falling into transference, repeating the illusion of the completeness of the sign. The winner is now himself locked in the Imaginary; the loser realizes he has been. Dupin as detective/analyst has a better understanding of the transferential structure of language and its effects. If a subject tries to deny the difference (retains the letter), there is a loss of contact with the Symbolic, hence of determined identity, even gender. The minister has turned the envelope inside out and addressed it to himself 'in an extremely delicate feminine script' (p. 65): the signifier is floating away from him. Sexuality (guaranteed only by difference) and textuality (the language system) are thereby equated, for each depends on a signifying system.

Lacan's reading of Poe's story, his purloining of the letter, has implications for the reading and writing process in general. The triangular structure within the text has shown itself to continue outside. Jacques Derrida has overtaken Lacan's reading (Derrida 1975), to be overtaken by Barbara Johnson in turn (Johnson 1977). The text (the letter) is not the property of a single subject, neither author nor reader. Lacan's disrespectful dismantling of Poe's story has revealed a new figure in the text, something hidden in full view as one reads. The reader/writer is an ostrich burying his head in a book.

The scenes as Lacan describes them are enacted in silence. What structures the uncanny repetitive movements are three glances: the characters are caught out by a look of desire. For Lacan desire is lodged to a degree in all that is seen, every observer taking his object-world for granted, and since the unconscious is inscribed in that desire there will always be a mis-seeing, a *méconnaissance*. Unconscious and repression, desire and lack – this dialectical opposition is present in every visual recognition. The pattern is exaggerated in the perversions: the exhibitionist seeking a perfect confirmation of his desire in the imagined desire of the other; the voyeur finding all his desire in his own looking, afraid to accept the Symbolic Order's dictum that it is not to be found there. Both perversions are denying the uncanny duality of all looking, all objectifications. Lacan identifies a 'scopic drive' for this lodging of desire in looking, a subject's search for a fantasy that represents for him/her the lost phallus. He calls the part of the object round which this fantasy is developed *objet petit a* (see 'Of the gaze as *Objet Petit a*' in Lacan 1977b). Freud was aware of such a drive, but stressed mainly its perverse aspects, whereas Lacan extends it to every act of seeing. The eyes, as one of the modes of access for libido to explore the world, become the instruments of this drive. A drive is not just pleasure-seeking, but is caught up in the signifying-system, characterized by the subject's first entry into that system. For Lacan this happens when the child learns to signify the presence and the absence of the mother. The sexual drive is now deflected from the child's primal object, the mother, into seeking an object always out of reach, to be found only by discovering its trace as an absence in every signifier. This signifying process comes to affect all looking, every recognition at once a finding and a failure to find.

Lacan explains this absence – that the fantasy is always missing from what is seen, that its absence looks through its wished-for presence – in the following way: 'When, in love, I solicit a look, what is profoundly unsatisfying and always missing is that – *You never look at me from the place from which I see you*' (Lacan 1977b, p. 103). The lover is narcissistically projecting an image of a desire that magically completes his own, that looks at him from the place where he wishes her to be; the absence breaks through the fantasy for he finds that she 'never looks at him from the place in which he sees her'. The 'place' is where he has placed her in field of the scopic drive, and she is discovered to be not there. The reality does not correspond to the wish, for her desires must be reckoned with. Lacan adds: '*what I look at is never what I wish to see*' (ibid.).

The eye is not merely an organ of perception but also an organ of pleasure. There is a 'dialectic of the eye and the gaze' (p. 102) – 'the eye' as caught up in the Symbolic Order and 'the gaze' as pursuing a narcissistic fantasy – for every object, subjected as it is to the scopic drive, partakes of the conflict between Imaginary fantasy and the demands of the Symbolic, the desire of the Other.

'I feel a great personal connection with Surrealist painting,' says Lacan, following on from his paper, 'Of structure as an inmixing of an Otherness prerequisite to any subject whatever' (Lacan 1970, p. 197). René Magritte's notorious picture *The Rape* is a case in point of an 'inmixing of an Otherness' as a dialectic of the eye and the gaze. The subject of the picture is apparently a face, framed in what is clearly a woman's hair, styled in what was then a consciously fashionable manner. It turns out, however, that the eyes are nipples, the nose a navel, and the mouth the pubic hair of a woman. If the cultural frame (the woman's hair) is ignored, the naked torso is plainly seen, hidden in full view. The picture is a metaphor for any gaze, signifying desire and an invasion of the other's desire ('The Rape'). The face, framed for culture by the hair, becomes fully sexual, a metaphor for desire being operative in everything. The face not being hidden is indicative of the public (not the pubic) personality, here unmasked, unveiled as the private(s). The (symbolic) eye (the painter's) has disturbed the (narcissistic) gaze of the viewer by turning the illusory eye in the picture into a nipple via a visual pun which removes the blindfold and makes the viewer see the ubiquity of the libidinous. He is caught out by his own looking; his eyes see themselves seeing themselves. This undermines the false idealization of the face, for it reveals that the body is operative at the level of the gaze. Only the fashioned hair gives the contextual clue that relates the cultural to the sexual.

Lacan's concept of the dialectic of the eye and the gaze undermines that view of art which takes it to be an imitation of life. There is no comparison of a representation with a putative reality: mimetic art is still presenting a fantasy, a favoured view of reality. There is no pure seeing. Lacan takes the artist to be saying: 'You want to see? Well, take a look at this!' (Lacan 1977b, p. 101). Art, says Lacan, combines a lure of the gaze (the *trompe l'oeil*) and a taming of it (the *dompte regard*). It tames (rather than consoles, as in Freud) because 'it encourages renunciation' (p. 111), calming the spectator by the turning of his gaze-fantasy into another look, in which there is the simultaneous awareness of desire and lack. Art encourages sublimation rather than idealization because the ideal object, being unrepresentable, is shown to be not hidden but absent. For Lacan, art has more the function of the analyst, offering itself as cause of desire and raising an ethical dimension: the semblance of the (lost) object, like the analyst's equivocal interpretation, provokes and opposes the inertness of the fantasy, producing the uncanny effect (see Adams 1996, for a further development in Lacanian art criticism on these lines).

As an illustration of the lure and the taming, Lacan cites Pliny's anecdote concerning the rivalry between the two Greek painters, Zeuxis and Parrhasios (pp. 103 and 111–2). Zeuxis painted some grapes and thought he had triumphed when they were so lifelike that birds came to peck at them, taken in by the resemblance. Parrhasios, on the other hand, painted a picture of a curtain, and Zeuxis, on coming to look at it, wanted to see what was painted behind it. Now Parrhasios was gleeful because Zeuxis had been taken in. Ernst Gombrich, who also discusses this tale, rightly points out that 'poor Zeuxis' was easily fooled because the likelihood of the painting just being of a curtain was extremely low, and therefore the representation need only be of the most rudimentary quality (Gombrich 1977, p. 173). Lacan (who translates the Latin *linteum*, 'curtain', as 'veil') makes a point similar to that of Gombrich but for a different reason. Neither in the case of the birds nor in the case of the man need the representation be exact: the birds would require only a crude stimulus to be taken in and it is not through a mimesis that the man was deceived. He was not taken in by the veil-as-representation, as he would have been had he imagined it to be a real present veil, but his gaze was lured into searching for the fantasy by the fascination of presence beyond absence. Parrhasios has triumphed for he not only did what Zeuxis did – produce a mimesis – but he performed a further sleight-of-eye, his eye seducing Zeuxis' gaze.

The victory of eye over gaze puts into question that theory in which imagination's task is pure disclosure, in that the ideal, the hidden picture, was shown to be not hidden but absent. The victory, however, is not meant to be one-sided, for the artist knows – and shows the spectator that he knows – that he himself suffers the same lack. He is not just an exhibitionist; he invites the spectator to share, not inner harmony, but desire and lack, not to compete in desire (as to who has the most immediate access to that harmony), but mutually to sustain a renunciation of a *fantasy*.

Lacan's theory of the lure of the Imaginary has been adopted in a critique of the cinema (for a later use of Lacan in film theory, see pp. 182–5). Christian Metz is a theorist and critic who has made systematic use of a combination of Freudian, Kleinian and Lacanian theory to account for what in his view is the peculiar fascination that the film has for the spectator, as the medium most appropriate for the luring of the gaze, and more successful in evading the Symbolic than other arts. The cinema, a field for the scopic drive, situates the spectator in a certain relation to objects such as Melanie Klein described, a relation which corresponds to Lacan's Imaginary. It is up to the film industry to induce 'filmic pleasure' rather than 'filmic unpleasure' by presenting its product as a 'good object', granting what is desired. The cinema lures the ego through being an image of its mirror-self; the screen is ready for narcissistic looking, a mirror for mirroring, thus a double of its double (Metz 1982, pp. 2–4). It is a Lacanian mirror in which the ego pursues its favoured image of itself, imagining that it is inserted into the Symbolic Order. There is no recognition of the screen as mirror-image, because the spectator is deluded into identifying with the camera. The 'all-perceiving subject' is an omnipotent eye, constituting the film within himself, in a pure act of perception (p. 48).

In stressing the importance of the look, Metz considers fetishism, voyeurism and exhibitionism, perversions of the sexual drive that underlie the 'scopic regime' of the cinema, and in these he finds its unconscious roots. Cinema is a series of substitutes that at one and the same time disavow that there is any lack, yet betray that there is because the absence of the (lost) object is conceded by the very nature of the photograph. The fantasy-objects within the film relate desire to the political economy (as in advertising; see the early use of Lacan in Williams 1978, pp. 60–6); it is in the interests of the film industry to keep this relation close. Hence it is essential for the fiction-film to erase the traces of its steps, to hide its lure and its means of production in the 'referential illusion' (Metz 1982, p. 185).

The relation between psychoanalysis and literature has changed as a result of the new developments in French psychoanalysis. Whereas the deliverances of classical psychoanalysis were used towards providing interpretations of actual texts, the effect of Lacan's work has been to revitalize literary theory. With the help of such new theoretical under- standing, approaches may indeed be made to actual texts, but it is as a result of the light they cast upon language and communication that they are most valuable. Lacan's 'Seminar on "The Purloined Letter"' (1972) is central to the (non-)application of his theory to literature, having implica- tions for both reading and writing. It elicits something from one text that can be extrapolated to authors, readers and texts in general.

The lure of all texts lies in a revelation, of things veiled coming to be unveiled, of characters who face shock at this unveiling. From the detect- ive story with its piecing together of clues by an all-seeing Dupin, to the romance with the discovery of the hidden heroine or hero, 'great expecta- tions' are subjected to sudden reversal. Oedipus the would-be detective expects to read the letter according to his narcissistic dream of kingly knowledge, but finds what is unveiled is his blindness. It is not only the characters who are beset by illusion: writer and reader find a lure and pleasure in the letter in which their unconscious is embodied. They can each play Dupin and Minister upon each other. One can have his desire while the other lacks, and vice versa: hence Lacan's claim that desire and lack are together shared by them both. In the pursuance of his desire, which is also the desire of the Other (that is, as specified by the Symbolic Order) the reader may explore the ground of images beyond what the text may *apparently* control. The Symbolic may be subverted, but only to the extent of seeing a hitherto unperceived figure, one hidden in full view. Image study in the past was made to subserve interpretation, often pursu- ing a so-called universal meaning. For Lacan new meanings are the shifts of desire in language, the question being whose desire shall purloin the letter.

But the answer cannot be entrusted to an agreement between two sub- jects, caught as they are in a specular relation. Psychoanalysis and the reading process (both inside and outside the clinical situation) require the awareness of the Other as a checkpoint. The grey area, the Möbius strip over which the purloining takes place, is unlike that of Green's or Winnicott's aesthetic play for two, because the power of the letter, of interest to kings and the police, implies an Other for both of them, not a transcendental signified, but language, of which it is not the case that only two can play. Lacan does not want analysis to become 'the relation of two bodies between which is established a phantasmic communication' (Lacan

1977a, pp. 90–1). The space of interpretation is not merely 'potential', because the interpretative play has to come to terms with the impossible Real (brute nature in self and world and their history), not only the Possible. This complicates the implication of any act of reading and writing, for it indicates that modern psychoanalysis may have a *general* task to play in theory, and not a particular one with regard to some lower-level problem. Instead of enlisting the critic as analyst/archaeologist digging for a repressed signified (Freud's main project in *Gradiva*), it involves the critic as analysand/rhetorician, attentive to the workings of the text (Freud's project in slips and jokes). What is wanted is not a spade, but a pen.

6.3 The turn of the reader/writer

The 'turn' of the reader/writer is here used in a double sense: first, because it is their turn to be considered as a site where meaning is produced and where the distinction between them is no longer a hard and fast one; and second, because with the influence of Lacan's definition of the unconscious as structured like a language, the phenomena of transference in reading become all-pervasive, the structures of desire in language turning (in the sense of affecting) reader and writer alike.

The division I have made between 'structural' and 'post-structural' is not a neat historical one. Lacan, for example, is equally part of the post-structural enterprise. The division I am making is based on a practice of reading, in so far as it concerns psychoanalytic criticism. In one case (this section) the focus is on the reader in the text, both text of life and literary text, both determined by history and hence already written before the subject arrives on the scene. It is the reader who is transformed rather than the text. In the other case (next section) the capture of the reader is not taken as final. She can by a dialectical play move the text on to a new meaning, undermining its old power and deriving new power by exposing the text as self-contradictory. Lacan's procedure is to challenge the misreadings of past readers of Freud, by focusing on Freud the semiotician as distinct from Freud the humanist (Ernst Kris), or Freud the biologist (Sulloway 1979); Jacques Derrida's procedure is to subject Freud's texts to the same scrutiny as any other text, reading Freud's revolutionary discoveries against him, using the very transferential structures that Freud discovered in language to undermine *his* system. Freud's texts too are at odds with themselves and cannot be frozen into a metapsychology.

In either case the reader/writer distinction is no longer valid because making sense of the sign-system implicates both: each is caught in the net of signs, is up against language. Reading, writing and criticism are part of a continuum whereby readers write in the act of reading and writers are shown to read in the act of writing. Barthes and Balzac are jointly implicated when the story *Sarrasine* is turned into *S/Z* (Barthes 1975; on this very point see Johnson 1978, p. 9: 'The difference between literature and criticism consists perhaps only in the fact that criticism is more likely to be blind to the way in which its own critical difference from itself makes it, in the final analysis, literary'). Texts can be made to turn upon themselves, meaning both less and more than the writer may have intended. The psychoanalytic concept of transference in its extended form (which I will recapitulate as I proceed) has changed the way in which the production of meaning is to be conceived. The examples about to be discussed are Roland Barthes' *A Lover's Discourse* (1979) and Shoshana Felman's 'Turning the screw of interpretation' (1977): both focus on the dilemma of the reader/lover in transference, albeit in different ways. Barthes is the reader of his own writing, self-consciously displaying the various effects of transference, and it is in this sense that he is performing a higher-level psychoanalytic criticism. Felman, while making a spectacular advance and attack on previous psychoanalytic criticism, is more orthodox in so far as she is working on the text of another writer.

A Lover's Discourse nicely illustrates the collapsing of the reader/writer/ critic distinction. In his introduction Barthes explains both his detachment from and involvement with the persona of the book:

> In order to compose this amorous subject, pieces of various origin have been 'put together'. Some come from an ordinary reading, that of Goethe's *Werther*. Some come from insistent readings (Plato's *Symposium*, Zen, psychoanalysis, certain Mystics, Nietzsche, German lieder). Some come from conversations with friends. And there are some which come from my own life (Barthes 1979, p. 8).

The 'I' of the text is both a person and a scene. 'I' is a problematic word; in 'To write: an intransitive verb?' (1972) Barthes examines its use. He wishes to show that a writer is not speaking from the position of a spontaneous bourgeois subject (the transitive 'I write the book'), but is rather subject to the system that places him, inseparable from his act, defined by the system (the intransitive 'I write'). To elaborate this he invents an image from grammar. Culture produces an illusory 'passive' *I*, the nature of which is wholly externally defined. The experiencing self produces an illusory 'active' *I*, the source of action appearing to be a pure ego without origin. The truth is half-way – a 'middle voice', Barthes' pun, since the voice is the very thing that is in question. He thereby shows a Lacanian sensitivity to the power of language over the body, for the pronoun 'I', 'the *je* and what is deprived of the mark *je*' (1972, p. 144), is one of the most powerful tools for the subjugation of meaning. There is that in the body which is not represented by 'je' in the ears of others, thus being deprived of expression.

In *A Lover's Discourse* the Imaginary is given a 'je' which will not fit the body. The lover is gagged by the Symbolic, yet trying to utter through forcing the Imaginary to follow the bourgeois signifier. The particular constraints forced upon the lover are the 'figures' that make him one (the 'fragments' of the discourse), not to be understood in a rhetorical sense. The figures are episodes, characteristic of a romantic lover's experience, self-enclosed courses of thought and feeling, rituals, obsessive fancies, to which the lover is bound: 'A figure is established if at least someone can say: "That's so true! I recognize that scene of language"' (1979, p. 4). Barthes wishes to offset the seductive influences of the figures of love, the chapters of cultural narrative imposed upon the subject, 'the *love story*, subjugated to the great narrative Other, to that general opinion which disparages any excessive force and wants the subject himself to reduce the great imaginary current' (p. 7). To make it impossible for the figures to fall into a conventional narrative he deliberately eschews an order of development by putting them in alphabetical order, a gesture of unlearning the ABC. To put something in alphabetical order that has some other order is deliberately to disturb it: the body's alphabet becomes the clearer as the culture's alphabet becomes blurred. Culture's version of the alphabet would have made the narrative flow. Nevertheless, he wants to sensitize the reader to the structure of these influences, however random they appear. It is not so much an individual psychology he is interested in, but the cultural fabrications, the traps there are for beings of passion. He notes the irrational swervings and sudden reversals which fail to break out of the given figure, as if the body was still showing its powers of resistance while helpless within the order, 'I am a Daruma Doll, a legless toy endlessly poked and pushed, but *finally* regaining its balance, assured by an inner balancing pin' (p. 141). This is part of a fragment under the title *This can't go on*. The titles and marginal notes have an effect he describes as 'à la Brecht', encouraging an alienation effect at the same time as an identification. The reader is to recognize the familiar schemes of emotion, the conventional sequences of thought, in order to distance himself from them. Hence the lover/writer and the critic/reader continually intersect.

The Barthesian lover does not have access to these alienation effects, safely tucked away as they are in titles, sub-titles and marginalia. He has to do the best he can, and this includes modelling himself on others. He needs a book to tell him how he feels. One might see him as having the same problem as E. T. A. Hoffmann's readerly/writerly cat:

> I decided that as a youth of erudition I should come to a clear understanding of my condition and began immediately, although with effort, to study Ovid's *De arte amandi*, as well as Manso's *Art of Loving*; but none of the characteristics of a lover given in these works seemed to fit me properly. It occurred to me suddenly that I had read in some play that an unquestionable spirit and a neglected beard are specific characteristics of a lover. I looked in the mirror. Heavens, my beard was neglected. Heavens, my spirit was unquestionable.
>
> Since I now knew that all was correct with the way I was in love, my soul was comforted (Hoffmann 1969).

In *A Lover's Discourse* a voice speaks about the Romantic novel *The Sorrows of Young Werther* in which a lover makes the description of his love all but a full-time occupation. Although Barthes' lover is struck only by Werther's passion for a woman he may not possess, it is worth noting that Goethe's epistolary novel revolves round a lover who also reads. He models himself on a Greek poet, Homer – in the spring and summer – and on a Celtic bard, Ossian (an impersonation of an impersonation, since the 'bard' was Macpherson) – in autumn and winter.

Barthes reads psychoanalysis. He knows that love, even and especially romantic love, is transference love. In the artificial hot-house conditions of the psychoanalytic encounter the old, the primal love, is reactivated, without having to wait for the right 'figure' (in Barthes' sense) to turn up.

In *A Lover's Discourse* the amorous subject addresses the (absent) mother. Here the archetypal lover/reader is the infant looking for links in the world/text which will bridge the gap left by the primal experience of separation. It is to be noted that Barthes sometimes adopts the benign perspective of Winnicott, at other times the dire perspective of Lacan, so that the concept 'Imaginary' is not purely Lacanian. In the figure 'Waiting', for instance, the lover knows that he is playing with reality (Winnicott's book is cited in a footnote). Waiting by the telephone for the 'call' of the beloved is like waiting for the mother to reappear:

> The being I am waiting for is not real. Like the mother's breast for the infant, 'I create and re-create it over and over, starting from my capacity to love, starting from my need for it': the other comes here where I am waiting, here where I have already created him/her. And

if the other does not come, I hallucinate the other: waiting is a delirium (Barthes 1979, p. 39).

This is a non-pathological form of playing out one's lack (with the sound of a voice), taking place in a moment prior to the constricting definitions of language. Other moments are not so benign and can only be endured by making a fetish of the play-thing. The figure headed 'The ribbon' designates a Lacanian moment, where the amorous subject becomes fixated upon every object the loved one has touched, as though it was a part of that body: 'Werther multiplies the gestures of fetishism: he kisses the knot of ribbon Charlotte has given him for his birthday, the letter she sends him (even putting the sand to his lips), the pistols she has never touched' (p. 173). Werther's kissing the ribbon is not simply kissing something that metonymically stands for Charlotte, for the lover is kissing what metaphorically – through its being a sign of absence – can stand for what the Mother lacks. This is no benign transitional object enabling the lover/ infant to effect his separation, but a pursuit of something he is unwilling to surrender, his narcissism. In the case of the transitional object the play is a game for two in which narcissism is modified by encounter with that of another: in the case of the *objet a* (Lacan is here alluded to) the fantasy pursued erases the beloved, who is repeatedly 'stifled' beneath the 'massive utterance' of the lover's discourse (p. 165, 'I am odious').

Another level of transference is that of the critic, who is both analysand and analyst. This joint function has already been discussed in the theory of André Green and in an example of Norman Holland's practice. In the present case a Lacanian model of transference is implied in that *A Lover's Discourse* is not just a matter of a pact between two subjects. Readers love texts, as Barthes shows in *The Pleasure of the Text*, and the *Lover's Discourse* demonstrates how that love can be a distorting infatuation, with the self caught in the existing, unsuspected signifying chain. Here is a writer giving the writer's game away in a game of his own, the writer's game being that of entrapping the narcissistic reader in a collusion of which even the writer is not fully aware. In showing how a text captures a reader Barthes enables *his* reader to escape capture both from transference and from the ideology that has contributed to it. He thus goes further than Lacan and further than Green. On the one hand he shows how 'writerly' texts set out actively to disturb the 'naive' reader's transference; on the other hand he shows how 'readerly' texts may be thawed from their classic crystallization in a discourse in which writers, readers and critics endeavour to prevent the fixation of the text, its freezing back into ideology.

In her article 'Turning the screw of interpretation' (1977) Shoshana Felman is concerned precisely with keeping the text open and on the move. Like Barthes she reveals the transference of which lovers and critics are unaware, both as readers within the text and as readers of the text. The story she investigates is Henry James's *The Turn of the Screw*. She shows how the discourse of the critics is caught up within the transferential structures of the story so that one set of unwitting analysands (the critics) are merely repeating the antics of another set of unwitting analysands (the characters). The act of interpretation ('turning the screw') links literature and psychoanalysis in a joint and hazardous enterprise, since both set the process of transference going, unbeknownst to naive and sophisticated readers alike, who believe there is a meaning there to be disclosed.

The setting of the story is a large country house, where a new governess takes charge of two young children in the absence of the owner, their uncle and guardian. She is aided by the housekeeper, Mrs Grose, and hindered by what she takes to be the 'ghosts' of two past servants, who appear to visit at intervals. The critical debate that Felman investigates centres around whether the governess is trying to save her charges from evil (the ghosts exist) or whether the governess is hopelessly neurotic (the ghosts are a projection of her repressed passion for the absent master). In a hundred-page virtuoso performance Felman shows the efforts on both sides to be doomed, already anticipated by the canny/uncanny textual strategies she uncovers:

> The reader of *The Turn of the Screw* can choose either to *believe* the governess, and thus to behave like Mrs Grose, or *not to believe the governess*, and thus to behave precisely *like the governess*. Since it is the governess who, within the text, plays the role of suspicious reader, occupies the place of the interpreter, to *suspect* that place and that position is, therefore, *to take it*. To demystify the governess is only possible on one condition: the condition of *repeating* the governess's very gesture. The text thus constitutes a reading of its two possible readings, both of which, in the course of that reading, it deconstructs (1977, p. 190).

Or perhaps we should say, Felman deconstructs, because, like Poe's Dupin, she 'knows *what to repeat*' (Johnson 1977, p. 496). She is the analyst, anticipating the capture of her analysand – readers, neatly turning their very misreadings against them, while making James, Freud and Lacan work for her own reading strategy, by citing them out of context, as part of a general intertext:

I didn't describe to you the purpose of it . . . at all, I described to
you . . . the effect of it – which is a very different thing (Felman
1977, p. 94, citing James, *The Sacred Fount*).

The unconscious . . . is most effectively misleading when it is caught
in the act (Felman 1977, p. 199, citing Lacan).

In Lacan's model of transference the analyst is 'absent' in order that
the analysand may do the analysing, refusing the place assigned to him
as 'subject presumed to know', playing 'dummy' instead (Lacan 1977a,
p. 229). Similarly, there is a master who will not play, both within the
story (the owner of the house to whom the governess addresses letters),
and outside the story (the author of the text who is addressed regarding
the meaning of his tale). 'The Master's discourse is very like the condition
of the unconscious as such: Law itself is but a form of Censorship' (Felman
1977, p. 145). Hence, quotes Felman, making the object-language of the
text act as her meta-commentary, ' "The story *won't* tell," said Douglas;
"not in any literal, vulgar way" ' (p. 106). The literal is the vulgar (what
Barthes calls the 'prattling text' (Barthes 1977, p. 5)), because it nails
signifier to signified, stopping the production of meaning, closing up the
gap that is the unconscious, the 'won't tell'.
    Felman gets down to the rhetorical functioning of the text, its deferring
of meaning through figures of desire, 'how' the story means, rather than
'what' it means (Felman 1977, p. 119). The Jamesian metaphor of seeing
is enlisted as a metaphor for transference, in that it becomes part of a
chain, seeing–reading–interpreting–viewing through the eyes of the unconscious, links by which meaning is transferred and agonized over: 'What
it was most impossible to get rid of was the cruel idea that whatever I
[the governess] had seen, Miles and Flora [the children] saw *more* –
things terrible and unguessable and that sprang from dreadful passages of
intercourse in the past' (Felman, p. 158, citing James). The business of
passing on the story involves both the actual transferring of a manuscript,
and the transference of love between the couples who pass it on, and this
in turn requires the exchange of looks: ' "Yes, she was in love . . . *I saw it,
and she saw I saw it*; but neither of us spoke of it" ' (Felman, p. 132,
citing James; her italics). The manuscript, since it was sent through the
post, had (presumes Felman) an address on it: the story of the governess
is a letter and a story about letters. Hence 'letter' becomes a metaphor of
the manuscript of the story and of the narrative as a whole, sent to the
reader. There is thus a parallel between the letters in the story we and
the characters never get to read and the story as a whole which defeats our

reading, but which nevertheless determines a story (for the readers in the text) and a history (for the critics in the world). The governess begins as detective and ends up as criminal, grasping a dead child. The reader begins as analyst and ends up as analysand, reactivating his past traumas. Instead of the reader getting hold of the story, says Felman, the reading effect is that of the story getting hold of readers, catching them out in a fiction of mastery.

This is an exemplary psychoanalytic reading, pursuing the interrelationship of psyche and text, without either one mastering the other, as was the case with classical applied psychoanalysis. Yet there are a few questions one might like to raise, which are not easily met. Where is the writer's transference in all this? James's repression is praised by Felman, but not analysed: 'James, like the Master in *The Turn of the Screw*, doesn't want to *know* anything about it' (p. 205); 'James's reader-trap' is 'a *trap set for suspicion*'; (citing James) 'an *amusette* to catch those not easily caught' (p. 188). Why is James out to catch readers? And why are we, with Felman, so gratified to be inscribed and comprehended by the text, for in the end we are no wiser than any other poor dupe that misreads, 'as we see the very madness of our own art staring back at us . . . the joke is indeed on us; the worry ours' (p. 207). But what if the governess, Mrs Grose, the children, the 'undead' servants, previous duped readers, James himself, do not like the place assigned to them in 'the text', and are waiting, like the characters in a fairy tale, to be finally disenchanted, freed from the game of servants and masters? It seems almost as if Felman, in her desire to put psychoanalysis and literature on an equal footing, had reintroduced (repeated) the hierarchies of master and slave in her reading. The text lies in wait, ready to occupy the subject. The scene of reading has become the story of the capture of the psyche.

7
Post-Structural Psychoanalysis: Text as Psyche

7.1 Derrida and the scene of writing

Unlimited ink has by now been spilt on Derrida's project. His sustained attack on the western metaphysical tradition is grounded in a notion of writing as devalued and repressed by that tradition. The main culprit singled out is philosophy with its desire to fasten words upon the world once and for all. What is at stake is not just writing with the letters of the alphabet, but any activity which sorts out the world into differing units. In the previous section the focus was on reading and writing as interdependent activities to the extent that both involve a continuing act of interpretation that is never final. Derrida's deconstructive approach to reading is already implicated in the critical practice of Barthes and Felman, but the Lacanian emphasis was more on the way both readers and writers were determined by the text, were being written by the very text they thought they were reading.

In his structuralist phase Lacan stressed the supremacy of the signifier in determining subjects in their acts. But for Derrida the signifier is not so supreme, and it is in pursuit of that argument that he substitutes and resubstitutes a set of terms of his own devising. These terms, to name only the most persistent, 'writing', 'trace', 'differance', 'dissemination', are designed to show the way any text undermines itself. Writing at once represses and reveals desire ('writing is unthinkable without repression' (Derrida 1978, p. 226)). Words, whether spoken or written, are subject to '*différance*', differing from and deferring any transient fixation of meaning. Derrida refers to this process as the sign being 'under erasure', the rubbing out being performed by past memories ('traces') in the unconscious, 'archives which are *always already* transcriptions' (p. 211), not copies, but unconscious interpretations. In Derrida's reading of Freud (to which I will be turning) the unconscious, through memories non-verbal as well as verbal, thus becomes active in the production of meaning, its traces being present in every word. Whereas for Derrida the unconscious is a weave of pure traces, for Lacan the unconscious is structured like a language. So wherein lies the difference? One is saying that the unconscious is operative in language all the time (seeing text as psyche). The other maintains that the entire unconscious is structured like a language (seeing psyche as text). It is a marked distinction of emphasis rather than a radical disagreement. Lacan places the emphasis on language's imposition of a mould which creates the unconscious, Derrida places it upon the unconscious's ability to escape the mould. Derrida is nearer to certain modifications made by followers of Lacan, in which the unconscious, 'rather than a language, is the very condition of language' (Laplanche and Leclaire 1972, p. 178).

The disagreement may in part be attributable to the difference of their interests, which makes it difficult to enlist them in the same venture, the investigation of the theory of the text. Lacan as a psychoanalyst uses texts as illustrative material for a theory of the genesis of the subject in relation to language (what makes a *subject* being his primary concern). Derrida as a philosopher looks at texts in order to undermine their power over subjects (what makes a *text* being his primary concern). This may be illustrated by their analyses of two literary texts, Lacan's reading of 'The Purloined Letter', and Derrida's reading of Kafka's parable 'Before the Law'. Where Lacan reads Poe's story as an allegory of the supremacy of the signifier, subjects being at the mercy of the law that made them, Derrida reads Kafka's story as a parable of a failure to exert one's freedom through the law, the point of the story being that the law is there for you. There is a pun in the title: 'before the law' can mean either prior to the law (you are the legislator), or up in front of the law (it legislates over you). In Kafka's story the man from the country allows the doorkeeper to bar the way, only to find out just before his death that the door had been there for him alone (Derrida 1982).

What Derrida derives from his reading of Freud is not only a deconstruction of Freud's texts but a self-reflection upon the very activity of deconstruction itself. It is Freud's discovery of the unconscious which has prepared the way both for a theory of textual deconstruction and for a deconstruction of the mode of that discovery. For Derrida, Freud becomes a Derridean *avant la lettre*, paradoxically, by showing this very idiom to be a mere figure of speech/writing. There is no 'before the letter': the subject *is* the subject of writing, both its product (as already written) and its producer (as rewriting the written). In describing the perceptual apparatus in terms which illustrate this double movement, 'Freud performs for us the scene of writing' (Derrida 1978, p. 229). The metaphors of which Freud avails himself describe a graphic system of representation; Derrida pursues these images of writing through a series of texts spanning thirty years:

> From the *Project* (1885) to the 'Note Upon the Mystic Writing-Pad' (1925), a strange procession: a problematic of breaching is elaborated only to conform increasingly to a metaphorics of the written trace. From a system of traces functioning according to a model which Freud would have preferred to be a natural one, and from which writing is entirely absent, we proceed toward a configuration of traces which can no longer be represented except by the structure and functioning of writing (p. 200).

That is to say, Freud's neurological metaphors, such as 'breaching' (*Bahnung*), can retrospectively be seen to perform the movements of writing, instituting 'differance' among a set of resistant neurones that 'breach' and thus record the traces in response to external stimuli, these traces continually left in the memory. They are not to be conceived of as emerging pristine at some future date. According to Freud they already exist loaded with feelings of fear and desire, but are open to further interpretation (as his example of 'Emma' shows (Freud I, pp. 353–4)). Like the dream-thoughts in Freud's theory of dream interpretation they cannot be directly transcribed, but have to be 'reproduced', *nachträglich*, after the event.

It is from Freud's 'Note upon the mystic writing-pad' that Derrida is able to develop the full potential of the metaphor of the psyche as a writing machine, one with a potentially disruptive element built in it. The 'mystic writing-pad' is a child's play-thing, still common today, used for rapid notes that can be quickly erased to enable later ones to be written. One writes with a simple stylus upon a celluloid surface under which is a piece of paper in loose contact with a waxen pad. The writing appears because of the temporary adhering of the paper to the wax.

Freud detects three particular analogies between this writing apparatus and the perceptual apparatus, to which Derrida draws attention: (1) the celluloid corresponds to the protection that the psyche institutes for itself against an excess of stimuli from without; (2) the fact that the paper is re-usable represents the endless capacity of the perceptual system for responding to sensory stimuli without becoming overloaded in any way;

(3) the impressions that actually remain on the underlying wax – 'legible in suitable lights', as Freud puts it (XIX, p. 230) – stand for unconscious traces which remain hidden in the unconscious. Derrida fixes upon the writing metaphor, especially through the third analogy, which brings out the continuous interaction of those hidden traces with the succeeding script. The unconscious is thus active at complex and profound levels as the marks of repression are inscribed. Blurrings and obliterations take place beneath the concealing paper. Derrida sees the possibility of the unconscious as thus active in all experience with the signifiers of the repressive order, a pointer to the deconstructive potential of all reading, which is only a form of rewriting, becoming 'legible in certain lights'.

One aspect of the model is singled out by Derrida for its inadequacy. In using a material metaphor for the psyche, Freud is omitting its spontaneity. Freud's use of the metaphor of writing points to what he has omitted: that the effects of history in experience must take the investigation outside that of a narrowly physicalistic psychology. The metaphor that Freud would finally have to cast away once his neurological theory had been achieved betrays the reason why this cannot be done. He did not see the significance of his own metaphor: that the unconscious is actively productive in the signifying system. The discoverer of the unconscious has had his own writings examined for their unconscious effects. Freud saw the mind as being inscribed upon by what it perceived. Thus a mechanical image of the brain was inadequate in itself to account for the influences of history.

As a general conclusion Derrida proposes that it is time for the signifier and all the forms involved in the construction of the signifier to become the focus of attention in order to resist the logocentric fixation upon plausible but illusory signifieds. The unconscious is hypersensitive to the signifying machines of repression. Derrida quotes Freud as noting the link of pen and penis, writing on white paper and sexual penetration, and praises Melanie Klein for her revelation of the way school activities – we might rename the three Rs as Reading, Writing and Repression – show the presence of strong unconscious investment. The teaching of reading and writing is in both method and content the establishment of the channelling of desire, and sexuality will invade them both. Derrida especially notes the ambivalence of Klein's good and bad objects co-present in the equipment of writing, an uncanny mingling, 'writing as sweet nourishment or excrement, the trace as seed or mortal germ, wealth or weapon, detritus and/or penis etc.' (Derrida 1978, p. 231). This is the theme of deconstruction itself – is literature a 'wealth' generously spread for readers or a 'weapon' to be used against the authority? Is writing the chief instrument of repression or is it the means by which the symbolic may be subverted?

7.2 The return of Freud: jokes and the uncanny

This double question marks the return of Freud in this book, in that it will be the occasion of reading him with a difference. He will be read not as in Part I for the content of his theory, but for the 'uncanniness' or 'canniness' of his writing, that is according to the way his writing reveals or conceals unconscious intention. Jokes and the unconscious go together, for the uncanny works like a joke, and the joke partakes of the uncanny: both participate in the double movement of the return of the repressed and the return of repression. On the one hand, both can appear to be a reassurance that desires will be satisfied; on the other, both can be an unexpected denial of what was hoped for.

One might sum up the Freudian development followed so far by seeing id-psychology as focusing on the return of the repressed, ego-psychology on the return of repression, and object-relations theory as uneasily trying to reconcile the two. Deconstructive readings of Freud try rather to reveal the tension, to elicit the contradictions that disturb fixed logical categorizations. Jonathan Culler's summary makes this abundantly clear:

> Freud begins with a series of hierarchical oppositions: normal/pathological, sanity/insanity, real/imaginary, experience/dream, conscious/unconscious, life/death. In each case the first term has been conceived as prior, a plenitude of which the second is a negation or complication. Situated on the margin of the first term, the second term designates an undesirable, dispensable deviation. Freud's investigations deconstruct these oppositions by identifying what is at stake in our desire to repress the second term and showing that in fact each first term can be seen as a special case of the fundamentals designated by the second term, which in this process is transformed. Understanding of the marginal deviant term becomes a condition of understanding the supposed prior term. . . . These deconstructive reversals, which give pride of place to what had been thought marginal, are responsible for much of the revolutionary impact of Freudian theory (Culler 1983, pp. 160–1).

Both Freud's full-scale investigation into *Jokes and their Relation to the Unconscious* (1905) and his more tentative inquiry into 'The uncanny'

(1919) have provided ample material for such deconstructive reversals. I shall begin with an account of Samuel Weber's reading of Freud's *Jokes*, because here the joke served as a pivot for a most searching investigation into the corpus of Freud's work, one centrally concerned with recovering the Freud that got lost in translation. In *The Legend of Freud* Weber sets out to show 'the conflictual dynamics of the unconscious' (1982, p. xvi) at work in the very theory of the unconscious itself. He argues that the duplicity Freud detects in the ego's attempts to systematize the external in response to its narcissistic desires will erupt in that theory itself. Although Freud's meta-psychological writings betray a tendency to underestimate the force of the unconscious (the crucial texts picked out are 'Project' (1895), *Three Essays* (1905) and *Beyond the Pleasure Principle* (1920); see, for example, Laplanche 1976), it is ironically his being drawn to the joke that points the way to the proper estimation of that force.

As we have seen earlier, ego-psychology assumes that the pleasure gained from the joke is due to its bringing about the play of energies in the psyche, for the ultimate benefit of the rational ego, which emerges refreshed and fortified. Deconstructive criticism of Freud, however, finds in his theory of the joke (1905) an anticipation of his theory of narcissism (1914), with a consequent shift of emphasis (Mehlman 1975; Weber 1977, 1982). The ego is no longer seen as a force that synthesizes and stabilizes, but as an ego committed to the affirmation of its illusory power.

Weber's *Auseinandersetzung* with Freud's joke theory ('analyzed into its components – that is, *auseinandergesetzt* – the word designates a process of decomposition or analysis'; used by Freud, and by Weber against Freud (Weber 1982, p. 24)), centres on his challenge to the distinction Freud upholds between the 'innocent' joke of pure pleasure and the 'tendentious' joke, the joke with a purpose. Before proceeding with Weber's analysis I need to clarify the organization and general presentation of Freud's argument.

Freud distinguishes three stages in the evolution of the joke, arising from a basis of primitive play. The first is at the level of the child's delight in games of recognition, which often manifests itself in verbal play, for 'children, who, as we know, are in the habit of treating words as things, tend to expect words to have the same meaning behind them' (VIII, p. 120). The pleasure of such recognition, Freud maintains, does not come from a sense of power but from a saving of psychic energy. This saving is in itself enjoyable (Weber presumes it 'saves' the effort of discriminating), so according to Freud 'the games founded on this pleasure make use of the mechanism of damming up only in order to increase the amount of such pleasure' (p. 122). This pretence of frustration on the child's part, making the play not quite so innocent, is a throw-away insight that should perhaps be rendered unto Freud.

The second stage of the joke's development moves it from the level of play to that of the 'jest' (*Scherz*). It entails making a concession to the growing demands of the intellect, which is not content to rest on the absurd chiming of words. There is a meaning, but it is of no consequence: 'the meaning of the joke is merely to protect that pleasure from being done away with by criticism' (p. 131). What distinguishes the jest from the joke proper (*Witz*) is that it is 'non-tendentious'; it has no axe to grind – its sole purpose is to give pleasure.

The third stage, then, is the joke proper, the 'tendentious' joke, in which there is a distinct purpose, taking the form of challenging either a person or a social inhibition. There are two forms, the hostile and the obscene, the first giving the opportunity to express 'aggressiveness, satire, or defence', the second 'serving the purpose of an exposure' (p. 97). The verbal play is now working in conjunction with this tendentious purpose. Freud envisages this type of joke as embedded in a three-person situation. The teller requires a listener as 'ally': the first and third person are thus linked in being in an alliance against the second person or object, the butt of the joke. As a prototype of the tendentious joke Freud cites the example of 'smut', the dirty joke, where the first and third person are enabled to share an imagined mastery over the forbidden and inaccessible sexual object, the woman, allowing a discharge of frustration in a seduction whose imaginary nature partakes of a fancied reality through being publicly shared (pp. 97–102). The alliance is confirmed by the spontaneous laughter in which the complicity of the third person in this mutual release of tension (the 'saving' of psychic energy) is made obvious to both. This 'economy of psychical expenditure' involves a double pleasure, the verbal play itself, which is the core (*Kern*), and the pleasure of lifting the inhibition, which is the casing (*Hülle*) (p. 138).

This is the point around which Weber organizes his *Auseinandersetzung* with the joke theory. His deconstructive intent is directed particularly at dismantling the distinction between the 'innocent' core and the 'tendentious' casing. Weber sees Freud's continual stress upon the playful aspect of the joke as negating a narcissistic desire, which takes the form of reducing all that is alien in the external to the sameness of unity. Even a rhyme exemplifies a determination to erase difference and establish sameness, as Weber puts it, serving 'the interests of the narcissistic ego bent upon reducing alterity to a variation of identity' (Weber 1982, p. 98). The example that comes to my mind here is a well-known post-Freudian Jewish joke which employs a Jewish practice of using a rhyming tag as a dismissive gesture, one that denies difference. It is about the Jewish mother, who, on being told about the Oedipus complex, says 'Oedipus-Schmoedipus – What does it matter as long as he loves his mother?' In the very rejection of the classification she is exemplifying the actual narcissistic idealization which it defines. The play on words can hardly be defined as innocent.

The joke is thus not merely a comforting collusion in which a temporary relief is effected from the demands of repression, but a place of conflict. Weber begins his unravelling of Freud's distinction by examining the position of the third person, the listener. He finds that it is curious, in that it combines a spontaneous unconscious element, namely the laughter itself, with a desire for complicity with the Other ('the third person'). There is an ambivalence in the 'third person' of the joke, for though, on the one hand, it represents the spontaneous breakthrough of the id in that bodily phenomenon of laughter, on the other, it partakes of the superego, which characteristically voices its demands in the public grammatical third person. The narcissistic confidence in the 'continuity of Self and Other' is reassured by the Other's complicity. The first and third persons are fused – id and superego become identical in the illusion of the joke. The third person is that nameless Other who is listening to you; the laughter is an id-confirmation of a superego agreement. The 'classical' double-bind (the way Freud sees the father's command to the son) in the superego's command to the ego – 'Be like me! Be yourself!' – is thus apparently resolved (p. 107).

The teller thus seeks a complicitous laugh for his tampering with the law. The readiness of the hearer to provide such a laugh, however, exposes him to being caught out by an unscrupulous teller. There are jokes which capitalize upon the joke situation itself, exploiting the hearer's willingness to challenge the taboo. Weber considers the most narcissistic of jokes to be the take-in joke or shaggy-dog story, in German *Aufsitzer* (metaphorical origin 'to straddle', literal meaning 'to dupe' (pp. 80–2)), mentioned by Freud in a footnote as 'idiocy masquerading in the form of a joke' (VIII, p. 138). The *Aufsitzer* is a joke on the hearer, who has been duped into the expectation of a 'good joke', namely one in which he is invited to join in the challenge to the taboo, but he is himself 'had', for there is no satisfaction to be gained. The teller enjoys a sense of control over the hearer, who has now betrayed himself in his readiness to break the taboo. By means of this trick the ego is able to 'install' the superego, without having to give up its narcissistic desire for a would-be-safe identity (Weber 1982, p. 107).

The border between the private and the public definition of the self is precisely one where the joke of the gap between interpretation and action can go several ways at once, for there is more than one interpretation of an action. Hence the joke cannot be seen either solely as a challenge to authority (Bakhtin's view of laughter; Bakhtin 1968), or as a 'social act' (Kris's view of laughter). It is neither solely 'weapon' of liberation from repression and oppression, nor solely part of the 'wealth' of nurturing culture (see Derrida above on 'writing'). Texts, and theories about texts, are always at the mercy of subversion from whatever direction, private or public, as Weber's deconstruction of Freud has illustrated. Freud's theory of the joke leads to 'the Joke of Theory' (Weber 1978, p. 28). It shows 'that what had been thought marginal' (see Culler above), here the shaggy-dog story, can lead to a redefinition of the general term 'joke'.

There is a link here with the uncanny, in that it too can be looked upon as a failure of theory in practice. This is certainly the burden of the many critical readings of Freud's essay in so far as he makes use of E. T. A. Hoffmann's story 'The Sandman' as a prime example. An early reading of this essay (Prawer 1965) pronounced Hoffmann to be master of the uncanny compared with Freud's rendering of him. This is still endorsed, but with a difference: take Freud's performance in the essay overall and he is reinstated as Hoffmann's equal. There have been at least nine recent readings of Freud's essay, all showing in various ways the unmistakable imprint of Lacan and Derrida, some of which I shall be citing. The general view is that it would indeed be a mistake to let Freud's analysis of Hoffmann be the last word on the uncanny. What is interesting is precisely the inadequacy of his interpretation, and how this inadequacy has produced a whole series of after-effects. As was the case with the stories of Poe and James, Hoffmann's tale and Freud's essay are yet another 'case' of a transference-story *par excellence*.

The consensus of critical readings of Freud's essay has it that 'The uncanny' (1919) reveals the founder of psychoanalysis in the grip of a repetition-compulsion and there is a general eagerness to display the effects (for a reading which makes this the central issue, see Cixous 1976). On the one hand, it is argued, Freud's paradigm for the uncanny, E. T. A. Hoffmann's story 'The Sandman', becomes a prime example of the return of *repression*, because Freud edits out its uncanny potential. On the other hand, Freud's essay as a (w)hole is held up as a prime example of the return of the repressed, because what is left out of the story returns to haunt the essay. Here, then, there is a failure of theory in practice, in that Freud represses the uncanny in Hoffmann, yet allows it to appear in his own text. How does this come about?

The notion of the repetition-compulsion is at the centre of what is probably regarded as Freud's most controversial work, *Beyond the Pleasure*

Principle, published in 1920, one year after 'The uncanny'. The compulsion to repeat was seen from the beginning as one of the commonest symptoms of neurotic behaviour, taking the form of obsessive rituals, recurring dreams, patterns of relationships, and manifesting itself, as has been shown throughout this book, at the level of transference. It was the need to find an explanation of such repetition phenomena 'beyond' the pleasure principle (because they were unpleasant) that led Freud to revise his earlier instinct theory and posit 'death instincts' in opposition to 'life instincts', for he could not deny the intensity, which he called 'daemonic', in such repetitions, which was closer to hate than to seeking after libidinal satisfaction (XXI, p. 119). The death instinct, arising from the organism's wish to return to a desireless stable state, can take the form of seeking to destroy, and in alliance with the sexual instincts (here associated with the life instincts), of a will to power, to sadistic or masochistic aggression (XIX, p. 163). The notion of a death instinct is not a comforting one, since it is a threat to the ego's narcissistic desire for omnipotence, and hence immortality, and yet, as it works in conjunction with the life instincts, it will keep desire circling round its (lost) object instead of becoming fixated on the self. It is this uncanny movement that critics have discerned in Hoffmann's and Freud's text.

Hoffmann's story is a complex narrative, beginning with three letters and continuing with a third-person narrator, who makes intermittent appeals to the reader. The plot concerns the fortunes of a student, named Nathanael, who is suffering from a haunting childhood memory, to do with a lawyer named Coppelius who used to come to the house on a mysterious errand, and whom the boy associated with the grim nursery tale of the 'Sandman', a bogey figure who threatens the eyes of children. Nathanael recalls how on one occasion he is caught spying and is manhandled and nearly blinded by Coppelius. The dreadful memory is revived by a visit from a seller of spectacles and telescopes, named Coppola, and by a figure associated with him, the Professor Spalanzani. Nathanael is caught between the desire for the latter's daughter, Olympia, and the girl to whom he is betrothed, Clara. Olympia turns out to be a mechanical doll and is torn to pieces before his eyes by the two men. A further incident, in which a variety of motifs combine, causes him to jump to his death.

In my retelling of the story I have deliberately dwelt on some features Freud left aside: the narrative complex and the repetition of violence. Freud's reading subordinates everything to a single thematic motif: the hero's fear of losing his eyes as equivalent to his fear of being deprived of his sexual organ. The threat of castration within the story is seen as actual. Nathanael is afraid of castration as a *real* event, believing that the dreaded figure of the Sandman has returned to punish his childish curiosity by robbing him of his eyes (penis). Freud notes a repetition: Coppelius (Sandman 1), Coppola (double of Sandman), and Spalanzani (double of double) arrive on the scene each time Nathanael is with a woman. The uncanny effect, Freud argues, refuting the psychologist Jentsch, is only peripherally due to the blurring of life/not-life in the doll: there is 'no doubt' that the uncanny feeling 'is directly attached to the figure of the Sandman, that is, to the idea of being robbed of one's eyes' (XVII, p. 230).

Freud's essay is far too long and rambling for an adequate summary here (for an attempt to trace its peregrinations see Cixous 1976), but an outline may be appropriate. The essay is divided into three sections whose subject matter overlaps, so I will merely indicate its nodal points, letting Freud state his intended mode of procedure, which already contains his conclusion:

> Two courses are open to us at the outset. Either we can find out what meaning has come to be attached to the word 'uncanny' in the course of its history; or we can collect all those properties of persons, things, sense-impressions, experiences and situations which arouse in us the feeling of uncanniness, and then infer the unknown nature of the uncanny from what all these examples have in common. I will say at once that both courses lead to the same result: the uncanny is that class of the frightening which leads back to what is known of old and long familiar (XVII, p. 220).

The first course involves tracing the connotations of the words *heimlich* and *unheimlich*. Here Freud finds that the distinction between them is not as exclusive as it may appear, but that the *heimlich* contains within itself a secret, in that the word signifies on the one hand the familiar and domestic, and on the other what is concealed and hidden, the two meanings coexisting: 'Thus *heimlich* is a word the meaning of which develops in the direction of ambivalence, until it finally coincides with its opposite, *unheimlich*' (p. 226). The second course involves taking a more tortuous path, one that branches out in two main directions. Freud is concerned with a close scrutiny of a variety of uncanny phenomena, and he proceeds by way of free association. In the first instance this leads to Hoffmann's 'Sandman', its uncanny effects – not so much the life-like doll, but the hero's fear of losing his eyes to the Sandman, then the motif of the double as the primitive man's 'harbinger of death', the compulsion to repeat, the dread of the 'evil eye' as part of an animistic world-view: 'the *unheimlich* is what was once *heimisch*, familiar; the prefix 'un' is the token of repression' (p. 245). The other direction Freud takes leads to the testing of this insight and the assuaging of a number of doubts, involving the role of repression in producing the uncanny. When do such bizarre motifs as dismembered limbs, being buried alive, death and the return of the dead, produce an uncanny effect and when do they not? And, at last, the crucial move from psychology to aesthetics, what is the distinction between the uncanny of immediate experience and the uncanny of fiction?

The core of the problem is the way the uncanny lies on that problematic boundary between fiction and reality which Freud has a positivistic leaning to keep firmly apart. It posed something of a problem for him when he found the 'primal scene' not to be a real event, but a retrospective interpretation (see 'From the history of an infantile neurosis', XVII), hence a fiction. He found the same principle to be in operation with the child's understanding of sexual difference, for only *nachträglich* did it infer that in the female there is a 'missing organ' to account for ('Some psychical consequences of the anatomical distinction between the sexes', XIX), another fiction. Freud's essay circles round the notion of the castration complex, which he sees as the source of the uncanny in Hoffmann's story. Having thus learnt that there is fiction in truth, as it were, Freud is bent on discovering the truth in fiction.

So what do the critics do with Freud? Again there is a certain critical consensus and it concerns both what Freud leaves out of Hoffmann's tale and what he leaves out of psychoanalysis. The two are related, for each is a consequence of the other. Freud's reading is neither an adequate literary reading nor an adequate psychoanalytic one. Hoffmann's story has a better account of the uncanny in it than the one Freud gives, both as regards literature and as regards psychoanalysis. But most interestingly, what Freud leaves out of Hoffmann transferentially strays into his long digressive essay.

Freud's omissions regarding literature can be summarized as follows (some are particularly acutely argued for by Hertz 1979, within a Bloomian framework, and by Kittler 1977, within a Lacanian/Foucauldian one). Freud has ignored the narrative strategies and textual devices employed (consciously/unconsciously) by Hoffmann. 'The Sandman' is in fact remarkable for the way it can be made paradigmatically to illustrate what psychoanalysis has to do with text structure. The return of the repressed works at the level of narration, plot and figuration. First, as regards narration, there is a narrator, not mentioned by Freud, who speaks of his desire and implicates both reader, author and character: not only the narrator, but also the hero has trouble in beginning. The way the story – finally – begins is via a 'feint in the direction of epistolary fiction', three letters whose 'real'/'fictitious' status is cunningly deployed by Hoffmann (Hertz 1979, p. 306), and totally ignored by Freud. Second, as regards plot, the story does not enact the return of the repressed solely in the figure of the Sandman. What is repeated is not only a content but a structure, a structure of delay, and what is delayed is death. This is the function of the repeated and different scenes of dismemberment, the unscrewing and re-screwing of the child Nathanael's limbs in the spying scene, the violent death of the father, the tearing apart of the doll, Nathanael's brains dashed out on the pavement. The plot thus performs a detour to death. Third, as regards figuration, this is perhaps the level at which the effect of the uncanny is most clearly perceived (for a brilliant analysis, on which I am here drawing, see Hertz 1979). To restore colour to fading images is to invest with desire. Both the narrator and Nathanael have trouble in describing the brilliant colours of their inner vision and feel impelled to add ever more colour to the narrative, to keep alive the images which torment them (and by further extension the reader), to stop them from fading, to play and replay the compulsive fantasy. Hence the images of glowing grains of coal, dazzling eye-glasses, blood-red rays, bleeding eyes, warm glances, soul-scorching words. Such figures of repetition (disregarded by Freud) are at their most uncanny when they are seen as '*merely* colouring, that is, when it comes to seem most gratuitously rhetorical' (Hertz op. cit., p. 301), for at that moment one does not know what it is that is doing the turning.

But Freud's sins do not end here, for there are also his omissions as regards psychoanalysis. In his insistence on the equation of eyes and penis he has coloured everything with the fear of literal castration, the loss of the male sexual organ: it is 'the violent and obscure emotion' excited 'by the threat of being castrated' that 'gives the idea of losing other organs its intense colouring' (XVII, p. 231). He thereby overlooks the point that eyes are the most powerful organs of desire and ignores the relation between perception and desire, in particular that moment when the child 'perceives' what the mother 'lacks'. The eye, therefore, takes on a special significance because it bears such a threat to desire, both for its role in this discovery and as an organ of perception, itself part of the satisfaction of desire. Loss of eyes becomes a metaphor for the dismembering of the self-image and subsequent loss of identity. Any adequate psychoanalytic reading would thus have to account not only for the return of the repressed in the form of the Sandman as oedipal father, but also in the form of Clara (and Olympia) as objects of desire which fail the hero, both in their own right (Clara refuses Nathanael's suffering, his 'text' – his poem; Olympia turns out to be an automaton), and by dint of his own blinded narcissism. The theory of narcissism, as one critic notes, is uncannily relegated by Freud to the status of three footnotes (Rubin 1982). In his reading Freud leaves out, represses, everything that Hoffmann allows to emerge, above all that which is a blow to narcissism. Hence the motif of Olympia as uncanny double is reduced to 'Nathanael's feminine attitude towards his father' (XVII, p. 232), or to an anthropological curiosity (alluding to Otto Rank). The double, once a comforting spare soul, became, at a later stage of civilization, 'a thing of terror' (p. 236). Freud makes no mention of the repeated images of death. He tries to re-automatize the uncanny, where Hoffmann de-automatizes it by letting death return (Meltzer 1982).

Freud produces an explanation for the uncanny in *experience*, as a resurgence of an infantile complex, or as a reviving of an animistic mode of perception, or both, but he has none for the uncanny in *fiction*. Fiction has more resources of the uncanny, but I was the first to explain it, says Freud, without saying it. What he has left out has returned as a supplement in his own text. Freud, in his essay, has 'disseminated' castration, in an infinite play of substitution (Derrida 1982, p. 268), by borrowing fiction – Hoffmann's story, plus a variety of literary examples and allusions – knowing (fearing) that there were supplementary resources to be found there, that fiction is required as a supplement to life. As he spins out his own narrative he seems to need more and more fiction in order to keep the uncanny off, perhaps hoping, like that archetypal storyteller Scheherazade, that death may be indefinitely postponed. In the course of his narration, however, Freud displays the very things he left out of Hoffmann's text: images of death and dismemberment, anxiety regarding priority (like the narrator in Hoffmann, who wants to be 'original'), the unbinding operations of the primary process. Death, the final castration, the uncanniest thing of all, can only return in fiction.

But it is castration that makes possible the play of substitution: though the father says 'no' to desire, the unconscious can get by. Thus, paradoxically, ambivalently, the failure of the object is both a blow to narcissism – a re-experience of primal lack – and a sign that the old rule for defining that object cannot hold and a new one must be substituted. Both objects and human desires undergo change. What Jean-François Lyotard calls the 'unpresentable' makes a sudden emergence out of the 'artifices' of the old objectifications, putting them in question; something is 'happening' which defies representation and conceptualization but which is unmistakably present nevertheless (Lyotard 1983, p. 338; and also lecture at Cambridge, 'The sublime and the avant-garde', 12 March 1984). The experience of the uncanny is an unconscious realization that such a change has come about. The breaking of existing categorizations can take the form of a disturbing fixity in behaviour and perception, repetitions obsessively held to, that evince their purposelessness, their irrelevance to desire. Bergson has noted how we are amused by self-defeating automatisms in another's behaviour. The winding-up of the doll Olympia in Hoffmann's story becomes comic by its clear metaphorical designation of that very source of the comic – that the subject is no longer guided by his own desires. The old mode of behaviour (what Freud calls the feminine attitude to the father) is no longer workable as a self-image, yet rigidly adhered to, out of fear. In literature, uncanny automata, mechanical dolls, machines out of control, become powerful metaphors for this inability to adjust one's objectifications or else for the rigidity of the existing order. The uncanny is the illusory aspect of all objects brought home to us: we cannot rely upon them as leading to the satisfaction of desire. The Surrealists took the failure of the category as a central theme of their manifestos. Surrealist art specializes in the uncanny object, the watch that melts (Dali), the pipe that proclaims 'Ceci n'est pas une pipe' (Magritte). The uncanny object brings home to us that all objects are in some sense 'transitional objects' (Winnicott), or in Klein's sense, 'good' and 'bad' at once, involving a sudden shift of desire.

Literature and the arts can present us with forms of the uncanny that life cannot, because the writer/artist has more access to illusion. He can contextualize as he wishes, choose whatever frame he likes (Magritte), discuss illusion (Hoffmann). Whereas in life one is at the mercy of repetition (the repeated detour to the brothel Freud relates in 'The uncanny'), the artist can play with the repressed. It is here that the uncanny rejoins the joke. Both the trickster and the artist can 'turn' the listener/reader and make her participate in a shift of desire. The result can be the changing of the old categorizations: the text may be reinterpreted, the painting reframed, the poem rewritten, indefinitely.

The uncanny and the joke have here been dealt with at length because they throw more light on literature and the arts than Freud's avowed positivist researches into the subject. Investigation of the uncanny has shown once again how a marginal term (something on the borders of aesthetics and psychology) can reveal itself as a special example of what is most general.

7.3 Bloom and the return of the author

I offer a special case of the anxiety of influence as a variety of the uncanny. A man's unconscious fear of castration manifests itself as an apparently physical trouble in his eyes; a poet's fear of ceasing to be a poet frequently manifests itself also as a trouble of his vision.

Bloom 1975, pp. 77–8

The anxiety of influence is Harold Bloom's version of the return of the repressed. In the context of post-structuralist theory it also marks the return of the author, who, in 1968, was declared to be dead by Barthes (see Barthes 1977). The author has risen from the dead and demands recognition, but his demand is made from the site of the poem itself and is addressed only to the elect: that is to say, a chosen poet/critic feels himself overcome by 'election-love' (Hebrew '*ahabah*'; Bloom 1980, p. 51), as if a divine gift was bestowed on him. The gift turns into a powerful fixation, which Bloom sees as analogous to the Freudian moment of primal repression: the unconscious of the young poet ('ephebe') becomes imprinted by that of the poetic father-figure ('precursor'). This sets off an intertextual rivalry, which is the Bloomian version of transference, implicating both poet and critic. Not only does the ephebe (mis)read the precursor but the critic (mis)reads the ephebe–precursor relationship. (I will be developing Bloom's concept of 'misreading'.) Criticism is thus what Bloom calls 'a rhetoric of rhetoric', a double misreading.

The challenge of a newcomer to the work of an established poet takes essentially the form of a turning of his meaning, a troping. This arises from the newcomer's reactions of defence against the strong paternal assertion, for each major trope identified by classical rhetoric can be matched, according to Bloom, with certain psychic defences (taken from Anna Freud's catalogue; Anna Freud 1966). If one maps Bloom's theory on a deconstructive reading of 'The uncanny', one can observe the end-process of what a later poet does to an earlier one. Freud is rated by Bloom as 'the strongest of the poets' (Bloom 1982, p. 144). The readings I discussed in the previous section saw Freud under Hoffmann's spell, suffering anxiety as regards death-as-castration. In Bloom's terms this would translate into a threat to his poetic strength and his priority. The final stage in which the anxiety of influence makes a newcomer into a 'strong' poet is marked by the moment when the precursor's image-structure appears uncannily in the newcomer's poem, as if it were now his. It is uncanny, because early and late have become reversed (the trope of *metalepsis*, in Latin 'transumption'). The defence mechanisms put in play are introjection (of the precursor's images) and projection (their reappearance as the newcomer's). The resultant 'revisionary ratio' (the changed relation between precursor and newcomer) is given the name *apophrades*, the return of the dead (1980, pp. 101–3; for a full and remarkably clear account of Bloom's map of 'misprision' – six defences, corresponding to six tropes, combined into six 'revisionary ratios', and finally paired into three 'poetic crossings' – see Leitch 1983).

The uncanny return of the precursor makes the latecomer seem to be the true author. It has been noted that 'Freud has hardly anything to envy in Hoffmann for his "art" or "craftiness" in provoking the *Unheimliche* effect' (Cixous 1976, p. 547). By the strength of his poetic will Freud has thus triumphed over time and death, for he has successfully troped against the precursor's id. According to Bloom, 'tropes are necessary errors about language, defending ultimately against the deathly dangers of literal meaning' (Bloom 1975, p. 94). Literal meaning is death because the movement of desire has been stopped. One might say that Goethe's Faust could only join the angels by a swerving away from literal meaning (the use of a subjunctive instead of an indicative). He got to heaven by turning a meaning, thus troping (tricking) his way to immortality, at the same time allowing Goethe to swerve from tragedy via a good joke.

Bloom reads Freud 'antithetically', that is as one strong poet reads another strong poet, against the establishment. According to Bloom's theory of misreading, this means reading him through his precursors as *Bloom* sees them, through Goethe, Shakespeare and Schopenhauer, etc., and not through Charcot, Janet, Helmholtz, etc., as Freud might fancy, or through Hegel, Nietzsche and Heidegger, as Lacan chooses to (Bloom 1982, p. 91). Since misreading is essentially *reading-through*, the result will always depend on the mediating influence. Hence my reading of Freud's reading of Hoffmann through Bloom is not the same thing as Bloom's reading of Freud's reading of Hoffmann through Goethe, Shakespeare and Schopenhauer.

So what does the antithetical Freud look like? Bloom claims that in the essay 'The uncanny' (from which it seems impossible to get away) Freud stumbled upon a psychology of the Sublime. But he only stumbles, because he can only see the dire aspect of the uncanny. He thereby chooses to ignore a well-established philosophical tradition of what Bloom calls the 'negative Sublime'. The classical emphasis on rule and order was gradually overtaken by the ascribing of the loftiest value to great feeling, instead of great thoughts. This allowed for feelings of terror to mingle with awe, via a narcissistic illusion of omnipotence. Freud himself succumbed to the negative Sublime and was trapped in its illusion of control, 'the pride of an originator who could say "I invented psychoanalysis because it had no literature", or even more ironically: "I am not fond of reading"' (pp. 206–7). Freud's 'strong' reading of 'The Sandman', Bloom argues, consists precisely of such a misreading of the Sublime, because he reduces the uncanny to an infantile and archaic complex. This makes him blind to the mode whereby the canny turns into the uncanny, that is by an act of the poetic will. I take it that he means that Hoffmann tropes excessively to hide the repressed, namely the return of death. It is the not-naming that counts, and which results in what Bloom in another context calls an overdetermination of language and an underdetermination of meaning. Freud repeats this configuration in transference to Hoffmann: the figural is a defence against death. The Sublime, as Bloom will argue, is the overcoming of the catastrophe of death, or rather of being born into death.

Bloom's Freud is thus very much the literary Freud. Bloom makes 'The uncanny' the occasion to link a group of Freud's metapsychological texts, concerned with the concept of defence, in order to argue for a 'catastrophe theory' of the imagination ('Freud and the Sublime', in Bloom 1982). These texts are for Bloom essentially about what happens when a poet/self (Bloom operates with selves rather than subjects) arrives on the scene, only to find his place already taken, the poem already written. He can only snatch victory from defeat by rising sublimely to the occasion. *Beyond the Pleasure Principle* overcomes the catastrophe of a drive that aims at death. 'On narcissism' overcomes the catastrophe of falling in love with the self. 'Negation' allows repressed images to get through by means of a misconstrual. *Inhibitions, Symptoms and Anxiety* provides a panoply of psychic defences, a veritable rhetoric for the psyche to defend itself against anxiety. 'Analysis terminable and interminable' provides the anxiety that leads to 'enabling fictions' (p. 115). Bloom does not forget the body: anxiety is unpleasure. Giving birth to poems is to relive the primal anxiety. Repression produces the rhetorical strategies for overcoming anxiety and is thus the necessary condition for producing poetry. The Sublime is the outcome of repression, not of sublimation because the energies are sexual and have not lost their desire-quality: the canny imagination produces poems.

It produces in particular what Bloom believes to be the dominant lyric form of what he grandly calls 'post-Enlightenment literature': the 'High Romantic Crisis-poem' celebrates the triumph of the poetic will. For Bloom it marks not only the birth of an individual poet, but also that of a poetic genre. It seems as if the Romantics had to overcome the rules of their neo-classical Fathers to follow (Mother) nature, the point being that they do *not* follow nature, and hence one might also see it, as Bloom does not, as a rebellion against the Mother. For Bloom, poets after Milton have to be 'strong' to fight against the tradition, competing against one another, instead of labouring in the service of representation. Inspiration no longer comes from nature but from another poet. For instance, Bloom cites four lines from *The Auroras of Autumn* by Wallace Stevens, one of his strongest poets:

> Out of the window,
> I saw how the planets gathered
> Like the leaves themselves
> Turning in the wind,

and comments, 'Stevens, out of his window, sees his own (and Shelley's) trope; the gathering planets are *like* the leaves turning in the wind. This giant perspectivizing shrinks the cosmos to one autumnal metaphor' (Bloom 1977, pp. 378–9). Poets/selves when they look out of the window do not engage in a pure act of seeing: what the poet sees is his own trope and that of another's. The view is obscured by representation itself, as in Magritte's picture, *The Human Condition*, where a canvas carrying the outside landscape obscures the view from inside.

According to Bloom, the meaning of a poem is another poem. 'The freedom to have a meaning of one's own . . . is wholly illusory' (Bloom 1979, p. 3). It is an illusion to be achieved against a prior plenitude of meaning, a meaning already 'authorized' by another. There is no benign play here: enter the 'bad-enough-child', not catered for in D. W. Winnicott's system, the poet–son who takes up a 'strong' stance in a space not so 'potential', a battleground already occupied, where a space for the imagination has to be cleared perforce. Since for Bloom poems are relational events, since his intertextual theory of poetry is so clearly object-relational, depending as it does on feats of introjection and projection, it is odd that he seems not to have made any reference to the British object-relations theorists. He is a great converser with other critics/analysts, and in the essay on Freud discussed above he holds converse with Derrida, Lacan, Laplanche, Anna Freud, Jung, Rank, Wollheim and Norman O. Brown, to cite just a few, but there is no mention of Winnicott or Klein. It is ironical that Bloom gives Anna Freud a key place in his canon, dedicated as her work is to unquestioned ideals of maturity, while Melanie Klein, with her feeling for the wayward and aberrant, is ignored. It is true that there are marked differences from Bloom, suggestive in themselves. Where Klein's reparation springs from a capacity to mourn, for Bloom the creative will is precisely the refusal to mourn. Yet the 'revisionary ratios' and 'poetic crossings' of the Bloomian ephebe look uncannily like the 'agonistic' movements (to borrow a term from Bloom) of the pre-oedipal Kleinian infant. Klein is herself a strong reader of Freud and merits a strong reading in turn. But perhaps this is already what has happened, since such readings can take effect without the reader's awareness. For the Mother has been displaced by the Father: the progenitors of the infant/ephebe have been shuffled. Bloom, with undaunted mettle, brings forth men-children only.

Bloom has provided a virtuoso critical practice which is workable and which makes room for the critic as brother–poet. This practice gives access to the tradition in renewed form, for it is to be won, in the Faustian sense, by effort and struggle. Most ingeniously, there is always an author-in-crisis, belated, wounded and mortal, and there is always a prior pleni-tude of meaning to struggle against. Thus the author returns, but with a difference. Bloom has brilliantly wedded the old orthodoxy with the new: there is a typology, but its archetypes are unstable; there is textuality, but it is the doing of persons, and not only that of the random effects of language; there is an author, but he is a pseudo-author; there is a myth, but it is grounded in psychology.

Yet there is something oddly self-validating about his practice: nothing is ever produced to upset the theory. Bloom adopts terms like 'post-Enlightenment' and 'Romantic Crisis-poem' without question. The crisis-poem takes for granted a unique self, always there, however divided, ready for a crisis, to turn into a strong or weak poet. Though it is a general truth that the meanings of a person in power can be subverted by someone without power, Bloom writes as if his poet–poet confrontation were *sui generis*. But the confrontation is not merely that of the defensive tropings on one set of isolated individuals against another: there are societies/cultures/histories involved. The firm presupposition of a-historical single selves, with their past crystallized around them, makes Bloom's critical practice self-validating in a trivial way, for he thereby keeps out meanings that cannot be directly lodged upon these selves. It is the institution itself which calls for an antithetical reading, including the institution of psy-choanalysis, and it is to such a reading that I now finally turn.

PART IV

8
Psychoanalysis and Ideology I: Focus on Subversion

8.1 Psychoanalysis as a discourse: sexuality and power

To speak of psychoanalysis as a discourse is to dispose of two contradictory assumptions: that it has sprung up as the fruits of genius at a particular moment in the history of the human sciences, or, as is still asserted, that it emerged in response to the specific needs of neurotic women in Vienna at the turn of the century. Both assumptions merely situate psychoanalysis in the domain of cultural history, whereas to call it a discourse is to situate it in a field which questions the very concept of history as traditionally defined.

Michel Foucault, historian of thought, has been writing since the 1960s on the subject of history as a discourse. By that, he means history as a set of linguistic practices which generate social and cultural activity, governed by rules that are unformulated and characteristically unrecognized by the speakers concerned. Thus rules of exclusion operate which keep out unqualified persons in fields such as law and medicine, and define what is to be considered irrelevant and unmentionable. Such activity is largely unconscious, creating what Foucault calls an 'archive', a kind of cultural unconscious to be sharply distinguished from the archetypal kind (Jung), since it is characterized by being subject to constant flux and change, to discontinuity rather than continuity. Certain forces of constraint will shape what is to serve as fact and truth in any particular discourse and what methods can be used to display them.

What keeps knowledge moving is the 'will to power' in the public arena of history. Foucault uncovers strategies of power within a discourse in order to show that power is inescapable because it is inextricably combined with the will to knowledge. Power, therefore, is not to be seen as simply oppressive, for it always has a double effect: it is bad in so far as it constrains both those at the top and those at the bottom in frozen gestures of domination and submission, but because this inevitably leads to counter-strategies of evasion and subversion it cannot help but also be productive:

> For, if it is true that at the heart of power relations and as a permanent condition of their existence there is an insubordination and a certain essential obstinacy on the part of the principles of freedom, then there is no relationship of power without the means of escape or possible flight. Every power relationship implies, at least in potential, a strategy of struggle, in which the two forces are not superimposed, do not lose their specific nature, do not finally become confused. Each constitutes for the other a kind of permanent limit, a point of possible reversal (Foucault 1982, p. 225).

Since every will to power cannot but meet with opposition from other wills, oppression must perforce open channels for its own subversion.

Psychoanalysis is a discourse of power which Foucault sees as having produced knowledge of both a general and specific nature. In this he provides ammunition for radical critics of psychoanalytic practice, such as Deleuze and Guattari, whose critique of society and textual criticism is to be considered next. As regards the general contribution made by psychoanalysis, he sees it as a master-science, in marked contrast to those who refuse to give it the status of a science at all:

> Psychoanalysis stands as close as possible, in fact, to that critical function which, as we have seen, exists within all human sciences. In setting itself the task of making the discourse of the unconscious speak through consciousness, psychoanalysis is advancing in the direction of that fundamental region in which the relations of representation and finitude come into play (Foucault 1974, p. 374).

Through challenging the very nature of representation, in revealing the unconscious elements within it, psychoanalysis calls all discourses into question. But this does not mean that it is itself immune to cross-questioning. With regard to its specific contribution, psychoanalysis has revealed the central importance of sexuality at a particular moment in western culture. In *The History of Sexuality* (1981) Foucault sets out to investigate why, since the Renaissance, sexuality has moved towards becoming the sole indicator of selfhood, how it has come to dominate not only discourses but institutions and practices. As an instance he cites the promotion of a 'children's sexuality' at a moment when family power was in decline and needed shoring up by giving the family special rights over the body and soul of its progeny. This then became the cue for the state professions to step in and offer their expert help, and thus began the age of psychiatry and the 'surveillance' of the body. The point Foucault wishes to make is that the resultant power-relations were not simply repressive but led to new knowledge via confession and self-revelation. From this it became obvious that knowing the body leads to a sensualization of power. Watching the forbidden creates pleasure, precisely the kind of prurience which D. H. Lawrence objected to, and which he saw as wholly negative. As will be seen in Deleuze and Guattari's account of Kafka, literature can be made to attest to the *productiveness* of this kind of perverse pleasure, in that power will thereby be disseminated, put into disarray, and not reinforced, as Lawrence would have it.

Foucault's position is counter to all those post-Freudian idealist sexologists, Wilhelm Reich, Herbert Marcuse, Norman O. Brown, who believe in the liberation of the body and the emergence of a true sexuality, away from the unnecessary repression exacted by a capitalist society, which forces its members to make work rather than love. For Foucault 'the good genius of Freud' has located sex as a strategy of power and knowledge at a critical moment in history (Foucault 1981, p. 159). The discourse of psychoanalysis is the modern form of the confessional: sexuality has become the secret which leads to the truth of man's being, a truth not on the side of freedom, but on that of power, the authority installed in the psyche. Deleuze and Guattari will turn from psychoanalysis as a discourse of power to schizoanalysis as a liberation of desire.

8.2   Deleuze and Guattari: schizoanalysis and Kafka

Gilles Deleuze, a philosopher, and Félix Guattari, a radical analyst who has been opposing orthodox psychiatry since the 1950s, are considerably less appreciative of Freud and psychoanalysis, although their enterprise is unthinkable outside that framework. They are a godsend to the critic surveying the scene of psychoanalysis and literature, who is engaged in anticipating objections from all sides. In exploding the whole oedipal apparatus they cater for a sizeable group of readers, but at the same time they give new fuel to the psychoanalytic critical enterprise because they are pouring new wine into old bottles. The 'schizoanalysis' of texts, as the example of Kafka will show, actually provides a *method* (even if this is not centrally relevant to their purpose), a textual critical practice which pays close attention to images and motifs, and which, unlike the New Criticism (for a classic example see Brooks 1968), gives the author a properly delimited place, one functionally related to the system of literary discourse as a whole (see Foucault 1980b, 'What is an author?').

'Schizoanalysis' is a mode of analysis which refuses the idea of an 'oedipalized' unconscious. For Deleuze and Guattari the process of 'free association', whereby a patient undertakes to speak whatever comes to mind, is an example of chaining desire to representations already singled out before desire ever had a chance to get going. The oedipal prohibitions are the very means by which desire is channelled towards the prohibited: 'The law tells us: You will not marry your mother and you will not kill your father. And we docile subjects say to ourselves: so *that's* what I wanted!' (Deleuze and Guattari 1977a, p. 114). They differ from the movement of anti-psychiatry as represented by Laing and his co-workers in not believing that there is a unitary and wholesome self that would emerge if only the narrow family network, together with a society which is seen as no more than an extension of the family, did not deform and distort it.

Anti-Oedipus: Capitalism and Schizophrenia (1977a) is a rebellion against psychoanalysis for presenting desire as rooted in lack. This is seen as a capitalist ploy, because the unconscious is being forced into a position where desire is characterized by insufficiency and hunger. Psychoanalysis has deformed the unconscious. Even though it is not to be held responsible for inventing the Oedipus complex, 'it merely provides the latter a last territoriality, the couch, and a last Law, the analyst as despot and money collector' (p. 269). Schizoanalysis *constructs* an unconscious, sees libido as still fluid, able to be directed into new channels, not already stabilized according to oedipal constraints. Deleuze and Guattari are not interested in a sexual liberation of any particular group, but in a general liberation of desire. Desire is a 'flow' (of libido) prior to representation and production. What has been 'territorialized' into Nation, Family, Church, School, Party, can be 'deterritorialized'. They maintain that, instead of there being these unifying totalities outside the body and a unique autonomous self within, 'the unconscious is an orphan' (p. 49). It is not bound to any particular social definition, but is produced in the body as an inescapable part of man within nature, needing the support of other bodies, equally partial.

Deleuze and Guattari postulate a material flow, a *hylé* as they term it (p. 36) – the Greek for a basic world-stuff – which the machines of the body cut into and divide up into partial objects. The unconscious is that part of the flux which escapes the sign-system. Hence their term 'partial objects' to stress that this system need not 'naturally' lead to whole objects. There is a pre-linguistic experience, which they regard as crucial; in this they differ from Lacan for whom the unconscious does not exist before language. For them, as for others discussed in this book (Lawrence, Ehrenzweig, Kristeva), desire is present from the beginning, whereas for Lacan there is a level of physiological need which pre-exists desire. They concede the need of a primal repression, without which an entry into the 'socius' (that is the community) would be impossible, but turn the full force of their attack upon the secondary repression, the preconscious investment of the libidinal flow that the capitalist world, via the shrunken oedipal family, has imposed upon its children. They praise Melanie Klein 'for the marvellous discovery of partial objects, that world of explosions, rotations, vibrations' (p. 44), but make a vital distinction. What Klein saw as an early oedipal pattern they see as obtaining prior to 'oedipalization': the parts are not fantasies derived from global persons but genuine productions, testifying to 'the absolutely *anoedipal* nature of the production of desire' (p. 45). The Kleinian unconscious is closer to the social nature of desire, whereas the Freudian unconscious is a capitalist construction, an internalized set of power-relations, the result of repression produced for capitalism by the family. Deleuze and Guattari believe that psychoanalysis aids and abets this process. They comment on the case-history of the psychotic child 'Dick' (see pp. 74–5): 'The psychoanalyst no longer says to the patient: "Tell me a little bit about your desiring-machines, won't you?" Instead he screams: "Answer daddy-and-mommy when I speak to you!" Even Melanie Klein' (ibid.).

Bodies are 'desiring-machines, because machines arrange and connect flows, and do not recognize distinctions between a person's organs, material flows, and semiotic flows'. According to Deleuze and Guattari, unconscious desire tends to one or the other of two poles, a schizophrenic one or a paranoiac one. The former is characterized by multiplicity, proliferation, becoming, flowing, a breaking of boundaries, and is constituted by partial objects, fragments of experience, memory and feeling, linked in chance and unexpected ways. The latter is marked by its unifying procedures, its search for order, similarity, wholeness, assuming identity and completeness of objects and selves within conforming constraints and recognized limits. At the schizophrenic pole there is a 'deterritorializing' tendency, shifting boundaries, transforming identities, ignoring the familiarly specified. At the paranoiac pole there is an incessant pressure to 'territorialize', to mark out and maintain the directions of desire. Deleuze and Guattari's 'material psychiatry' becomes a political factor in the active undermining of such territorializing.

There is, however, a problem concerning their project as a whole. Whereas Foucault sees psychoanalysis as a discourse of power which brings in the beneficial side-effects of more knowledge, Deleuze and Guattari see it as entirely harmful. They fully acknowledge the presence of oedipal repression, but they stress that in all cases it is possible and needful to get away from it. They rely upon the concept of the 'schizo' as part of their attack upon the system, for they wish to prove (unlike Laing) that it is not the case that society has driven him 'mad', but instead that he has miraculously escaped the effects of the bourgeois repression-by-signifier and may therefore be held up as representative of a potentially desirable and natural human condition. Instead of Freud's distinction between neurotic/normal and psychotic/mad they distinguish between schizo/normal and paranoiac/mad. Both sets of terms equally belong to a discourse of sanity and madness, precisely what their politics of desire would seem to want to deconstruct. To point to a negative of a hated positive as an escape is still to be bound to the patterns supposedly false (see Rajchman on this issue, 1977, pp. 54–5).

This leads to the problem concerning their project as a whole. The question arises of whether it is possible to conceive of reform as a matter of opposing a given 'norm' to a given 'deviation', since this is to do no more than perform the definitions laid down by the ideology currently in force. It is difficult to see how any dialectical change can come about with such a view, for it inevitably confines political action to a re-action in the form of fixed confrontations. Moreover, it is hard to see how there can be any substance in the claim that the unconscious possesses a single utopian truth, a true reality, as if each body were not recalcitrant in its difference; nor, looking at the other side of the equation, is it conceivable that the existing structures of the 'socius' can be abandoned without a remainder. It is rather the case that 'the unconscious in Freud does not speak the language of the Other but speaks "many dialects", which cannot be composed or translated into a *single* language' (Rella 1994, p. 29). The myth of the new nomad moving beyond frontiers may itself be considered as a lingering sign of an ineradicable colonialism: 'What in fact, is more rhizomatic, more uncontainable, overflowing and uncontrollable than imperialism itself?' (ibid., p. 43). Mundane reality indicates that ethical and political dialogue is as interminable as analysis and that there are no edenic guarantees beyond the symbolic.

So where does literature come into all this? In the effects they produce in literary texts Deleuze and Guattari's views are at their most attractive.

Their engagement with the play of the text and the imagination of the author tempers the extravagance of their view by introducing a distinctly dialectical element. Literature is like schizophrenia in that it breaks out of the system: 'an author is great because he cannot prevent himself from tracing flows and causing them to circulate, flows that split asunder the catholic and despotic signifier of his work, and that necessarily nourish a revolutionary machine on the horizon' (Deleuze and Guattari 1977a, p. 133). But the author cannot do it without some help. So now yet another type of reader is required, the desire-liberating reader, the schizoanalyst, whose task it is to convert the text into a desiring-machine, or better still, into a revolutionary machine. For Deleuze and Guattari the work of Franz Kafka particularly lends itself to such an enterprise:

> Kafka's machine plugs desire into the premonition of a perverse bureaucratic and technocratic machine, a machine that is already fascist, in which the names of the family lose their consistency in order to open onto the motley Austrian Empire of the machine-castle, onto the condition of Jews without identity, onto Russia, America, China, continents situated well beyond the persons and the names of familialism (1977b, p. 123).

Their study is entitled *Kafka: Pour une littérature mineure* (1975; page references are to the German translation, 1976). Deleuze and Guattari are not using the term 'minor literature' in its accepted sense, that of relatively unimportant works. For them it means the literature of a minority which must needs use the language of a majority from which it feels alienated. There are three characteristics: the 'minor' writer will use words of the 'major' language in 'deterritorialized' ways, shifting meanings across customary boundaries. The individual case presented in 'minor' literature, in particular the familial triangle, is directly connected to and determined by political events outside; it will become the expression of alternative possibilities, new ways of viewing communal life. Contrast this with 'A dissenting opinion on Kafka' (Edmund Wilson) from the 1950s (just after the defeat of an oppressive regime, that of the Nazis), which places him as minor in a pejorative sense, seeing both him and his characters as nothing but victims:

> The denationalized, discouraged, disaffected, disabled Kafka, though for the moment he may frighten or amuse us, can in the end only let us down. He is quite true to his time and place, but it is surely a time and place in which few of us will want to linger — whether as

stunned and hypnotized helots of totalitarian states or as citizens
of freer societies, who have relapsed into taking Kafka's stories as
evidence that God's law and man's purpose are conceived in terms
so different that we may as well give up hope of ever identifying the
one with the other (Wilson 1962, p. 96; orig. publ. 1950).

Deleuze and Guattari's schizoanalytic project actively opposes such a
critical assumption. They reject the whole idea of the domination of a
'subjugated group' via a group-fantasy, myths and propaganda of all kinds.
The work of the unconscious endeavours to ensure that the fantasy of
subjugation (the ideology that has kept desire under constraint) is transformed into one of revolutionary potential for a 'subject-group' (the power
to liberate those so oppressed). For them Kafka's text performs this operation by showing how desire exists simultaneously in two forms of the
law, a 'paranoiac transcendental law' (the oedipal system) whose action
is to mark out and rigidify into separable and recognizable units, and an
'immanent schizo-law' (the rightful demands of the unconscious), which
loosens what has been made rigid, erases the marks, and discovers what
has been left undefined. Both forms are co-present in Kafka, but what
Deleuze and Guattari are bent on demonstrating is how at every point the
schizo-law disassembles the paranoiac law, how writing breaks up the
codes of language. They engage in a virtuoso textual and scholarly performance which is in nice contrast to their revolutionary enterprise, and
which provides new access to Kafka as a writer, particularly as a comic
writer, often acknowledged, but never adequately demonstrated.

   The two states of law present in the text correspond to two states of
desire. One law channels desire into the production goals of the capitalist
system: the Oedipus complex ensures that the law gets inside the subject and sets up a paranoiac structure of competition. This law is 'transcendental' because the interdiction seems to be coming from some ideal
source outside the self. But this law is constantly undermined: for every
assembling of the fascist machine, the political machine, the bureaucratic
machine, a simultaneous disassembling goes on via the operations of an
anti-law, which subverts the repressive representations from within the
system, hence an 'immanent' law. According to Deleuze and Guattari,
Kafka's work is a 'rhizome' (Deleuze and Guattari 1976, p. 7), a favourite image of theirs: a fertile tuber that sprouts a dozen unexpected plants
out of concealment. Thus certain elements found together in Kafka's
work enact a constant dialectic of repression and expression of desire,
but these elements are not in any simple binary opposition because they
constantly combine and recombine with others. Typically, there is a kind

of submission ritual which finds every possible way to get itself represented. Its favoured representations are the bowed head and the framed photograph. The two together have the effect of neutralizing and blocking desire. The framed forbidden photo that one may not touch, may not love, that can only satisfy desire through the look, and the head kept down by means of roof or ceiling, together function as images of repression. This effect is reversed by a set of counter-images, a general raising of limbs and eyes, of objects raised high (spires and turrets), accompanied by the random sounds of music, all of which function as images of the lifting of repression. Deleuze and Guattari are far from wishing to practise yet another form of image criticism; what they are after is the recapturing of pre-linguistic experience, unconscious investments of the sensory field (sounds and sights), which stimulate resistance to repression, liberating desire (1976, chapter 1, 'Content and expression').

Whereas childhood memory is 'hopelessly oedipal', reterritorializing by constantly saying 'father!' and 'mother!', the deterritorializing is done by what Deleuze and Guattari call 'blocks of childhood', pointing to a field of unbounded sexual and social activity, play with sisters, friends and all kinds of companions. These memories, 'higher intensities' not bound by the oedipal experience, make no distinction between the child and the adult. Deleuze and Guattari cite an incident in *The Castle*, where men are sitting in washtubs, splashing among the suds, while solemn-eyed children look on or, an unpleasant converse, a scene in *The Trial*, where two warders are beaten, an event conceived in a manner and tone (the men react with childlike pain and fear) which suggest that children are being punished. These 'affectations' (*Manierismen*), as Deleuze and Guattari call them, are to be seen as a hallmark of Kafka's style, for with this 'childhood affectation' goes another, a 'politeness affectation', for instance the excessive politeness and worldliness of the two carefully cleansed and exquisitely dressed executioners who collect and prepare Joseph K. for his end. The first affectation reflects an endeavour to return to the free sensuous experience of childhood in the 'flows' of the soapy water. The second affectation is a false representation of an authority which seems intent on the well-being of those in its power while exercising that power in its ultimate form: the executioners, for example, walk Joseph K. up and down to keep him warm, then place a stone under his head for comfort.

Together they constitute — as two poles of affectation — the schizo-clownishness so typical of Kafka. The schizophrenic is well-acquainted with both, it is his mode of deterritorializing society's given. Kafka has utilized them — or so it seems to us — in a most

admirable way, in his life as in his art: the machinic art of the
marionette (chapter 8, 'Blocks, series, intensities', p. 111).

The clown represents the fearful authority in a comic manner by carica-
turing its apparent ceremonious concern for the private wish.

Deleuze and Guattari are intent upon showing that unconscious investment of desire in the social field, the so-called 'higher intensities', have
primacy over narrow familial investments of desire, made in the name of
Oedipus. All desire is first and foremost social production. Throughout
Anti-Oedipus they argue that, before sexuality has gone through the process of secondary repression, it is all a flow of unbound libido, 'a body
without organs' (they quote Artaud). The 'body without organs' means
that the body has not yet been subjected to limiting definitions of its parts;
it has not yet been transformed into a single unit within a state-system,
accepting its castration. Marxism and psychoanalysis have both made the
same discovery of the pattern of production that has emerged in capitalism, but Marxism ignores desire while Freudianism has hampered the
class struggle in chaining desire to the family. Kafka's work is revolutionary for Deleuze and Guattari, because their schizoanalysis reveals the
unconscious investments of desire as more powerful than those induced
by the state-system. That is to say, desire is not tied to a particular representation of power: bodies and objects are constantly on the move, thwart-
ing capitalism in its efforts to maintain its representations. Desire refuses
a final embodiment in a particular power-machine; it will always find a
way out (*Ausweg* – a key word in Kafka's writings).

Kafka's way out is to write. The letters, stories and novels articulate
this theme in three distinct ways. In the famous letter to his father Kafka
abjures Oedipus by projecting an absurd father-image into the world at
large, for his 'writing-machine' constantly converts the familial triangles
into an infinitude of legal, economic, bureaucratic and political triangles,
turning the threatening into the comic.

In his stories he stages a transformation process in parallel, a double
flight. On the one hand there is the becoming-beetle, -ape, -mouse, anything rather than becoming-bureaucrat, -policeman or -judge. On the other
hand there is the reverse effect of the becoming-human of the animal, the
ape who wants to find a way out. The simultaneous transformation of
human into animal, and animal into human, functions both as an escape
from and a reassertion of the oedipal system, because the animals, in their
effort to imitate their supposed superiors, also suffer from oedipalization,
particularly the dog, 'the Oedipus-animal *par excellence* (chapter 2, 'All
too great an Oedipus', p. 23).

In the novels the flight from oedipal authority is achieved through the disassembling of the great power-machines. The single subject (the protagonist Karl or K.) is always at the centre of a vast complex, in contact with a variety of 'machinic' sections (a metaphor for the human beings and objects which constitute the power-structure). The machine, whether technocratic (*America*), or legal (*The Trial*), or bureaucratic (*The Castle*), is governed simultaneously by social and erotic forces: each section of the machine has its own erotic component. As a bank official K. is in touch with one particular woman, as a witness with another, as a defendant with another still. People are assigned to different parts of the machine, where they make love, work or argue. The buildings themselves are part of a vast topography of desire, rooms whose entrances and exits lead from one section to the next in unexpected ways, a continuum of moving barriers. The law machine consists of chambers, books, judges, women, pornographic law. The unexpected irrupts in the office next door or in doorways. Desire dwells within the law: where there is power there is sensual satisfaction to be had. Power produces gains of pleasure through surveillance, an inevitable form of voyeurism (Foucault 1981). Desire itself is deterritorialized and cannot judge, for the judges are full of desire. The verdict gets postponed. Authority is always in a different part of the desiring machine. A series of triangles proliferates in Kafka's text: three bank clerks, three lodgers, three voyeurs, three bureaucrats. No triangle is eternal. The women, too, although assigned to specific sections, 'overflow' the precise position allocated them; they have 'connections' with the total power structure and that is why they can 'help' K. They function at the intersection points of the great machine. The washerwoman makes love to the student in the doorway of the law court, a woman extracts K. from the chamber of the advocate. The women are part-sisters, part-servants, part-whores, occupying positions that are anti-marriage and anti-familial. Like Foucault, Deleuze and Guattari believe that: 'As soon as there is a relationship of power, there is a possibility of resistance. We are never trapped by power: it is always possible to modify its hold, in determined conditions and following a precise strategy' (Foucault 1980a, p. 13).

Deleuze and Guattari's schizoanalytic criticism may be seen as a bold attempt to deterritorialize psychoanalytic criticism. They substitute a provoking textual practice which recovers some of the scandal which psychoanalytic criticism lost in its various stages of naturalization, on its way from id- to ego-psychology. They subvert its representations, playing havoc with so-called typical symbols. They refuse to believe that desire is forbidden from the start. Theirs is an attempt to make reading into a revolutionary political activity, discovering omissions, non-sequiturs, mismatch between style and purpose in texts and patients, more radical than deconstruction in the refusal to reassemble the text, more radical than Lacan in seeing the patient as a 'body without organs' (as essentially uncoded) rather than as a text. The revolutionary writer/reader conducts experiments, trying to find a way out of the given representation. Desire has to begin with a line of flight, a deterritorializing move. Yet the problem of how to escape remains, for the way out of representation inevitably leads through it. Hence there is an ironic success in their schizoanalysis of Kafka's text, because it becomes a new form of traditional literary criticism. Schizoanalysis rebels against psychoanalysis, yet like psychoanalysis it finds itself in literature, finds its own strategies anticipated in it. So it is interesting finally to turn back to *Gradiva* and see what happens to this text when appropriated by a schizoanalytic literary critic.

8.3 *Gradiva rediviva*: towards a way out

For Freud, Jensen's *Gradiva* is a story that neatly illustrates the 'cornerstone' of his theory: the return of the repressed (see pp. 26ff.). He is able to turn the story into an allegory of psychoanalysis: one character, the heroine, is able to perform a successful analysis on another character, the hero, 'curing' him of his 'delusion'. Freud called his piece of psychoanalytic criticism *Delusions and Dreams in Jensen's 'Gradiva'*. In *Anti-Oedipus* Deleuze and Guattari write: 'Never was Freud more adventurous than in *Gradiva*' (1977a, p. 352). How can this be? Surely they cannot approve of the psychoanalytic rehabilitation of the central character. Nor do they. But the very effect that caught that character's attention, a desire caught by the movement of a limb, is the place where schizoanalysis wants to install itself, where it wants to take up the battle with psychoanalysis. In an article called 'The fiction of analysis' (1977), Sylvère Lotringer, a French critic, develops the hint dropped by Deleuze and Guattari. He takes up where Deleuze and Guattari left off, wondering 'whether the revolutionary aspect of *Gradiva* comes from Freud or from Jensen' (Lotringer 1977, p. 173). What is this revolutionary aspect? It is the ' "Gradivian" gait', which Freud wants to see as the return of a repressed complex. But there is actually nothing in the text to indicate why the hero, Norbert Hanold, should have a repressed complex about women (ibid., pp. 175–6). Fastening on this omission, Lotringer refutes Freud's textual analysis step by step. His central argument is that Norbert's interest in the gait of Gradiva is not a fetishistic fixation on a woman's foot. What captures him is an image of the freedom of walking, a movement of the body, a 'walking-towards':

> Nomadic form, without specific territory, and from no definite epoch: transhistoric. And the archaeologist is moved not by formal beauty nor even by the woman's (indifferent) face, but rather by the vertical position of her right foot. The representation of someone *in motion*. This is moreover the name with which he dubs her: Gradiva, 'she who walks in splendour' (p. 177).

Norbert's restlessness to get away from his native city and to visit Pompeii is not the response to the return of the repressed in his dream, but the desire to get away from his narrow familial world. The couples in Pompeii that arouse his hatred do so not because of incest-anxiety but because he wishes to get out of the oedipal world into a wider social field. Archaeological excavation need not be a metaphor for the digging up of Norbert's repressed childhood, nor need his love of knowledge be desire for oedipal sexual knowledge: 'the libido does not have to be desexualized or sublimated, i.e., repressed in varying degrees, in order to cathect the socio-historical arena' (p. 178).

The revolutionary element is that the 'Gradiva-effect' is one of deterritorialization. The movement of the foot has little to do with its being that of a woman: 'Gradiva is the proper name of a singularity without individuation, a delimitation of the global person . . . a moving region to which sexes, qualities, and races come each in turn to communicate' (p. 178). Where Freud saw the foot as a fetishistic fixation of one unable to move to the genital stage of oedipal development, Lotringer argues for the case being the reverse of a fixation, the foot's movement being the significant feature. Instead of being a delusion, a turning away from reality, it represents Norbert Hanold's attempt to throw off the restrictions of the oedipal family. The motion of the foot is the flow of libido, a movement of desire: 'What then is an *active* fantasy if not libido in full flow storming the walls of representation and overthrowing all the significations that attempt to shackle it' (p. 186). Norbert's own journey re-enacts this search to overthrow. Pompeii is no longer the ground for precisely named objects but a place where naming has to begin anew. Lotringer quotes from Jensen's text:

> Anyone who harboured a desire for such a comprehension had to stand alone, among the remains of the past, the only living person in

the hot noonday silence, in order not to see with physical eyes nor hear with corporal ears. *Then something came forth everywhere without movement and a soundless speech began*; then the sun dissolved the tomb-like rigidity of the old stones, a glowing thrill passed through them, the dead awoke, and Pompeii began to live again (ibid.).

Noon is the hour of the god Pan, the Greek god of *hylé*, the flowing source of all being. Is this just another Lawrentian celebration of a life force? (Deleuze and Guattari frequently cite Lawrence with approval.) Lotringer sees it rather as a material process, 'a cosmic enunciation free of all subjective appropriation' (p. 187). The becoming impersonal of the person, the 'machinic "it" ', is like the awakening of the dead that Jensen describes, a resurrection of what Deleuze and Guattari call 'the body without organs'. Depersonalization is here seen as a redemptive experience because it liberates man/woman from the repression of civilization. Indeed, civilization is redefined and seen as part of desiring production.

Gradiva is thus read through *Anti-Oedipus*. Zoe Bertgang, Norbert's childhood sweetheart, does not become the walking *woman*, but rather *walking* woman, the flow rather than the gender-identification being the key element in the fantasy. Lotringer indeed sees Zoe as an agent of repression in the text, for in 'curing' Norbert, acting as his analyst, she returns him 'to becoming-sensible . . . to becoming-husband' (ibid.). Thus the oedipal unconscious wins over the anti-oedipal 'productive' unconscious; the repression is reinforced. For Freud the delusion was a turning away from reality, but the schizoanalytic critic goes beyond even those psychoanalysts and critics who see illusion and play as a means of mediating the Real. For him 'delusion' need not be a delirium but may be the awakening of a sixth sense.

Both readings, the psychoanalytic and the schizoanalytic, call into question the nature of representation while allowing new forms of it. Freud's reading avoids the challenge coming from the ambiguous wish: the returning repressed must be pacified and returned whence it came. Lotringer's reading, on the other hand, centres on the radical implications of the ambiguous representation, thereby revealing a particular repression to be counter-productive, and pointing to the possibility of a way out of 'the text', both story and system.

9
Psychoanalysis and Ideology II: Focus on Dialectic

9.1 Psychoanalysis and the theatrical: the dance theatre of Pina Bausch

What is the relation of psychoanalysis to theatricality and to representation in general? Theatricality becomes the operative factor both in the consulting room and on the stage, since both are what Jean-François Lyotard has called 'disreal spaces' (1989, p. 156), in the sense that in each representations are tried out and the question arises of what is 'real' outside representation. Both in the analysis and in the drama there recur the crises that bespeak underlying conflicts of interpretation. The recognition of the implications of theatricality for life as such came relatively late, although the *theatrum mundi* analogy – 'All the world's a stage, / And all the men and women merely players' – has been a platitude for centuries. This recognition emerged in the wake of Freudian theory but via a circuitous route which entailed working through a mimetic fallacy. Just as there was an assumption which entailed the imitation of a pre-given reality at the level of consciousness, so too, by the same token, the unconscious was taken to be mirrored in the latent structure of a work, rather than being implicated in that very mimesis through the operations of the narcissistic subject in which both performers and spectators are involved.

Of particular relevance to this investigation is Freud's essay, 'Psychopathic characters on the stage' (see pp. 29–32 in this book), of which a

Some of the material in section 9.1 appears in different form in *Analysing Performance: A Critical Reader*, ed. Patrick Campbell, Manchester and New York: Manchester University Press, 1996.

sophisticated and extended version can be found in the work of psycho-analyst and critic André Green (see pp. 91–5 in this book), who develops the notion of theatre as 'the best embodiment of that "other scene", the unconscious' (Green 1979, p. 1). Just as the child is faced with the riddle of its parents, so the spectator is confronted by the enigma of being misheard and misunderstood. Every theatrical work is a riddle for the spectator and the invitation to solve it leads her/him to take up certain positions. The barrier of the edge of the stage sends the spectator's gaze back to her/himself as source, thus establishing a relation between subject and object and stimulating the hope 'that the secret behind the moment of disappearance of the repressed objects will be revealed' (ibid., p. 3), that the objects of fantasy will no longer be subject to repression. Art offers a lure, setting up a new category of object in the field of illusion, whereby the desired objects remain occult, available only in masked distorted form, to be appropriated in a way that does not disturb either the creator's or spectator's narcissistic idealization. Fantasy helps the creator/spectator couple to form a narcissistic pact: the objects are ejected and disappropri-ated by the artist in the hope that the spectator will appropriate and pro-cess them. The 'upsurge of desire that gave them birth' (ibid., p. 24) is repeated by each spectator, thus continually validating the narcissistic idealization of the creator via a series of mutual 'trans-narcissistic' desire-fantasies (see above p. 92). Hence the enjoyment gained is surreptitious, effected as it is through the displacements of sublimation inherent in the work of art (Freud 1908, IX), which enable it to negate the action of repression and afford a 'bonus of pleasure'. Green compares this with the symptom, which yields a certain unpleasure when, as a return of the repressed, it irrupts into consciousness, since forbidden satisfaction car-ries with it a need for punishment (Green 1979, pp. 22–3). The moment of catharsis, too, is a pleasure tinged with pain, involving an identification with the hero (pity) and his masochistic movement (terror). While this development of what might be called Freud's emerging psychoanalytic spectator theory in one sense breaks with Aristotle's poetics of the drama, in that the socially undesirable emotions are played with rather than got rid of, in another sense it is on a par with Aristotle, in that the process is still adaptive and maintains the status quo. The cathartic function is still the assuaging of unsatisfied desires, thus staying within the parameters of classical psychoanalysis.

Post-Freudian criticism takes a different reading from Freud, dispens-ing with the notion of art as luring the spectator into a collusive pact. In his essay, 'Theatricum analyticum' (see p. 31 of this book), Philippe Lacoue-Labarthe (1977) uses an advanced reading of psychoanalysis to overturn the would-be reassuring nature of a simplistic catharsis theory, which assumes the audience's passification in relation to the demands of the symbolic and hence a reconciliation to their fate. Such an assumption implies a classical theoretical dependence on a pleasure principle versus a reality principle, since it is based on the notion that a better catharsis is obtained through the recognition of the repressed unconscious impulse (pleasure principle) being opposed by a conscious one (reality principle); the result is a saving of libido, of economic expenditure, as Freud has it. This poses the question of the relation between the two processes. Lacoue-Labarthe argues that there is something theoretically prior to these principles. The communal belief in the Symbolic, enshrined in language, hides the fact of death and the cessation of desire which it nevertheless endlessly promises to fulfil: the unbinding play of the death drive introduces the notion of deferral with its element of risk. The reality principle does not provide a haven. The theatrical cannot help but show this disruption at the heart of drama, so that the effect is not simply an exorcism of anger, fear and resentment, but a recognition of the risk that is at the heart of all play, with its 'economy of difference and deferral' (Lacoue-Labarthe op. cit., p. 133).

This economy of play, is not, however, the reassuring play of an anaesthetizing form, but 'real' play, which, like the child's 'Fort/Da' (Freud 1920, XVIII, pp. 10–14), involves renunciation. The price of subjecthood is living out the real of the drives within the symbolic net. However, there being no simple opposition between a pleasure principle and a reality principle, real effects break out in both, producing a dual risk, in that neither inner nor outer, libido nor law, are stable elements. Instead of two opposed principles, there is a dialectical interplay that results from the ongoing repositioning of the symbolic net upon a basically unconceptualized ground, the Real. To enter the symbolic dooms us to repetition: to desire and to the sacrifice of desire. But whereas desire is 'noisy' when directed outwards in the guise of Eros as a part of the noise of life, desire is 'silent' when working inwardly in the guise of the death drive. In the latter case it is 'unmarked' (Phelan 1993), *unvorstellbar* /'unrepresentable' (Freud), 'unpresentable' (Lyotard 1983) and can only be theatricalized as the repeated attempt to re-present itself. Within the Dionysian/Apollonian struggle (Nietzsche) there is something that cancels the very notion of a utopian presence as promised by the symbolic, leaving only the possibility of 'the impossible ethical trial of the abyss' (Lacoue-Labarthe op. cit., p. 139). Time continually erodes all presence and necessitates beginning over again in the very face of death. Death is 'the empty form of time' (Deleuze 1994, p. 112); it is not simply something to which the living tries to return, but that of which the living tries to divest itself by means of repetition and differentiating modes of experience in its repeated attempts to enter the Symbolic. Theatricality thus turns up in the inescapable dialectic of the drives.

In the repetitions that are basic to performance there is a re-presenting of the recurrences to which the unconscious is bound. So what is being repeated? The trance of the transference is the vital affective means which tempts the subject into modifying those repetitive somnambulistic acts which mark the refusal to engage in the Symbolic. According to Cornelius Castoriadis (1994), psychoanalysis is a poetic practice faced with what Freud called an impossible task, the enabling of the patient to become autonomous largely through self-reflection upon the automatism of the unconscious. The dance theatre of the German choreographer Pina Bausch engages the spectator in this problematic in that it presents figures attempting to execute social roles and failing to do so. What we get to observe is the theatrical in everyday life.

Bausch's company was formed in the early seventies when she took charge of the Dance Theatre in Wuppertal, a small town in the Ruhr, since when her group has appeared all over the world. The works are long, often up to three or four hours. The scenes to be described are from a two-hour-long film, made for German Television (Zweites Deutsches Fernsehen) in 1993, her first venture into cinema. In it she uses the same principle of montage as she does in her stage performances. One difference is that, while her stage action is always decentred, several things going on simultaneously, the camera focuses on one image at a time. An analogous decentring effect appears, however, because there are no shot-reverse shots which show where the camera's look is coming from and hence the viewer is uncertain of where to insert him/herself into the fantasmatic scenarios. Otherwise Bausch uses the same principle of montage, alternating between swift cuts and agonizingly long ones, producing an associative but discontinuous linkage of scenic material. As in a psychoanalytic session, time is relentlessly subjectivized, stretching out in endless repetitions only to be suddenly and brutally cut. In both her theatre and film work there is a calculated lack of fit between decor, recorded music and speech or body language.

Bausch has always used concrete materials on the stage, whose sound and smell can be perceived – leaves, flowers, earth, grass, water – in order to estrange the familiar. These invasions of the real are doubly effective when the use of film enables her to go outside. The model animals she hitherto used on the stage are replaced by actual animals, sheep, goats, dogs and birds, acting as obstacles or milling around helplessly. She deals with that which won't be turned away, such as time, space, snow, earth, motion, weight. Her scenarios are, for example, set in actual time, which means lengthy and sometimes boring repetition, but it shows her subjects to be really exhausted by their futile efforts. She shows the traumatic element at the very core of the Symbolic by staging scenarios in which her subjects imaginarily act out nameless anxieties and confront specific fears. In the midst of a somnambulistic performance, when they are in thrall to the Other, to that which has determined them without their knowing it, the Real takes them by surprise. As traumatized figures, unaccountably driven, they stumble around, in a void filled with alienating music, either sentimentalized tunes, part of their would-be familiarity, or primitive chants of a disconcerting unfamiliarity. They are caught up and trapped by mud, stones and leaves, automatically impeded by machines that are out of control or coming too close for comfort. The opening sequence is of a woman struggling with a huge garden-vacuum, blowing masses of leaves randomly about, now and again taking a pot-shot at them from a pistol held in her hand; another scene is of a radio-controlled helicopter, emitting a menacing noise and zig-zagging in front of a man in a long billowing dress, standing on a dais with her/his back against a wall. There are also figures, obsessively engaged with the challenges of weight and space: for example, a long slow sequence of a man struggling with the dead weight of a large wardrobe, which he is endeavouring to carry across a wide green plain, his burden comically sliding off him over and over again, to the sounds of a wailing primitive chant; the next take is of a featherlight dancer, draped in veils, endlessly and silently turning cartwheels as if the body's desire to return to an imaginary weightlessness must be confirmed. Then again, in another sequence, this fantasy is denied by the Other's demand that the subject take its place in the symbolic: the legs of a dancing pair are cut off by the camera as they uncannily and parodically perform a ballroom dance which bawdily suggests a sexual encounter.

The film is entitled *Die Klage der Kaiserin* ('*The Plaint of the Empress*'): an empress has power within the Symbolic, but this 'empress', appearing in various guises throughout the film, is a figure who has given up on her desire and continually protests and fills the air with idle chatter, unable, like everyone else in it, to perform an act of mourning, exhibiting the kind of uncanny anxiety that, according to Heidegger, is caused by 'nothing', by what the would-be authentic self has not yet done.

Pina Bausch's figures show a world where there are no consoling 'transitional objects' in which inner and outer reality can coincide in a playful illusion. In her world the symbolic injunction of language will never match the real body without a measure of fixed trangressive fantasy. What makes Bausch's work so compelling is that her dancers demonstrate, in a what might now be called a post-Brechtian way, how the unconscious shows itself unconsciously: the docility of the figures comes about because the subjects do not know that the orders come from an Other. As actors they do not 'demonstrate' their unknowingness. Their somnambulistic behaviour reveals the unconscious effects of law and language on the body. The entry into the Symbolic generates transgression, which, as the performances amply illustrate, is 'enjoyed' in the symptom: the symptom yields surreptitious enjoyment and enables the subject to avoid the Real of lack. Hence enjoyment is not spontaneous but marked with prohibition. 'Enjoying your symptom' is covertly living out your transgression, allowing the element of the Real to slip into language by surreptitious means (Žižek 1992a, p. 14). The symptom is the resistance to the Other, the tell-tale sign of the law's implementation.

Performance theatre challenges any simple notion of mimesis, whether applied to the conscious or the unconscious. The discontinuities in the narratives of the subject, which displace the big narratives and grand illusions of the past, betray the theatrical nature of reality: the subject is theatrical through and through. The post-Freudian theatre, in the wake of Lacan, reveals theatricality as a necessary element in the construction of the subject. Its effect is to make the subject (artist and spectator) experience the gap between the body as a discursive construct and its felt embodiment in experience, between the representational (reality) and the Real, and to expose it to continual risk of further re-presentation.

9.2   Psychoanalysis and music

The gap between discourse and experience turns up again in the attempt to impute an organic structure to music. There is a desire to give a timeless symbolic perfection to the sonority of music, turning it into a music of the spheres, removed from the concreteness of the mundane world. Traditional music criticism has favoured unifying explanations which betray a rationalist prejudice, a 'constative' illusion, a term borrowed from J. L. Austin, applying to utterances that are true or false, as against 'performative', applying to those that are successful or unsuccessful (see Kramer 1995, p. 11, from whom the argument that follows is in part derived). What is in play in both music and language is an endless series of performatives. Modernist musicology, however, has been bound to 'a logic of alterity', defined as the imposition of a set of distinctions by which 'a normative unitary self, invested with universal significance' is given a privileged place, constituted by such oppositions, as, for instance, masculinity versus femininity, white versus non-white, hetero- versus homosexuality, and higher social class versus lower (ibid., pp. 34–5).

The question is, then, how music too has been drawn into this logic. On the one hand, its form was thought to have been delineated by the idea of a completeness of structure, every note in a great work having its organic place in a total system. Even the journey of every work conceived within the tonal system away from the tonic and back seems to emphasize this totality. The sonority of music has to be kept within bounds by the form because it appears to be searching out an alien otherness. Kramer here refers to Nietzsche's *The Case of Wagner*, a diatribe at the feminized submissiveness Nietzsche detects in Wagner's music, with which never-theless he cannot help betraying a fascination, in particular with the *Liebestod* in *Tristan und Isolde*. Such invectives against the Dionysian in music are not uncommon at the turn of the century, significantly often taking the form of giving voice to horror and disgust. The fusion that music invites produced a wide range of unease about emotional excess (Thomas Mann's work is cited as representative). Kramer interestingly associates this excess with the Kristevan notion of the 'abject', that which represents a fusion with the mother that must be rejected in order that the subject can maintain its own boundaries (Kristeva 1982, p. 10).

This fear of the Dionysian represents a determination to keep music in an unworldly realm, uncontaminated by contemporary influences and existing subjectivities. In particular, there is a hidden agenda in which music and language are regarded as remote from each other: where music is regarded as open to the ineffable, language is confined to the constative dimension, thereby being denied access to music. Here we move into both psychoanalytical and epistemological terrain, in that this begs the whole question of how reference is achieved, for language is as much alienated from any of its objects as it is from music. Moreover, as psychoanalysis shows, language cannot be exhausted along its constative dimension: Freudo-Lacanian psychoanalysis, as has been argued in this book, makes no distinction between poetic and ordinary language, between the perfor-mative and the constative. Music, like speech, is polysemic; the synchronics of language (*la langue*) are open to the diachronics of speech (*la parole*).

The very immediacy of music is a 'performative effect', an immediacy which 'empowers persons, institutions, social groups in control of its pro-ductions' (Kramer, ibid., p. 17). As a 'cultural trope' it is always found within a system of social forces, figuring the social construction of the subject. What traditional criticism does is to deny that music is a cultural trope, a view that has been perpetuated in the conservatoires and academies in order to keep music as a structured aesthetic object, untouched by suspect external influences. Hence the subject is supposedly insulated from the threat of the other, a listener enjoying his/her submissiveness to formal control in a masochistic way 'as a reward for his deliverance from worldliness' (ibid., p. 65).

A similar denial can be detected within the history of music itself. At the end of the seventeenth century music was still able to embody the utopian hope that individual and society, love and law, body and Symbolic might be brought into harmony. Slavoj Žižek (1997) instances the finale of Act II of *The Marriage of Figaro*, where the differing voices can arrive at a harmonious resolution, neither losing individuality nor dislodging the communal ideal. Pre-modernist music makes appeal to the 'big Other' in the guise of the Lady of courtly love, the revered King, the adored God, to respond to the entreaty and grant the longed-for bliss: 'music is an attempt to provoke an answer from the Real', in the hope of closing the lack that the Symbolic has instituted; music calls on a quasi-divine figure, either religious or amatory, who would appease the subject's longing for an ecstatic dissolution (Žižek 1997, p. 192). Such a finally fulfillable *jouissance* is what the Symbolic gives an illusory promise of, this being the answer that is continually demanded of the Real.

To pursue Žižek's argument: by the time Beethoven is writing, this utopian vision cannot be securely maintained; with the advent of Wagner's *Die Meistersinger von Nürnberg* it is under threat (the opera actually being about a song under threat). But the clearest indicator of this shift in vision is the changing status of melody. Emerging at its most popular and appealing in Viennese classicism, where it recalls past happiness, melody falls back in the nineteenth century with the bleak realization that the promised bliss had never been achievable in the first place. In the Romantic period music begins to speak not of a loss, but of 'a loss of a loss': where classicism is about 'a loss of what one had', romanticism 'is a loss of what one never had' (ibid., p. 195; Žižek here draws on Rosen 1996).

Where Kramer has shown that traditional and modernist criticism have pursued an ideal of unity and closure, keeping remote the threat of history, Žižek detects the same syndrome operative in melody. The symptoms of abjection that Kramer detects in nineteenth-century responses to musical excess find a parallel in the melancholy which Žižek locates in many Romantic and late-Romantic composers. The melancholy arises from the refusal to accept that there is a void in the place of what was yearned for. The melancholy yearning becomes a yearning for the void itself, the cessation of all desire, mobilizing the death drive towards this end. The refusal to yield up this blank longing is the Romantic gesture *par excellence*, turning the longing itself into a fetish object, of which the final 'Ewig, ewig' of Mahler's *Das Lied von der Erde* and the last movement of Tchaikovsky's 'Pathétique' Symphony may serve as examples. There is a kind of narcissistic indwelling upon the original gaze which has now lost its ideal object. This quest for a lost *jouissance* is particularly evidenced in opera, where the object, initially a (mother's) voice, whether desired by aficionados of opera or by characters in the libretto, becomes the loss of that voice: 'to identify with the lost vocal object is to become loss oneself, to become supreme purification, to *be* silence; in other words, to die' (Poizat 1992, p. 104).

Although some composers (Žižek cites Rachmaninov) are locked in the refusal to give up this object-less longing, there are others in whose work the realization of the disappearance of the ideal begins to show itself. Their music reflects this in 'the structural failure of full melody' (Žižek 1997, p. 197); the interruption or disappearance of melody becomes a figure for the vanishing of the ideal. Žižek takes the example of Schumann in whose *Lieder* there is a deliberate failure of the melodic line which manifests itself in the well-known form of a dialectic between voice and accompaniment. The voice is no longer in unquestioning command of a full and complete melody – with the accompaniment no more than what its name implies – but it yields to the melodic line in interruptions and cessations, with the piano sometimes taking over the main melody from the voice. Sometimes there is also an effect of a suppressed melody, indicating a reluctance to dwell upon a longing for its own sake, an acceptance of symbolic castration, an acknowledgement that the lack is constitutive of subjecthood. According to Žižek, this disappearance of the voice is to be seen as profoundly anti-humanist, since the subject has lost its illusion of singularity, seeing its existence as 'virtual', a fictive construct over a void (ibid., p. 204).

In following the reception of the *Lied*, Kramer distinguishes two modes of response, one that uncritically enters into the nostalgic world of the song and one that is conscious of seductions that now verge on the obsolete. The nostalgic world is one of 'birds and blossoms, sighs and tears, *Heimweh* and *Heimkehr*, the turns of all natural cycles . . . a scene of love and death removed from history' (Kramer, p. 143); what hides within this world is 'the authority of the modern nuclear family' (p. 144), which positions the listener as oedipal subject. To enter the nostalgic world is to run the risk of becoming a melancholy subject (by Žižek's definition): Kramer's recommended strategy is to detect the authoritarianism that resides in the seduction. The example given is that of Mendelssohn's Goethe songs, in each of which there is a female voice ostensibly asking for a sign of love, the price of which is her submission to a master on whom she as disciple is dependent, which not only signals Mendelssohn's own tutelage to Goethe but the whole problematic of the tutelage relationship in Germany at that time, resting as it did on the Greek prototype.

Such a distanced form of reception, in which awareness of cultural tropes is a part of the process of musical appreciation, is an act of performative listening, whereby the beguiling seductions are displaced and their new pathos now become an element in the aesthetic experience. A psychoanalytic music criticism inflected by the postmodern will endeavour to discern the traces of instability and fragmentation that underlie the supposedly timeless ahistorical music of the spheres.

9.3 Psychoanalysis and popular culture: Slavoj Žižek

The idea that art is always both cultural trope (figuring what the social requires of us) and sensuous aesthetic object (with a 'life' of its own) is perhaps most strikingly evidenced in popular culture, where the first aspect is generally ignored and therefore the relation between the two is rarely inquired into. Perhaps the most remarkable intrusion of psychoanalytic criticism to enter this field in the last ten years or so has been that of Slavoj Žižek, the nucleus of whose work is still in his book, *The Sublime Object of Ideology* (1989).

What is the 'sublime object of ideology'? At its simplest it is that which we most ardently desire, imagining it to be in the possession of the Other; this object, beyond everything else, is what is unconsciously believed will fill the void at the core of being. This void is the effect of the constitution of the subject in language out of the real of the body with all its undirected drives, which language vainly tries to bring entirely within its laws. The subject owes its existence to those laws before it can even question them. The dilemma arising therefrom, as Žižek sees it (following the later Lacan), is that the subject finds itself confronted with a *fait accompli*, as having already chosen to yield up its incestuous object, the mother, and, what amounts to the same thing, to submit to the law of language, the Father's Law. This 'choice' is to be regarded as a 'forced' one, summed up as *le père ou pire*, the father or worse (Žižek 1992b, pp. 75–6; Lacan 1971–2), the worse 'choice' being to stay out of the Symbolic, as a psychotic, thus losing the very possibility of choice. The subject is therefore alienated from its very inception, hence designated as a barred subject ($), one whose signifier will never match its signified. Hence the subject is condemned to a repetition in which the ideal order of the Law forever fails to 'integrate some "impossible" kernel of the Real' (Žižek 1992b, p. 79). This part-failure of subjectivization produces a void that the subject continually tries to disguise from itself with the support of fantasy, in an attempt to assuage an internal antagonism arising from the impossibility of symbolizing that kernel. The fantasy invariably takes the form of believing that it is in the Other that 'the fullness of enjoyment' is to be found (Žižek 1990, p. 254). The 'sublime' object of ideology is an object which, be it in life, in art or in popular culture, is elevated into possessing in its very being the attributes that are felt to be painfully missing in the subject.

At the same time as sustaining this idealization the subject projects its own internal antagonisms outside itself onto an external adversary; the more intense this antagonism, the more it blinds the subject to its own internal, irreparable split. Social fantasies, similarly, chart attempts to fill out the void at the heart of the social structure (Žižek here refers to the work of the political theorists Laclau and Mouffe, 1985). As a gross example there is the Fascist attempt to attribute the distance between the promised utopia and a society riven by strife to an external factor, the Jew: 'it can be easily shown how the figure of the Jew is a symptom in the sense of a coded message, a cipher, a disfigured representation of social antagonism' (Žižek 1989, p. 126). The Jew had for economic and religious reasons already existed for centuries as the embodiment of Christian negativity. The National Socialists were able to build on this, first, by displacing class antagonisms onto the supposedly rich Jews, and then, by attributing to them a whole series of contradictory features: 'Jews are supposed to be dirty *and* intellectual, voluptuous *and* impotent' (ibid., p. 125). Typically, the object of racial hatred is regarded as stealing the subject's enjoyment. The social fantasy as such can be seen to parallel the primal internal fantasy which hides the internal antagonism.

Social fantasies need not, of course, only take such pathological forms. In popular culture these structures can be seen to be equally operative, even if the ideological effects do not have such immediately disastrous consequences. What is the disturbance around which these popular cultural forms revolve? The motive force is the same as for the blatantly political: to provide a fantasmatic cover for the split in the subject, its constitutive void which never ceases to try to inscribe itself. In his book, *Looking Awry: An Introduction to Jacques Lacan through Popular Culture*, Žižek (1991a) shows how the Real through its resistance to direct description distorts both the operations of the Symbolic and the mundane realities that the Symbolic appears to uphold; the book is an account of the strategies adopted by readers and audiences to enable them to ignore the Real of their desire.

In his analysis of popular culture, Žižek discusses the move from one mode of crime fiction to another in order to illustrate 'two ways to avoid the Real of desire' (1991a, pp. 48–66). He examines the two main types of detective story, the logic-and-deduction form and the hard-boiled private eye one. The first is characterized as going from the 'lawless sequence' to the 'lawful sequence', with normality re-established by the detective (analyst) through his re-reading of the murderer's false narrative, discovering the truth *in the very mode of its false telling*, a misleading narrative projected by the murderer (patient?). The second is seen as revealing the detective, not as detached spectator, but as drawn into the false narrative, involved with the disturbing events he himself relates.

The classical sleuth notices that something does not quite fit into the frame of the apparent reality: the 'clue' makes evident that the unity of the scene is only imaginary, only apparently natural. The scene of crime is a scene of 'free association' analogous to the scene of analysis, beginning with a traumatic shock – a sequence of lawless events emanating from the Real – which cannot be made to fit into symbolic reality. The clue is an image of pathological excess, a trap set for speculation, a field of meaning meant to lure. Each element 'means' in relation to another; nothing means in itself but in its intention to mean for someone else, to deceive. As a result of this deception the suspicion falls upon a group of suspects, bound together by their putative guilt: the killer attracts to himself the desire of the group to find a scapegoat – a libidinal gain for the reader to offload his or her personal guilt, for which the sleuth provides the justification in pointing the finger of blame. This is the first of the two ways in which the subject is able to avoid the Real of its desire.

The reader/analysand expects the detective/analyst to be the 'subject-supposed-to-know' (Lacan's term for the patient's imputation of knowledge to the analyst), and thus to see the true meaning in the false appearance, to transform the random lawless sequence into an ordered lawful one. The fact that the classical detective routinely receives payment confirms his place in the symbolic structure, thus enabling him to maintain an 'ex-centric' position (ibid., p. 75). The hard-boiled private eye, on the other hand, gets tied up in the libidinal circuit. Unlike the classical detective, he is not immediately concerned with payment; he is pursuing an individual ethical course through a corrupt world, whereby he cannot help but incur guilt. By the end of the story he has settled his debt, often in an ambivalent confrontation with a *femme fatale*. This wry absolution is the second of the two ways in which the subject (author/ character/reader) avoids the Real of his/her desire, sustaining the illusion that the ideal form of the Law has integrated the 'impossible' kernel, that the Real has been brought back within the scope of the Symbolic.

In *The Sublime Object of Ideology* Žižek, in a similar vein, uses Hitchcock's films to reveal the nature of the 'MacGuffin', the little bit of the Real that destabilizes the balance of the Symbolic, disrupting 'the homeostatic indifference of relations between subjects' (1989, p. 183). According to Hitchcock, a MacGuffin is an object which is nothing in itself, but which is of vital importance to the characters, who are therefore either in pursuit of it or trying to hold onto it. Like the Real, this object is only to be grasped through its effects: for example, the cigarette lighter in *Strangers on a Train* functions as the guarantee which maintains the murderous agreement, proposed to the protagonist, Guy, by the murderer, Bruno – the theme of which is a transference of guilt, a central motif in Hitchcock's universe (Žižek 1991a, p. 74). What is frightening is the emergence within the Symbolic of this unwanted Real guilt (when Guy's unpleasant wife is murdered), intensified by the Other (the police) being in pursuit of the 'innocent' Guy. By the conclusion of Hitchcock's films this guilt has invariably been purged (often at the expense of the woman; see Modleski 1989), leaving the spectator with the inner antagonism anaesthetized.

Such a scrutiny of popular culture as a rich source of social and political fantasy epitomizes the dialectical approach adopted by the artists and critics considered in this part of the book, providing evidence that there is a dynamic between regarding art as an ideological construct and art as an aesthetic object. In both popular and highbrow culture a new reading can include the suspect fantasies as part of the total aesthetic experience, whether it be the longing for complete symbolic confirmation or the horror of what is concealed by the fantasy. The dialectical approach has been carried further in a remarkable way by feminist psychoanalytic criticism, with a crucial stake in its outcome.

PART V

10
Feminist Psychoanalytic Criticism

This section will examine contemporary issues concerning a viable feminist critique of literature and the arts. Psychoanalytic criticism and feminist criticism did not properly join forces and become textually and politically sophisticated until the early eighties, the heyday of post-structuralism. Since then, feminist psychoanalytic criticism has become an ever-expanding field. Feminist interventions in the production and reception of the arts have made a distinct contribution towards revealing art to be a cultural practice that has historically excluded the subjectivities of women: much of feminist criticism has been a concerted effort to challenge the representation of woman as constructed within a patriarchal symbolic. Feminist literary and art criticism, and feminist film criticism have a particular investment in the exploration of sign systems in order to discover how woman is signified, how she came to be positioned in pre-ordained social roles – daughter, wife, mother – within the restrictions of an inherited patriarchal circuit. Hence, psychoanalysis as the only discourse offering a theory of the subject of the unconscious has been crucial for feminists and indeed for all those who want to situate themselves outside a rigid definition of sexual difference: the unconscious, however theorized, is the ground from which such rigid definitions might be questioned and disestablished. Nevertheless, feminists have not been slow to undertake systematic critiques of Freud's repeated efforts to define femininity (see, for instance, Kofman 1985 [1980]) and have been equally assiduous in launching ambivalent critiques against Lacan (Gallop 1982; Grosz 1990). This is not the place to make a special case for those feminist analysts and theorists (Irigaray and Cixous for instance) who have made distinguished contributions though their revisions of Freud's view of women but whose impact on the psychoanalytic criticism of the arts has so far been indirect.

One of the currents of feminist psychoanalytic literary criticism that produced a strong following in the eighties took its impulse from object-relations theory, particularly with regard to relations between women, most notably those of mothers and daughters. Running counter to Freudo-Lacanian theory, it took as its themes plenitude rather than lack, connection rather than castration, celebrating the pre-oedipal closeness between mother and daughter rather than the oedipal loss (see Hirsch 1992). The source for these investigations was mainly the novel, but there was also a crucial examination of Freud's self-confessed inadequacy 'in Dora's case', as a collection of essays came to be called (Bernheimer and Kahane, 1985), which re-read the case-history arguing that he misinterpreted Dora's desire through his patriarchal prejudice. A more recent example focusing on women's oppression takes up the distortions of hysterical narratives that result from the intrusion of the woman's speaking voice into the text of the novel, revealing 'the passions of a narrative voice disordered by its own productions', failing to keep control as it tries to portray women in revolt (Kahane 1995).

In this section I take on some of the major issues of current contention between psychoanalysis and feminism. This is not intended as a survey of the whole field because I believe that the general issues I want to engage with here are best presented by focusing on a select group of topics centrally concerned with sexual difference. I begin with Lacan's sexuation formulas in an attempt to clarify how women and men have to deal differently with the failure of the Symbolic. I argue, with particular reference to the feminine, that the formulas provide an asymmetrical schema of how sexual identifications are in play both in life and art.

10.1 The critique of the phallus

In the Freudian universe of discourse sexual difference is neither reduced to a biological given nor wholly constituted by social practices. A great conceptual difficulty for psychoanalysis, but also a central part of its theoretical importance for feminism, is its tenet, now reduced to a cliché, that anatomy alone does not determine sexual identity, this being a matter of identifications. Neither can sexual difference be reduced to the social alone even though the child's identification with one or the other sex is

Some of the material in section 10.1 appears in different form in *Coming out of Feminism?* ed. Mandy Merck, Naomi Segal and Elizabeth Wright, Oxford: Blackwell Publishers, 1998.

both variable and subject to social convention. So, if male/female sexualities are not essential categories and masculine/feminine not just historical constructs, what creates sexual difference?

For Freud it was the meaning ascribed to anatomical differences, of male and female sexual organs when interpreted in terms of presence and absence. As a consequence, neither sex is complete: males suffer from castration anxiety, females from penis envy. This part of the Freudian doctrine has produced much incredulity and offence because it invited and still invites so literal an interpretation.

Lacan, by considering psychoanalysis as a sexuation process, takes psychoanalysis a step further. But his theory of sexuation, the origin and development of sexual difference within the field of language, has really not fared much better. Initially hailed for its decisive turn from biology-as-destiny to the constitution of the subject in language, his theory all too soon lost its popularity with feminists as his various statements on Woman and the emphasis in his earlier work on the phallus as signifier of difference became as contentious as Freud's several treatises on femininity and his pronouncements on penis envy. Feminists of all kinds declare war on the phallus as master-signifier. Even though they may well recognize that 'phallus' is here used figuratively instead of literally (the penis) they still find objectionable the use of the figure derived from that bit of a man's body. Although there are good historical reasons for the use of the term 'phallus' inasmuch as the phallus has played the role of penis in the cultural fantasies and imagination of the West, from, for example, the Dionysian mysteries to the fantasies revealed in early psychoanalytical case histories, the algebraic signs of the sexuation formulas cannot be given a signified which can be culturally monopolized. In these formulas it becomes evident that the phallic function, the function of castration – the sacrifice demanded by the Symbolic – applies in different ways to both sexes, that it is not the case that the woman has lost something which the man does not have to lose, and that neither sex can have or be everything.

Until recently not a great deal of Lacan's work has been available in translation, and hence critical comment in the Anglophone world was largely restricted to the essays from the fifties in *Écrits*, particularly his essay 'The Signification of the Phallus' (Lacan 1977a [1958]; see, for instance, Silverman 1992). There is now a complete translation of *Encore*, Lacan's Seminar XX (1998 [1975]), where he puts forward his formulas for defining the masculine and feminine position in the sexuation process. In his first theory of sexuality in the 1950s, Lacan, taking his cue from Freud, centred on the function of the phallus as distinguishing between the sexes, seeing the man as wanting *to have* the phallus, the woman as wanting *to be* the phallus, which does not imply at all that the two sexes can be regarded as complementary since masculinity and femininity, as will be seen, rely on completely different dynamics. Although the being/having dichotomy gives two clear types of sexual position, this indicates no more than two imaginary modes of identification by means of which each sex wards off castration. 'Waiving the phallus' (Adams 1992), rather than waving it, is the fate of man and woman alike.

My discussion is based on chapters VI and VII of *Encore*, 'God and ~~Woman~~'s *jouissance*' and 'A Love Letter' (chapter VII includes the formulas) (Lacan 1998 [1975]). My aim is to show to what extent the feminist critique of the phallus is based on a misunderstanding of what the sexuation process implies.

Lacan uses symbols from a modified form of the predicate calculus as he is dealing with the application of binary definitions to a hitherto disorganized part of existence, the distinguishing of entities in sets being common to language, mathematics and sexual difference. The formulas show each group as embodying an existential and a universal proposition which are in a contradictory relation to each other.

In each case there is a failure of the Symbolic, but it is a different failure for each sex. The failure is a question of the degree to which *jouissance*, the satisfaction of the drive, is accommodated for each sex within a given symbolic system. The logic of sexuation divides the field of speaking beings in two:

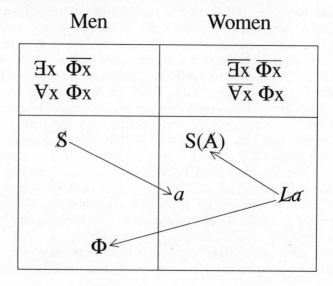

In the top half of diagram 1 there are four propositions, two existential
(∃) and two universal (∀).

The male existential (∃X $\overline{\phi}\overline{X}$) can be rendered as 'there is an entity x
that says "no" to the phallic function'; the male universal (∀X ϕX) as 'all
x's are subject to the phallic function'.

On the female side there are also two contrasting propositions: the
female existential ($\overline{\exists}\ \overline{X}\ \ \overline{\phi}\overline{X}$), 'there is no entity x that says "no" to the
phallic function'; the female universal ($\overline{\forall}\ \overline{X}\ \ \phi X$), 'not all of x is subject
to the phallic function'.

The phallic function (ϕ) is the castration performed by the Symbolic.
As a product of this procedure the (imaginary) phallus comes to signify
the prohibited *jouissance* – the greater part of drive satisfaction that is forbidden to all subjects. This is the sacrifice demanded of men and women
alike for entry into the Symbolic, for the very assumption of subjecthood.

All speaking beings inscribe themselves in whatever way they want,
regardless of their biological sex. The inscription is the result of an identification. For the male side the identification coincides with the phallic
function; the exception of the primal father (see below) demands sacrifice and unites the group. For the female side woman is 'not-all' identified
with the phallic function; she says yes *and* no, yes *or* no to it, the female
formula demonstrating the undecidability and impossibility of totalizing
the woman. Femininity is not organized as a universal function as is
masculinity; hence 'not-all' the woman is subject to the phallic function.
The woman's side exists, but not as a defined set as that for man, and this
is why Lacan uses the hyperbole '*The* Woman does not exist'.

She has an additional possibility, as the lower diagram shows: she is
bound to castration through her subjection to the phallic function, but
she is also related to the signifier of the barred Other (S(Å). A stands for
'*Autre*'), a paradoxical statement because to admit a lack in the Other is a
recognition that the promised rewards of the Symbolic are not guaranteed.
As a consequence, she has a connection to the Real, a supplementary
jouissance, one not related to the castration enjoined by the phallic function – a *jouissance* that castration forgets. For the man, a surplus *jouissance*
– what he is denied by castration (shown by the barring of the subject, $\mathcal{S}$)
– is trapped by the object a, a fantasy concealing his lack that is the
inevitable outcome of being subjected to the phallic function.

The phallic function applies to all, guaranteed by the one exception
of the Father (linked to the primal Father in Freud's *Totem and Taboo*
(1912, XIII)), who appears as exempt from castration, and hence is
the source of the law of castration that bears on the desires of all others.
Since Woman, however, is not completely defined by the phallic function,

La (~~The~~) is crossed out, indicating that she does not form a set, having access to two modes of *jouissance*, a sexual and an asexual kind.

All speaking beings end up by being castrated, giving up a part of their *jouissance*; the male identification too is bound to fail since the phallus does not give absolute power. In the case of both male and female beings, there is a failure with respect to the Symbolic: woman's failure is with the signifier and man's failure is with the object. The man pursues a fantasy by which means he attempts to totalize the woman as the absolute Other, the one who lacks nothing: the woman is tempted into a 'masquerade', a performative act in which she attempts to become the fantasy for the man. Both attempts are a denial of lack and fail because of the invasion of the Real into the Symbolic. Thus, the logic of sexuation produces two sets of speaking beings that are not in a complementary relation to each other. Each sex is lacking but it is not a penis they lack, even though the phallus is used as a metaphor, stands for the phallic function, for that which enjoins separation and constitutes a subject.

Note that the formulas do not plot which sexual position the subject may take up; they are not hetero-sexuation formulas. What they reveal is the historical limits of the possibility of change, not a particular subject's object-choice, which can go across biology. And whatever the biology of human beings might become in the far-flung future, their society will still demand a binary of some kind, the equivalent of a 'castration' by means of which identifications would be constituted. For Lacan these formulas are concerned with how a speaking being experiences sexuality on the level of the psyche. They have nothing to do with biological sex, neither with the love of a man for a woman, nor that of a man for a man, nor that of a woman for a woman. This implies that a biological male can function according to the female side and a biological female according to the male. Following this line of reasoning a Lacanian feminism would imply a fundamental recognition of the singularity of the feminine element.

10.2   The problem of masquerade

The diagram has shown that woman is not in a complementary relation to man and hence the discordance of the sexes shows itself in pretence and masquerade. In a celebrated article Joan Riviere (1929) introduces

Some of the material in section 10.2 appears in different form in the *Cambridge Companion to Brecht*, ed. Peter Thomson and Glendyr Sachs, Cambridge: Cambridge University Press, 1994.

the idea of womanliness as a performance that itself constitutes womanliness within the social; as Emily Apter comments, 'There is no absolute femininity beneath the veil, only a set of ontologically tenuous codes that normatively induct the feminine subject into the social practice of "being" woman through mimesis and parroting' (Apter 1992, p. 243). Riviere's example is the female intellectual who excels at playing both a male and female role in her life. One such woman, a patient of Riviere's, followed a day spent after a successful public performance by a night seeking reassurance for what she felt to be her inappropriate behaviour. She obtained this reassurance by being flirtatious and seductive. She wished to hide her masculinity in a dual attempt to ward off her belief that she had stolen the father's penis and to defend herself against the feared retribution. Thus, argues Riviere, womanliness could be put on both to hide the phallic position and to forestall reprisals for taking it up (Riviere 1929, pp. 304–6). But is there a distinction between genuine womanliness and the pretence? No, says Riviere, they are the same. There is a capacity for womanliness, but it can only manifest itself in this defensive way. 'Femininity is nothing but the mask itself, or the mask is itself the truth of femininity as a phallic emblem' (Brousse 1991, p. 124).

It is inevitable that the masquerade, particularly because of its dramatic nature, has become a recurring topos in art. In Brecht's *The Good Person of Szechwan* (1970 [1943]) the figure of masquerade is not only the central theme but invests the very structure of the work. I shall dwell at some length on this piece, not only because it brings out so forcibly the predicament of women under the patriarchal system but also because it shows the failure of the classic Marxist discourse to confront this issue.

As a woman, Shen Te is already implicated in a masquerade: she is the 'good woman' wanting to live up to being 'an Angel of the slums' (Brecht, p. 106), thereby placating her suitors and the father-gods, who respectively derive economic and moral advantage therefrom. The appearance of her male half, Shui Ta, is a defence against the failure of this masquerade, thus reversing the strategy of Riviere's patient, whose 'feminine' impersonation (coquetry/being the phallus) came to the rescue of her 'masculine' one (success and achievement/having the phallus).

Shen Te is split into the good exploited female and bad exploiting male. In her first masquerade, as Shen Te, she is attractive for her very helplessness and innocence, while as Shui Ta, her second masquerade, she is attractive for her power. Divided by these masquerades, she occupies the hysterical position in that she endeavours to perform (both in the sense of functioning in and acting out) the historically specified mode of symbolic identification for the woman. Although for Brecht her profession

'demonstrates' economic necessity ('Let me admit: I sell myself in order
to live', p. 10), for the gods, to whom she makes this admission and who
cautiously pay her for their overnight lodging, she is a lure and forbidden
source of (obscene) enjoyment: 'But please let nobody know that we paid.
It might be misinterpreted' (p. 11).

Shen Te is placed in a subordinate position by a number of different
systems and not just by a single mechanism, that of a woman with property within capitalism and its market economy. Her oppression is three-
fold: economic as a prostitute, psychic as a romantic beloved, social as a
pregnant mother. Moreover, the various reactions to her in each of these
positions ally with each other to disempower her in specifically concrete
ways. Where in her 'masculine' masquerade Shen Te is immediately
accepted as a shop/factory owner, in her 'feminine' masquerade she is
repeatedly called to account. Shui Ta as a man inspires confidence without further credentials for being 'sharp as a knife' (p. 16) and for his
'decisive action' (p. 29), while Shen Te as 'Angel of the slums' is used
and exploited both by her fellow citizens and by her lover. The gods, the
Other, desire her to 'freely follow the impulses of her gentle heart' (p. 22)
and Shen Te's desire accords with this, declaring that 'to love, honour and
cherish a husband would be very pleasant' (p. 10). But although as rejected
lover she weeps, as mother she vows to be 'a tiger, a savage beast/To all
others if need be. And/It need be' (p. 77), which means further 'masculine' masquerade. It is not that Brecht is unaware of the sexist behaviour of Shen Te's lover (Yang Sun: 'You want to appeal to her reason!
She hasn't any reason!' (p. 53)), but that he sees this sexist behaviour
as economically determined, rather than discursively constructed, as an
effect of capitalist rather than gender oppression.

For Lacan, the unsymbolizable remains of the living body and its experiences, real (material) lack, is the inevitable consequence of the loss of
the primal object – the mother – and an inescapable part of the constitution of the subject. Both the Imaginary (from the viewpoint of the subject)
and the Symbolic (from the viewpoint of society) operate as if there were
no lack, the Imaginary by a fantasy of plenitude (e.g. Shen Te's romantic
love and maternal joy), the Symbolic by appearing to promise fulfilment
(the gods as perceived by Wang and Shen Te). But at least two songs in
the play admit the bankruptcy in the Symbolic. 'The Song of the Smoke',
features lack (*Mangel* translated as 'hunger') as lack of hope (pp. 19–20),
while 'The Song of Green Cheese' ('*Das Lied vom Sankt Nimmerleinstag*'
– 'Never-Never-Day') declares through five stanzas that only 'when the
moon is green cheese' will the earth become a paradise (pp. 68–9). In
these songs the lack in the Other is of course figured as an anti-myth, as a

challenge to bourgeois inertia and complacency. Brecht, however, prefers to perceive lack as principally in the capitalist system rather than in the Real of the subject, that portion of being that falls outside the Imaginary and Symbolic, 'the traumatic kernel the symbolization of which always fails' (Žižek 1991, pp. 197–209). Shen Te cannot find a signifier which is her own, she cannot say it 'all' (p. 108), she cannot represent herself in the Symbolic as either 'good' or 'bad'. Her sobbing is a testimony to the failure of either Shen Te or Shui Ta to fill the lack with words (p. 92).

Shen Te breaks apart through trying to carry out the mandate of the gods: she can neither be the 'good person' producing Imaginary plenitude, nor can she stop trying to fill out the void in the Symbolic, the lack in the Other. When her second masquerade fails, her hysterical position comes to the fore, for she resists the specified Symbolic identification of 'good person': 'But do you not understand that I am the wicked person whose many crimes you heard described?' (p. 106). She perceives that in order to survive she must sustain a dual masquerade, spoken by the Symbolic when called upon to help, speaking from the Imaginary when in love: 'goodness to others/And to myself could not both be achieved./To serve both self and others I found too hard' (p. 105). Shen Te is a hysterical subject by the end of the play, asking – Why me? Why do I have this mandate? What does the Other want of me?

Shen Te's idealization of the phallic, bourgeois hero and Yang Sun's response to her 'womanly' masquerade testify to the precariousness of the feminine, which also implicates Brecht as male author unable to extricate himself from his masculinist discourse. *Pace* Brecht, what Shen Te's dilemma shows is that there is no essential femininity behind the phallic mask, but a woman 'accommodating rather: to the point where there is no limit to the concessions made by any woman for *a* man: of her body, her soul, her possessions. Powerless with respect to her fantasies which are less easy to control . . . she prepares herself on-the-off-chance, so that her inner fantasy of Man will find its hour of truth' (Lacan 1990, p. 40). This preparing of herself is what masquerade is about and which the illusory effects of the cinema are particularly apt to explore.

10.3 The feminist critique of the cinema

In their use of psychoanalytic theory feminists have paid particular attention to the function of the image, the gaze, the producer and the spectator, for all of which the locus of the cinema may be regarded as paradigmatic. The conjunction of psychoanalysis and the cinema first emerged as a powerful form of ideological criticism through the publication of the British film journal *Screen* in the mid-seventies and eighties, continuing in the later seventies also through the North American feminist film journal, *Camera Obscura* (see particularly Bergstrom and Doane 1989). This criticism announced itself in an early use of Lacan's concepts of the mirror phase and the Imaginary, and his development of the Freudian drive and the split subject. For an account of its inception and its subsequent and crucial feminist trajectory I have drawn on a number of sophisticated versions (see in particular Kaplan 1990 and Penley 1989).

Much of seventies' criticism took off from the work of Christian Metz (1982 [1977]), discussed p. 110), who theorized the contribution made by psychoanalysis to an understanding of how film and cinema worked at an unconscious level. In particular he discussed the way the 'scopic regime' of the cinema leads to mechanisms of voyeurism and fetishism: cinema becomes a desiring machine by bringing into play the 'scopic drive'. What is the scopic drive? In Lacan's rethinking of Freud the gaze and voice are both first incorporated by the infant in concrete response to the mother's recognition of it; in Lacan's mirror phase the mother is already implicated through being present in the infant's perception of itself, which includes being held. The result is a locating of the subject in the field of the Other, the social. From then on the scopic drive (associated with the eye) essentially involves the subject's constituting itself in relation to others: 'what is involved in the drive is making oneself seen (*se faire voir*). The activity of the drive is concentrated in this *making oneself* (*se faire*)' (Lacan 1977b, p. 195). Thus, in the scopic fantasy the subject exists only in relation to an imaginary gaze, the (m) Other's.

With this notion of the gaze, feminist film criticism comes into force, but there is still a theoretical difficulty owing to the fact that feminist psychoanalytic film critics conflate a notion of the 'look' with that of the 'gaze'. The French term *'le regard'* serves for either, but the translators of Lacan use 'gaze', while those of Sartre use 'look'. In Sartre's thinking *le regard* (look) is on the side of the subject; while in Lacan's later thinking *le regard* (gaze) is on the side of the object, in the field of the Other (for further elaboration see Evans 1996, pp. 72–3). Thus, it has to be made clear that in the discussion of what came to be known as the cinema's specular regime the look is identified with the camera and the camera is on the side of the subject.

Psychoanalytic film criticism sees the cinema spectator as positioned by the cinematic apparatus, which includes a darkened room, larger-than-life figures overhead, and methods of classical editing which 'suture' the spectator into the filmic narrative in analogy with the Lacanian mirror phase. 'Suture' is a metaphor taken from surgery for the uniting of two body surfaces, especially the stitching together of the edges of a wound. According to Metz, the primary identification is with the spectator's own activity of looking, not with the persons on the screen: the cinematic signifier constructs a fetishistic relation for the spectator to the frame, the characters, the story, and even to the cinematic institution itself. Since in classical Hollywood cinema the camera is usually controlled by a male director, the spectator's perception is joined to the orchestration of the male look, which leads us to the point of feminist intervention.

Feminist film criticism came into its own with the appearance of a celebrated essay by Laura Mulvey (1989a [1975]), which inaugurated a strong feminist investment in questions of representation. She argued that the look is linked to the discovery of sexual difference, the woman's lack of a penis. In Hollywood cinema from the thirties to the fifties various glamorous images of women were destined to fill this lack, such that the woman becomes a substitute for the imaginary phallus, provoking and satisfying the male viewers' voyeuristic and fetishistic needs. As Mulvey famously formulated it, this makes the man the active bearer of the look and the woman its passive object (Mulvey op. cit., pp. 18–19). In identifying with the camera held by a male director, the spectator identifies with the male look. The spectator is thereby sutured into the film from an unavoidably masculine voyeuristic position. An important corollary of this analysis was that Mulvey theorized pleasure as a negative term, a mark of the spectator's collusion with an oppressive sexual system. With the appearance of this article the film became a feminist weapon *par excellence*, such that 'feminism and psychoanalysis became tools in an absorbing act of decipherment for Mulvey's film theory and for its discovery of "active spectatorship" which aimed to lay bare "the social unconscious under patriarchy"' (Lebeau 1995, p. 38).

The late eighties and early nineties, however, saw the launching of a late Lacanian critique of the use made of Lacan in Metz's and Mulvey's analyses, which now sees these analyses as grounded in a misconception of Lacan's notion of the gaze, as presenting the subject as too much determined by the image on the screen. In her article, 'The Orthopsychic Subject: Film Theory and the Reception of Lacan', Joan Copjec (1994 [1989]) argues for a distinction between the screen conceived as a mirror (derived from the Lacanian mirror phase) and the mirror conceived as a screen (to be derived from a proper understanding of the Lacanian gaze). The problem arises because the Lacanian gaze has been confused with the Foucauldian 'panoptic gaze' which defines the perfect visibility of woman under patriarchy and 'of any subject at all' (Copjec, p. 17): the panoptic apparatus of the nineteenth century denies the existence of what lies outside the visible and the known (Foucault 1980c [1972], pp. 146–56). This is not to say that this apparatus ignores the fact that individual subjects are in conflict as to what constitutes knowledge, but rather that the apparatus assumes that a determinate knowledge, totally defined, can be arrived at as the outcome of such conflicts. The Lacanian system, to the contrary, shows that what is produced by a signifying system can *never* be determinate. Conflict here does not arise 'from the clash between two different positions, but from the fact that no position defines a resolute identity' (Copjec, p. 18), that no definitive knowledge can be arrived at.

The new view of the cinema as an apparatus was radical to the extent that it put paid to a theory of representation grounded in a reality presumed to be already there before the discourses which help to construct both it and the spectatorial subject. The concept of 'apparatus', as Copjec shows, came in the wake of Gaston Bachelard and Louis Althusser, who both traced discourses to their historical determinations. As a consequence, the imaginary dimension revealed in Lacan's mirror phase was taken as a necessary ideological founding of the subject, who was thereby seduced into an illusion of his/her own mastery of the image. But the trouble with this argument is its seeing ideology as all-embracing, for then the subject becomes no more than a determinant of the social system, a puppet. Although, following Metz, film criticism turned away from a naive mimetic theory (that of image matching reality), it still operated with the narcissistic link between image and spectator. The image that the subject is ideologically induced to project continued to be taken as a pure match for the subject her/himself. The result was that the conflation of the 'reality effect' (the image of the world as the subject sees it) and the 'subject effect' (the image that the subject has of itself) produced the illusion that the subject is fully visible to itself (Copjec, p. 22).

In Seminar XI (Lacan 1977b [1973]) Lacan theorizes the distinction between the eye and the gaze (discussed above, pp. 107–10), showing that the speaking subject can never be wholly trapped in the Imaginary; the process that brings the ideological operation of subject-construction about cannot be assumed to work without any error. For Lacan, misrecognition is inseparable from the very process of construction, for the subject can never locate itself at the point of the gaze: 'at the moment the gaze is discerned, the image, the entire visual field, takes on a terrifying alterity' (Copjec, p. 35), an invasion of the uncanny. The field ceases to be a mirror and becomes a screen. Hence it is theoretically inadequate to concentrate on the spectator's imaginary identifications when the emergence of alterity disturbs the distinction between object and subject, 'between what "I" look at and what "I" am' (Lebeau, p. 42). The 'old' new film theory treats identification as recognition and thus misses the invasion of otherness. Within Lacan's three orders, the Imaginary, Symbolic and Real, the Real always has the last word, or rather goes beyond the last word; any representation partakes of the nature of the signifier and therefore always refers beyond itself.

The cinematic illusion is no meaningless phantasmagoria, but is traversed by the signifiers that the ideology has released into the visual field. Yet these signifiers cannot be solely confined by that ideology. Where the Foucauldian view sees the signifiers as opaque to the subject, wholly monopolizing its gaze, this very attention allows the subject to project beyond this opacity, to sense that which is missing in the mundane interpretations of the signifiers – the breakings-through of the ignored or 'impossible' Real. The Real is 'impossible' from the standpoint of the Imaginary that the ideology has in its grip, but its existence makes itself felt all the more terrifyingly other because of its absence from the spectator's illusory world. Therefore, the screen, instead of being merely a mirror for the narcissism of the subject, becomes a screen – an alien opaque element that meets and challenges the gaze of the subject.

Magritte's picture *Dangerous Relationships* can be used as a metaphor for Copjec's argument. In the picture a naked woman hides behind a mirror. But the mirror thus used as a screen betrays her desire to be seen, for in the mirror we see the back of the naked woman herself. She hides (masquerades) as feminine while wanting to be looked at as the phallus. She solicits the gaze by an affectation of modesty, but the screen/mirror not only does not conceal but reveals what it should not: that in her feminine masquerade she is phallic.

In line with these theoretical re-visions, feminist film criticism of the nineties has turned away from a central concern with the mechanisms of fetishism and voyeurism towards the constructions of fantasies and to what it takes to keep the dialectic of subject and Other constantly in view. One of the most recent and striking developments of feminist film criticism has been the attention paid to the *film noir*, a type of Hollywood film of the forties and fifties, retrospectively made into a genre (for my brief account of *noir* criticism I draw on Cowie 1993 and Doane 1991). There are two aspects of this genre, which together make up its ideological appeal for feminists: one is its formal devices, the other its scenario. The formal devices articulate the enigmas proposed by the scenario. A chiaroscuro visual style of white light and black shade in an urban setting defines the mood for the duplicitous action whose motor is the femme fatale. How does the *film noir* position the spectator and what fantasies does it have to offer through its devices, plot and characters? On the one hand the film presents itself as a masculine genre. A male hero is struggling with other men trying to overcome alienation in a corrupt system, lured by a dangerously deceptive woman: 'the power accorded to the femme fatale is a function of fears linked to the notions of uncontrollable drives, the fading of subjectivity, and the loss of conscious agency – all emergent themes of psychoanalysis' (Doane 1991, p. 2). So one way of looking at *film noir* is to see the woman's destruction by the plot or by the male hero as retribution for having aroused his passive desire, for having enthralled him with the promise of love, for entrapping him with her dangerous sexuality. On the other hand – and against seeing *film noir* as a specifically masculine genre – women take up active roles in these films, even and especially where their desire is sinister, and they finally incur punishment. However, since the fantasy of the promiscuous woman is inscribed in the oedipal scenario, the pleasures of the forbidden are shared by both feminine and masculine subjects.

This, then, runs counter to Mulvey's classic argument, that within patriarchy cinematic pleasure is invariably dominated by the male look; it is also governed by the woman's unconscious fantasy which partakes of the forbidden. For what becomes evident in *film noir* is that the femme fatale's active desire manifests itself in her endeavour to draw the man into her circuit. The *film noir* epitomizes the problem of masquerade in that the woman as fantasy object is drawing on her phallic attributes to make herself desirable, but nevertheless this identification can also be an active place offered to the female spectator who can enjoy it deconstructively.

10.4 Desiring woman: Mary Kelly's *Post-Partum Document* and *Interim*

'Above all I am trying to picture the woman as subject of her own desire'

Mary Kelly *Woman – Desire – Image*

The artist Mary Kelly has drawn attention to the continuity between her two projects in terms of treatment of subject matter and the visual similarities of a series of images; in each project she has followed what she calls an 'ethnographic' procedure, 'the artist as participant observer, recording the "rituals" of maturity and ageing' (Kelly 1993, p. 353). Being a mother and being in the place of an ageing woman are perhaps the two most vulnerable positions that a woman may sooner or later occupy. More specifically, the experiences Kelly records in both works are a mother's and ageing woman's difficulties in situating herself in a predominantly patriarchal and masculinist world. To this end the artist deliberately fails to provide portraits in the form of photographs or images that could be ideologically appropriated. Her stance as artist is unusual in that her installations are made up both of images that mimick and mediate 'life/live' experience and an exploratory theoretical commentary upon it. An 'installation' uses the gallery format in a parodic kind of way, knowing itself to be an exhibition of artefacts, but aware that these cannot be preserved and commodified in the traditionally hallowed way. Like 'found art' it provides a frame for subjective finds and offers them up to the spectator for work, rather than, as Brecht would put it, for 'gawping' at romantically (Brecht 1967 [1919], p. 70).

Post-Partum Document, an exhibition of a mother's celebration of and mourning for her dyadic relation with her infant son, has two aspects to each of its six sections: 1. objects (in the first instance, stained nappy liners) with accompanying charts (measuring the solid foods gradually introduced), hung on walls behind glass; 2. a theoretical commentary making use of modern critical theory, particularly psychoanalytic theory from Freud to Lacan. Seen generally, the combination of, on the one hand, sensuous traces and intimate confessional material and, on the other, linguistic notations with measurements of diet charts brings home to the spectator that every experience is already 'contaminated' by theory and every theory 'contaminated' by experience. The real being of the child and mother cannot be adequately captured by the knowledge that is painstakingly and painfully applied to it.

The first three sections of the installation record the stages of separation after birth: weaning from the breast to analysing faecal stains (caption: 'What have I done wrong?'; Kelly 1983, p. 39); weaning from the stage of the child's babbling to that of its use of grammatical language (caption: 'Why don't I understand?'; p. 71); weaning from the symbiotic union to analysing the child's early scribbles (caption: 'Why is he/she like that?'; p. 91). The next three sections deal with more advanced difficulties of separation, involving the child's attempts to find its place in the oedipal triangle (caption: 'What do you want?'; p. 107); its early scribbles and letters (caption: 'What am I?'; p. 159); and the mother's dialectic of desire involving the re-experience of archaic separation anxieties (caption: 'What will I do?'; p. 187).

What Kelly articulates is the inevitably traumatic separation of mother and child, an anguished replay of the mother's own prior experience with her mother and her intimate recollections of this rupture: 'the mother-and-child relation in its social and psychic interplay cannot be pictured, for it is a process, like the dream or a fantasy of which we can have knowledge only through its traces, its coded signs' (Pollock 1988, p. 169). Kelly's work bears out the Lacanian principle that 'the child is a phallicized object that can only be located by means of its appearances in fantasy' (Brousse 1991, p. 125). The lack of a signifier for woman in the unconscious (her 'negative place' as shown by Kelly) finds a solution in her being a mother, which paradoxically, in being phallic (like masquerade) locates the woman on the male side of Lacan's sexuation formula: 'Motherhood necessarily implies a phallic investment in the child, giving it a libidinal value, and therefore requiring a fantasy' (Brousse 1991, ibid.).

Critical response is divided as to whether to absorb the experience as a purely negative entry into a historical Symbolic which prevents the mother from having any subjectivity, or whether to see it as a trans-historical Symbolic moment which allows for the imaginary pleasure a woman has in mis-recognizing her infant as part of herself. Kelly's work seems to invite the viewer to move compassionately between the two perspectives. There is a cultural critique of the slights and deprivations of motherhood in the patriarchal Symbolic but also an acknowledgement that mother and child are necessarily subject to the Symbolic as a system of difference. According to the Lacanian perspective, which Kelly largely adopts via a series of advancing Lacanian diagrams, the Symbolic is lacking, although it holds out the promise of plenitude to get the subject to enter it, and demands an acknowledgement of lack and consequent sacrifice. But Kelly's work also shows and articulates that there is a certain amount of perverse pleasure to be had from this sacrifice: 'perhaps it is precisely the replay, the repetition, the representation of moments of separation and loss which captivates us more than the promise of plenitude' (Kelly 1984, p. 31). She acknowledges the relation between the loss of narcissism (in this case, the loss of symbiotic union with her child) and castration. Kelly is asking whether pleasure could be produced differently for women, 'perhaps by representing a very specific loss – the loss of her imagined closeness to the mother's body . . . that which was assumed to be outside language, unspeakable, invisible, unpresentable . . . to have the child as phallus, to be the phallic mother, or perhaps to have the mother in being once again the child' (Kelly 1984, ibid.). This is a provocative response to the question she posed elsewhere (1996, p. 128), reiterated twice since by others (Pollock 1988, p. 86; Apter 1991, p. 97): 'How is a radical, critical and pleasurable positioning of the woman as spectator to be done?'

In *Interim* Kelly explores another critical moment in a woman's life – another crisis of the body – the arrival of middle age as an interim stage

for women, a stage between child-bearing and old age. She calls it 'interim'
to indicate that it is a pause for a new awareness rather than (merely
biologically speaking) the end of a sequence. As presented in New York
in 1990 the installation consists of four main parts entitled *Corpus, Pecunia,
Historia, Potestas*. I shall only be discussing Part I, *Corpus*, first shown in
Edinburgh, London and Cambridge, and recorded in catalogue form (Kelly
1986). Elsewhere Kelly describes her project as follows:

> *Corpus* makes explicit reference to Charcot's now famous photo-
> graphs of female hysterics by using the titles of 'the five passionate
> attitudes' (Menacé, Appel, Supplication, Erotisme and Extase) to
> announce the work's five sections. Citing the attitudes provided a
> means of linking popular discourses of the body with those of psy-
> choanalysis as well as placing psychoanalysis itself within a histor-
> ical context by referring to the founding moment of Freud's theory
> (Kelly 1991, p. 60).

By this means she emphasizes how the French nineteenth-century neuro-
pathologist J. M. Charcot, in focusing on the visible symptom, theatricalized
the young women he treated for hysteria, the five passionate attitudes
cited above being adopted by the hysteric in her hallucinatory phase.

The objects of *Corpus* consist of photographs of five pieces of clothing
(with the titles of the five passionate attitudes as quoted above), shown in
three different foldings/attitudes. The viewer can read two histories into
the exhibits: the 'hystery' of psychoanalysis, which learned to read the
symptoms of its female patients; and the discourses of popular culture,
such as fashion, medicine and myth, which have done much to oppress
women in a patriarchal system. Each object – a leather jacket, a handbag,
a pair of boots, a black negligée, a white embroidered dress – is fastened
to a perspex panel and paired with a framed text. The first object in each
case appears neat and crisp, the second rumpled and distraught, the third
tied up, as if ready to be put away. The framed text, which accompanies
the image, is handwritten and records the fragmentary conversations of
women of middle age, using the popular discourses relevant to the image
with which the writing is paired: 1. the discourse of fashion and advertising; 2. the discourse of the body and medicine; 3. the discourse of a
vulgarized romance and fairy tale.

Kelly wants 'to release the so-called "female" spectator from her hysterical identification with the male voyeur' (ibid., p. 65). She argues that
to have pleasure in looking is to be actively desiring, but a woman would
like to see herself as others see her, and this involves her in an identification

with a masculine position. The 'female' spectator (who could also be a man in the feminine position) is perhaps defending herself against the masculinity involved in the act of looking by 'trying on the "mask(s) of womanliness" as Joan Riviere described it' (ibid., pp. 65–6; Riviere 1929, p. 306). The process of identification might be reversed by allowing the enigma of femininity to show on the surface rather than be concealed, for the female spectator can identify with the 'masquerading' objects in the installation rather than with the woman 'behind' them: it is significant that in *Corpus*, as in the other installation discussed above, there *is* no woman behind the image, no photograph to collude with the spectator's fantasy.

In her Introduction to *Post-Partum Document* Kelly points out that the mother's way of saving treasured possessions connected with her child is a way of allowing Winnicottian transitional objects to harden into fetishes, to which the objects in the installation bear witness. Moreover, there has recently been clinical support for such a view (see Welldon 1988, p. 72). What is clear is that female fetishism has become quite an issue for feminism (see Schor 1985, 1992; McClintock 1993; Gamman and Makinen 1994). Kelly has been hailed for articulating in her work a specifically female form of fetishism in response to Freud's account of it as an exclusively masculine perversion (1927, XXI, pp. 147–57). Rather than 'rehash the evidence of visual exploitation of women by men', feminists have tried to revise the male bias in the perversions, in particular, the 'implicit valorization of phallic potency' that there is in fetishism (Apter 1991, p. 98).

More recently Kelly has distanced herself from this approach and prefers to see a procession of psychic identities that will call for different fantasies at different stages of life, some of which might involve fetishisms, which implies that fetishism would mean something different at each stage. Interviewed by Apter Kelly (1993), commenting on *Interim* in general, reflects on the different psychic identities (masquerades?) that mark the time of a woman's life. The so-called young woman takes up an imaginary position which enables her to participate in a narcissistic fantasy: she is herself the phallus. For the reproductive woman/mother, on the other hand, the infant is the imaginary object, signifying that the mother is occupying the active, desiring position: the child is now the phallus. The post-reproductive woman/mother of mid-life will then look for various substitutes for the child. Returning to *Interim*: if the first two paired panels of each section of *Corpus* suggest a woman's carefully groomed, much advertised looks and the second the gradual dissolution of those looks, then it is the third pair in each of the five sections which

gives an ironic distance to the ubiquity of 'masquerade' and questions
woman's relation to her image. Each object, caught in crumpled bondage
behind glass, accrues to itself an uncanny life which resists reification by
any look whatsoever: 'the third image, with its explicit sexual reference
to a discourse of perversion, opens up the question . . . of female sexual
desire' (Mulvey 1989b, p. 154).

But does this imply an invitation to the viewer to come up with a
positive image for woman, 'a feminine imaginary, the demand for a feminine gaze in which we might bask?' (Adams 1991, p. 92). Not so. Mary
Kelly's work, in Adams' remarkable reading, is rather like the discourse
of the analyst, in that her aesthetic project, like the analyst's clinical one,
is precisely to prevent the viewer/analysand from succumbing to 'the
Other of *jouissance*, a primal Other, a presymbolic Other' – the Lacanian
object *a*, that obscure object of desire, which is ironically embossed on
the walls in another section of *Interim*. In *Corpus* – that incorporeal
exhibition that interrogates a woman's desire – the marks and creases
in the clothing articles testify to the draining away of (feminine) enjoyment, and yet this subjective destitution, which also marks the end of
an analysis for male and female subjects alike, is precisely what makes
it possible to scrutinize the masquerading objects and to endeavour to
detach the desiring subject from them.

Conclusion

Psychoanalysis as a clinical practice has been concerned with those bodies whose entry into the social is particularly fraught with difficulty. In its investigation of these cases it was confronted with the very principle of the genesis and construction of the subject. Freud discovered that psychoanalysis has to deal with the body caught up in the tropes and figures of language. To free the patient of his or her most debilitating symptom, to release the flow of desire where it has got trapped, the analyst relies on the patient's living response. Nevertheless, both analysands and readers (and all analysts and critics are both of these in the first instance) are engaged in pursuing undecidable meanings: ambiguity, ambivalence, fantasy, illusion and play are their joint stock-in-trade.

That psychoanalysis should become controversial was inevitable. The patient with his symptom is an example of inadequacy at the meeting-place of body and society. Where this inadequacy is to be lodged, in the body in question, or the society of which it is a member, or both, cannot be decided unequivocally. The trope, the figure of speech, has been seen as a mechanism of subversion, or defence, or even both. Such multiple meanings arise because at the interface of body and society conscious and unconscious hold place together; for Lacan language creates the two in one operation. An incessant struggle is at work in language because it is at once cause and effect of the subject's desire.

These theoretical implications have gradually led away from the enclosed space of psychoanalytic criticism to a broader terrain. I do not myself think that applied psychoanalytic criticism is either intrinsically wicked or totally without relevance to literature, even if literature is being 'used' to prove psychoanalytic claims. After all, psychoanalysis is also 'used' to show how clever literature is. To the familiar Freudian and Jungian criticism, concerning itself with the psychosexual or archetypal fortunes of the author or character or both, can now be added other applied criticisms analysing the figurations of the text in terms of the identity problems of the characters and their author. Such contributions will obviously vary in the rigour of their execution, but at their best, as I hope to have shown with the example of Bonaparte, they might be seen as the 'popular' literature of psychoanalysis, as 'texts' in their own right, often done better by the psychoanalyst than by the critic who tries to emulate her.

At the other end of the scale there is the impressive way in which psychoanalysis and deconstruction have combined in French and American criticism, particularly in feminist criticism, so much so that psychoanalytic theory has been absorbed in the rhetoric of deconstruction, as shown in the ever escalating readings of the seminar on 'The Purloined Letter'. This kind of criticism, focusing as it does on what is repressed in our culture and in the psyche, is unthinkable, unwritable, and, perhaps more to the point, unreadable without a proper understanding of psychoanalytic concepts as distinct from the bandying about of psychoanalytic terminology. Without such an understanding the new and original ways in which Freudian theory has been assimilated into literary criticism cannot be grasped and adequately criticized. For the traffic has not gone one way only: there is a body of work which does not regard Freudian theory as canonical but instead interrogates literary texts (Deleuze and Guattari on Kafka) and psychoanalytic texts (Derrida on Freud's *Beyond the Pleasure Principle*) for revisions of that theory so that the theory comes to be modified by the texts themselves.

This book tries to provide a framework within which such different types of criticism might be read and understood. To assess the persuasive force of a text is to discover in what ways writer, reader and critic, and analyst, analysand and society can enter into transforming relationships that necessarily involve structures of desire. Three elements in particular were shown to characterize these transformations. First, there is the question of the mechanisms of language. What Freud detected in dreams – the figurations of the unconscious in its evasions of the censor – was seen to be operative in texts in general. The demonstrations of both id- and ego-psychology of the working of psychic mechanisms contribute to the understanding of desire in language. They cannot be dismissed just because we happen to disagree with the conclusions drawn.

Second, there is an overlap in the 'reader theory' of psychoanalysis and literature. As has been seen, the assumptions of classical criticism, that the text is the patient and the reader the analyst, no longer hold: the case is rather that the text is the analyst. The reader-cum-critic's position is then far more complicated for she is subject to the effects the text produces in her as reader, and at the same time is committed to the analysis of these same effects as critic. Such transference phenomena have much to contribute to the old problem of 'aesthetic distance', for this is also what the analyst and analysand have to achieve in order to bring the analysis to a successful conclusion.

Third, there is the force of history as it affects the participants in both the analytic and the literary situation. There is no simple choice between the author or critic as master of the text, and the text as master of the author or critic, because such choices leave out the field over which interpretative play must range, the field of human action from which history is derived. History is both cause and effect, determining subjects and being determined by them. It is a field not directly accessible: to negotiate it both psychoanalytic and literary readers have to resort to play, fiction and illusion.

Literature and the arts are generally valued for their 'aesthetic ambiguity'. This does not exist of itself, but is an aspect of interactions between persons. The convergence and divergence of desire over a knot of understanding emerges as the essential feature of the psychoanalytic encounter and can be extrapolated to the aesthetic interaction. This is why the best psychoanalytic model of the aesthetic interaction is the joke, for it not only typifies the interchange of conflicting interpretations along with other psychic phenomena such as dreams or symptoms, but it is also to be distinguished for the peculiarity of its structure and effects. As with the aesthetic text, the joke offers a site for struggle which involves not only two participants but their relation to language and power. Aesthetic response is the joint and agreed releasing or confirming of repression. While there is a risk involved – who will have the last laugh? – neither author nor text nor critic can reign supreme forever. Psychoanalytic critics and theorists cannot claim that the theory of the joke is theirs because a particular joke has served their turn.

The joke of language appears in the Russian tale that is my epigraph: it provoked a ready laughter recently at the National Theatre. The pretence is that there is no desire in language, no unconscious, no body. If there are no desires, then there is no point in speaking: since there are desires and they do not converge, some bodies may be forced into an untimely exit. Under Stalin's absolute law the teller of the tale, Daniil Kharms, was arrested and put to silence. Equally, where there is no law whatsoever, the body in pieces may be all that remains. At both extremes ambiguity is cancelled out. Psychoanalytic criticism explores texts for the (ambiguous) 'free' associations that tell of the struggle between a body and the society on which it depends.

References

Adams, Parveen (1991) The art of analysis: Mary Kelly's *Interim* and the discourse of the analyst. In *October*, 58, special issue: 'Rendering the Real', 81–96.
—— (1992) Waiving the phallus. *Differences*, 4:1, pp. 78–83.
—— (1996) *The Emptiness of the Image: Psychoanalysis and Sexual Difference*. London and New York: Routledge.
Althusser, Louis (1977) Freud and Lacan. In *Lenin and Philosophy and Other Essays*. London: New Left Books, pp. 88–108.
Apter, Emily (1991) Fetishism and visual seduction in Mary Kelly's *Interim*. In *October*, 58, special issue: 'Rendering the Real', pp. 97–108.
—— (1992) Masquerade. In *Feminism and Psychoanalysis: A Critical Dictionary*, ed. Elizabeth Wright. Oxford: Blackwell, pp. 242–4.
Bachelard, Gaston (1938) *La formation de l'esprit scientifique*. Paris: Vrin.
—— (1968) *The Psychoanalysis of Fire*. (Orig. *La psychanalyse de feu*, Paris: 1938). Boston: Beacon Press.
—— (1969) *The Poetics of Space*. (Orig. *La poétique de l'espace*, Paris, 1958). Boston: Beacon Press.
—— (1971) *The Poetics of Space*. (Orig. *La poétique de l'espace*, Paris: 1938). Boston: Beacon Press.
Bakhtin, Mikhail (1968) *Rabelais and his World*. (Orig. *Tvorchestvo Fransua Rable*, Moscow: 1965). Cambridge, Massachusetts: MIT Press.
Barthes, Roland (1972) To write: an intransitive verb? In *The Structuralist Controversy*, eds Richard Macksey and Eugenio Donato. Baltimore and London: Johns Hopkins University Press, pp. 134–45.
—— (1975) *S/Z*. (Orig. Paris: 1970). London: Jonathan Cape.
—— (1976) *The Pleasure of the Text*. (Orig. *Le plaisir du texte*, Paris, 1975). London: Jonathan Cape.
—— (1977) The death of the author. (Orig. La morte de l'auteur, *Mantéia*, 5, (1968)). In *Image–Music–Text*. London: Fontana/Collins, pp. 142–8.
—— (1979) *A Lover's Discourse*. (Orig. *Fragments d'un discours amoureux*, Paris: 1977). New York: Hill and Wang.
Beckett, Samuel (1973) *Not I*. London: Faber and Faber.

Benjamin, Walter (1982 [1936]) The work of art in the age of mechanical reproduction. In *Illuminations*, ed. Hannah Arendt, trans. Harry Zohn. London: Jonathan Cape, pp. 219–53.

Bennett, Andrew (1995) *Readers and Reading*. London and New York: Longman.

Bergstrom, Janet and Doane, Mary Ann (1989) The Spectatrix. Special edition of *Camera Obscura*, 20/21.

Bernheimer, Charles, and Kahane, Claire (eds) (1990) *In Dora's case: Freud – Hysteria – Feminism*. New York: Columbia University Press.

Bersani, Leo (1986) *The Freudian Body: Psychoanalysis and Art*. New York: Columbia University Press.

Bloom, Harold (1975) *The Anxiety of Influence: A Theory of Poetry*. London: Oxford University Press.

—— (1977) *Wallace Stevens: The Poems of our Climate*. Ithaca, New York: Cornell University Press.

—— (1979) The breaking of form. In *Deconstruction and Criticism*, eds Harold Bloom, Paul de Man, Jacques Derrida, Geoffrey Hartman and J. Hillis Miller. London: Routledge and Kegan Paul, pp. 1–37.

—— (1980) *A Map of Misreading*. Oxford and New York: Oxford University Press.

—— (1982) *Agon: Towards a Theory of Revisionism*. Oxford and New York: Oxford University Press.

Bodkin, Maud (1934) *Archetypal Patterns in Poetry*. London: Oxford University Press.

Bollas, Christopher (1976) Melville's lost self: *Bartleby*. In *The Practice of Psychoanalytic Criticism*, ed. Leonard Tennenhouse. Detroit, Michigan: Wayne State University Press, pp. 226–36.

Bonaparte, Marie (1949) *The Life and Works of Edgar Allan Poe*. (Orig. *Edgar Poe: Étude psychanalytique*, Paris: 1933). London: Imago.

Bowie, Malcolm (1979) Jacques Lacan. In *Structuralism and Since: From Lévi-Strauss to Derrida*, ed. John Sturrock. Oxford: Oxford University Press, pp. 116–53.

Brecht, Bertolt (1967 [1919]) *Trommeln in der Nacht*. In *Gesammelte Werke*, vol. I. Frankfurt-am-Main: Suhrkamp Verlag, pp. 70–124.

—— (1970 [1943]) *The Good Woman of Szechwan*, in *Collected Plays*, vol. VI (1), eds John Willett and Ralph Mannheim. London: Eyre Methuen.

Brooks, Cleanth (1968) *The Well-Wrought Urn: Studies in the Structure of Poetry*. London: Methuen.

Brousse, Marie-Hélène (1991) Feminism with Lacan. In *Newsletter of the Freudian Field*, 5:1/2, pp. 113–28.

Castoriadis, Cornelius (1994) Psychoanalysis and Politics. In *Speculations after Freud: Psychoanalysis, Philosophy and Culture*, eds Sonu Shamdasani and Michael Münchow. London and New York: Routledge, pp. 1–11.

Chasseguet-Smirgel, Janine (1981) *Female Sexuality*. (Orig. *La sexualité féminine, recherches psychanalytiques nouvelles*, Paris: 1964). London: Virago.

Cixous, Hélène (1976) Fiction and its phantoms: a reading of Freud's *Das Unheimliche*. *New Literary History*, 7, pp. 525–48. (Orig. La fiction et ses fantômes, *Poétique*, 10 (1972), pp. 199–216).

Clancier, Anne and Kalmanovitch, Jeannine (1987) *Winnicott and Paradox: From Birth to Creation*. Trans. Alan Sheridan (Orig. *Le Paradoxe de Winnicott*, Paris: Payot, 1884). London: Tavistock Publications.

Copjec, Joan (1994 [1989]) The orthopsychic subject: film theory and the reception of Lacan. In *Read My Desire: Lacan against the Historicists*, Joan Copjec. Cambridge, Massachusetts: MIT Press, pp. 15–38.

Cowie, Elizabeth (1993) *Film Noir* and women. In *Shades of Noir: A Reader*, ed. Joan Copjec. London and New York: Verso, pp. 121–65.

Culler, Jonathan (1983) *On Deconstruction: Theory and Criticism after Structuralism*. London: Routledge and Kegan Paul.

David, Nicolette Miranda (1995) *A Kleinian Dynamics of Reading: Dante, Ponge, Rilke and Sarraute*. Ph.D. thesis, University of London.

Deleuze, Gilles (1994) *Difference and Repetition*. Trans. Paul Patton. London: The Athlone Press.

Deleuze, Gilles, and Guattari, Félix (1976) *Kafka: Für eine kleine Literatur*. (Orig. *Kafka: Pour une littérature mineure*, Paris: 1975). Frankfurt-am-Main: Suhrkamp Verlag.

——— (1977a) *Anti-Oedipus: Capitalism and Schizophrenia*. (Orig. *L'Anti-Oedipe*, vol. I, *Capitalisme et schizophrenie*, Paris: 1972). New York: Viking Press.

——— (1977b) Balance-sheet program for desiring machines. *Semiotext(e), Anti-Oedipus: From Psychoanalysis to Schizopolitics*, 2, pp. 117–35. (Orig. Bilan-programme pour machines désirantes, *Minuit*, 2 (1973)).

Derrida, Jacques (1975) The purveyor of truth. *Yale French Studies*, 52, pp. 31–112. (Orig. Le facteur de la vérité, *Poétique*, 21 (1975)).

——— (1978) Freud and the scene of writing. In *Writing and Difference*. (Orig. *L'Écriture et différence*, Paris: 1967). Chicago: Chicago University Press.

——— (1982) *Dissemination*. (Orig. *La dissémination.*, Paris: 1972). Chicago: Chicago University Press.

Doane, Mary Ann (1991) Femmes Fatales: *Feminism, Film Theory, Psychoanalysis*. New York and London: Routledge.

Ehrenzweig, Anton (1970) *The Hidden Order of Art: A Study in the Psychology of Artistic Imagination*. London: Paladin.

Ellenberger, Henri F. (1970) *The Discovery of the Unconscious: The History and Evolution of Dynamic Psychiatry*. New York: Basic Books.

Ellmann, Maud (ed.) (1994) *Psychoanalytic Literary Criticism*. London and New York: Longman.

Empson, William (1930) *Seven Types of Ambiguity*. London: Chatto and Windus.

Evans, Dylan (1996) *An Introductory Dictionary of Lacanian Psychoanalysis*. London and New York: Routledge.

Faris, Wendy, B. (1995) Scheherazade's children: magical realism and postmodern fiction. In Zamora and Faris, eds, pp. 163–90.

Felman, Shoshana (1977) Turning the screw of interpretation. *Yale French Studies*, 55/56, pp. 94–207.

——— (1980) On reading poetry: reflections on the limits and possibilities of psychoanalytical approaches. In *The Literary Freud*, ed. Joseph H. Smith. New Haven and London: Yale University Press, pp. 119–48.

Fischer, Jens Malte (ed.) (1980) *Psychoanalytische Literaturinterpretation*. Tübingen: Max Niemeyer Verlag.

Foucault, Michel (1974) *The Order of Things: An Archaeology of the Human Sciences*. (Orig. *Les mots et les choses*, Paris: 1966). London: Tavistock Publications.

——— (1980a) The history of sexuality: An interview. *Oxford Literary Review*, 4, pp. 3–19.

Foucault, Michel (1980b) What is an author? In *Textual Strategies: Perspectives in Post-Structuralist Criticism*, ed. Josué V. Harari. London: Methuen, pp. 141–60.

—— (1980c) *Power/Knowledge: Selected Interviews and Other Writings, 1972–1977*. Brighton: Harvester.

—— (1981) *The History of Sexuality*, vol. I. (Orig. *La volonté de savoir*, Paris: 1976). Harmondsworth: Penguin.

—— (1982) The subject and power. In Hubert L. Dreyfus and Paul Rabinow (eds), *Michel Foucault: Beyond Structuralism and Hermeneutics*. Brighton: Harvester Press, pp. 208–26.

Franz, Marie-Louise von (1972) *Problems of the Feminine in Fairy Tales*. Dallas, Texas: Spring Publications.

Freud, Anna (1966) *The Ego and the Mechanisms of Defence*. (Orig. *Das Ich und die Abwehrmechanismen*, Vienna: 1936). New York: International Universities Press.

Freud, Sigmund (1953) *The Standard Edition of the Complete Psychological Works* (24 vols). (Orig. *Gesammelte Werke*, vols I–XVIII, London and Frankfurt-am-Main: 1940–68). London: Hogarth Press and the Institute of Psycho-Analysis.

—— (1895) *Project for a Scientific Psychology*. I, pp. 281–397.

—— (1893–5) *Studies in Hysteria*. (with Josef Breuer), II.

—— (1900) *The Interpretation of Dreams*. IV and V.

—— (1905) *Three Essays on the Theory of Sexuality*. VII, pp. 123–246.

—— (1905) *Jokes and their Relation to the Unconscious*. VIII.

—— (1905/6) Psychopathic characters on the stage. VII, pp. 303–10.

—— (1907) *Delusions and Dreams in Jensen's 'Gradiva'*. IX, pp. 1–97.

—— (1908) Creative writers and day-dreaming. IX, pp. 141–54.

—— (1910) 'Wild' psychoanalysis. XI, pp. 219–30.

—— (1910) Leonardo da Vinci and a memory of his childhood. XI, pp. 59–138.

—— (1912) *Totem and Taboo*. XIII, pp. 1–161.

—— (1913) The claims of psycho-analysis to scientific interest. XIII, pp. 165–92.

—— (1914) On the history of the psycho-analytic movement. XIV, pp. 1–66.

—— (1914) On narcissism: an introduction. XIV, pp. 67–104.

—— (1915) Repression. XIV, pp. 141–53.

—— (1916–17) *Introductory Lectures on Psycho-Analysis*. XV and XVI.

—— (1918) From the history of an infantile neurosis. XVII, pp. 1–124.

—— (1919) The uncanny. XVII, pp. 217–56.

—— (1920) *Beyond the Pleasure Principle*. XVIII, pp. 1–64.

—— (1923) *The Ego and the Id*. XIX, pp. 1–66.

—— (1924) The economic problem of masochism. XIX, pp. 155–72.

—— (1925) A note upon the 'mystic writing-pad'. XIX, pp. 227–34.

—— (1925) Negation. XIX, pp. 235–40.

—— (1925) Some psychical consequences of the anatomical distinction between the sexes. XIX, pp. 241–60.

—— (1926) *Inhibitions, Symptoms and Anxiety*. XX, pp. 75–176.

—— (1926) Psycho-analysis. XX, pp. 259–70.

—— (1927) Fetishism, XXI, pp. 147–57.

—— (1928) Dostoevsky and parricide. XXI, pp. 173–96.

—— (1930) *Civilization and its Discontents*. XXI, pp. 57–146.

—— (1933) Preface to Marie Bonaparte's *The Life and Works of Edgar Allan Poe: A Psycho-Analytic Interpretation*. XXII, p. 254.

—— (1933) *New Introductory Lectures in Psycho-Analysis*. XXII, pp. 1–182.

—— (1937) Analysis terminable and interminable. XXIII, pp. 209–54.

—— (1940) An outline of psycho-analysis. XXIII, pp. 139–208.

—— (1940) Splitting of the ego in the process of defence. XXIII, pp. 271–8.

Frye, Northrop (1957) *Anatomy of Criticism: Four Essays.* Princeton, New Jersey: Princeton University Press.

—— (1978) Forming fours. In *Culture and Literature,* ed. Robert D. Denham. Chicago: Chicago University Press.

—— (1981) *The Critical Path: An Essay in the Social Content of Literary Criticism.* Bloomington and London: Indiana University Press.

Fuller, Peter (1980) *Art and Psychoanalysis.* London: Writers and Readers Publishing Company.

Gallop, Jane (1982) *The Daughter's Seduction: Feminism and Psychoanalysis.* Ithaca, New York: Cornell University Press.

Gamman, Lorraine, and Makinen, Merja (1994) *Female Fetishism: A New Look.* London: Lawrence and Wishart.

Gargano, James W. (1967) The question of Poe's narrators. In *Poe: Twentieth-Century Views,* ed. Robert Regan. Englewood Cliffs, New Jersey: Prentice-Hall, pp. 164–71.

Gombrich, Ernst (1977) *Art and Illusion: A Study in the Psychology of Pictorial Representation.* London: Phaidon Press.

—— (1983) Freud's aesthetics. In *Literature and Psychoanalysis,* eds Edith Kurzweil and William Phillips. New York: Columbia University Press, pp. 271–92.

Green, André (1978a) Potential space in psychoanalysis: The object in the setting. In *Between Reality and Fantasy: Transitional Objects and Phenomena.* New York and London: Jason Aronson.

—— (1978b) The double and the absent. In *Psychoanalysis, Creativity, and Literature: A French–American Inquiry.* New York: Columbia University Press, pp. 271–92.

—— (1979) *The Tragic Effect,* ed. Alan Robert. (Orig. *Un oeil en trop,* Paris: 1969). Cambridge: Cambridge University Press.

Greenacre, Phyllis (1970) The transitional object and the fetish, with special reference to the role of illusion. *International Journal of Psychoanalysis,* 51, pp. 442–56.

Grosz, Elizabeth (1990) *Jacques Lacan: A Feminist Introduction.* London and New York: Routledge.

Hartmann, Heinz (1964 [1955]) Notes on the theory of sublimation. In *Essays in Ego-Psychology.* New York: International Universities Press, pp. 215–40.

Hawthorne, Nathaniel (1978 [1850]) *The Scarlet Letter.* New York and London: W. W. Norton.

Hermann, Ann (1990) Travesty and transgression: transvestism in Shakespeare, Brecht and Churchill. In *Performing Feminisms: Feminist Critical Theory and Theater,* ed. Sue-Ellen Case. Baltimore and London: Johns Hopkins University Press, pp. 294–315.

Hertz, Neil (1979) Freud and the Sandman. In *Textual Strategies: Perspectives in Post-Structural Criticism.* London: Methuen, pp. 296–321.

Hirsch, E. D. (1976) *The Aims of Interpretation.* Chicago: Chicago University Press.

Hirsch, Marianne (1992) Object-relations-oriented criticism. In *Feminism and Psychoanalysis: A Critical Dictionary,* ed. Elizabeth Wright. Oxford: Blackwell, pp. 280–84.

Hoffmann, E. T. A. (1969) *Selected Writings of E. T. A. Hoffmann,* 2 vols, eds Elizabeth C. Knight and Leonard J. Kent. Chicago; Chicago University Press. The

Sandman, I, pp. 137–67 (orig. 1816); *The Life and Opinions of Kater Murr*, II (orig. 1820–1).

Holland, Norman N. (1968) *The Dynamics of Literary Response*. New York: Oxford University Press.

—— (1975a) *Poems in Persons*. New York: W. W. Norton.

—— (1975b) *Five Readers Reading*. New Haven and London: Yale University Press.

—— (1978) Poem opening: An invitation to transactive criticism. *College English*, 40:1, pp. 2–16.

—— (1980) Recovering 'The Purloined Letter'. In *The Reader in the Text*, eds. Susan R. Suleiman and Inge Crosman. Princeton, New Jersey: Princeton University Press.

—— (1982) Why, this is transference, nor am I out of it. *Psychoanalysis and Contemporary Thought*, 5, pp. 27–34.

—— (1993) Psychoanalysis and literature. *Contemporary Psychoanalysis*, 29:1, pp. 5–21.

—— (1997) An intellectual autobiography. Internet site http://www.clas.ufl.edu/users/nnh/autobios.htm.

Jacobi, Jolande (1968) *The Psychology of C. G. Jung: An Introduction with Illustrations*. London: Routledge and Kegan Paul.

Jakobson, Roman, and Halle, Morris (1956) *Fundamentals of Language*. The Hague: Mouton.

Johnson, Barbara (1977) The frame of reference: Poe, Lacan, Derrida. *Yale French Studies*, 55/56, pp. 457–505.

—— (1978) The critical difference. *Diacritics*, 10, 2–9.

Jones, Ernest (1949) *Hamlet and Oedipus*. London: Victor Gollancz.

Jones, Richard M. (1978) *The New Psychology of Dreaming*. Harmondsworth: Penguin.

Jung, Carl Gustav (1972a) *Two Essays on Analytical Psychology*. (Orig. *Über die Psychologie des Unbewussten*, Zürich: 1943). Princeton, New Jersey: Princeton University Press.

—— (1972b) On the relation of analytical psychology to poetry. In *The Spirit in Man, Art and Literature* (orig. Über die Beziehungen der analytischen Psychologie zum dichterischen Kunstwerk, Zürich: 1931). Princeton, New Jersey: Princeton University Press, pp. 65–83.

—— (1976) *Symbols of Transformation*. (Orig. *Symbole der Wandlung*, Zürich: 1952). Princeton, New Jersey: Princeton University Press.

—— (1978) *Man and his Symbols*. London: Picador.

Kahane, Claire (1995) *Passions of the Voice: Hysteria, Narrative, and the Figure of the Speaking Woman, 1850–1915*. Baltimore and London: Johns Hopkins University Press.

Kaplan, E. Ann (1990) Introduction: From Plato's Cave to Freud's Screen. In *Psychoanalysis and Cinema*, ed. E. Ann Kaplan. New York and London: Routledge, pp. 1–23.

Kaplan, Morton, and Kloss, Robert (1973) *The Unspoken Motive: A Guide to Psychoanalytic Literary Criticism*. New York: Free Press.

Kelly, Mary (1983) *Post-Partum Document*. London and New York: Routledge.

—— (1984) Woman – Desire – Image. In *Desire*, ed. Lisa Appignanesi. London: Institute of Contemporary Arts Document, pp. 30–1.

—— (1986) *Interim*. Kettle's Yard Catalogue for the exhibition of 20 September to 24 October, 1986.

References 201

—— (1991) Re-presenting the body: On *Interim*, Part I. In *Psychoanalysis and Cultural Theory*, ed. James Donald. Basingstoke: Macmillan and the Institute of Contemporary Arts, pp. 59–67.

—— (1993) The smell of money: Mary Kelly in conversation with Emily Apter. In *Fetishism as Cultural Discourse*, eds Emily Apter and William Pietz. Ithaca and London: Cornell University Press, pp. 352–62.

—— (1996) Desiring Images/Imaging Desire. In *Imaging Desire*. Cambridge, Massachusetts: MIT Press, pp. 122–9.

Kharms, Daniil (1974) Ministories. In *Russia's Lost Literature of the Absurd: Selected Works of Daniil Kharms and Alexander Vvedensky*, trans. and ed. George Gibian. New York: W. W. Norton.

Kittler, Friedrich (1977) Das Phantom unseres Ichs und die Literaturpsychologie. In *Urszenen*, eds Friedrich Kittler and Horst Turk. Frankfurt-am-Main: Suhrkamp Verlag.

Klein, Melanie (1977 [1937]) The importance of symbol formation in the development of the ego. In *Love, Guilt and Reparation and Other Works, 1921–1945*. London: Hogarth Press, pp. 219–32.

Kofman, Sarah (1985 [1980]) *The Enigma of Woman: Women in Freud's Writings*. Trans. Catherine Porter. Ithaca and London: Cornell University Press.

Kramer, Lawrence (1995) *Classical Music and Postmodern Knowledge*. Berkeley, California: University of California Press.

Kris, Ernst (1964 [1952]) *Psychoanalytic Explorations in Art*. New York: Schocken Books.

Kristeva, Julia (1980) *Desire in Language: A Semiotic Approach to Literature and Art*. Ed. Leon S. Roudiez. New York: Columbia University Press.

—— (1982) *Powers of Horror* (orig. *Pouvoirs de l'horreur*, Paris, 1980). Trans. Leon S. Roudiez. New York: Columbia University Press.

Kuhns, Richard (1983) *Psychoanalytic Theory of Art: A Philosophy of Art on Developmental Principles*. New York: Columbia University Press.

Lacan, Jacques (1970) Of structure as an inmixing of an Otherness prerequisite to any subject whatever. In *The Structuralist Controversy*, eds Richard Macksey and Eugenio Donato. Baltimore and London: Johns Hopkins University Press, pp. 186–200.

—— (1971–2) '. . . ou pire'. Unpublished seminar.

—— (1972 [1966]) Seminar on 'The Purloined Letter'. *Yale French Studies*, 48, pp. 39–72.

—— (1977a [1958]) *Écrits: A Selection*. London: Tavistock Publications.

—— (1977b [1973]) *The Four Fundamental Concepts of Psycho-Analysis*. London: Hogarth Press.

—— (1988a [1975]) *The Seminar of Jacques Lacan, Book I: Freud's Papers on Technique 1953–1954*. Ed. Jacques-Alain Miller. Trans. by John Forrester. Cambridge: Cambridge University Press.

—— (1988b [1978]) *The Seminar of Jacques Lacan, Book II: The Ego in Freud's Theory and in the Technique of Psychoanalysis, 1954–1955*. Ed. Jacques-Alain Miller. Trans. Sylvana Tomaselli. Cambridge: Cambridge University Press.

—— (1990 [1974]) *Television*. Ed. Joan Copjec. Trans. Denis Hollier, Rosalind Kraus and Annette Michelson. New York and London: W. W. Norton.

—— (1998 [1975]) *The Seminar of Jacques Lacan, Book XX Encore, 1972–1973: On Feminine Sexuality, The Limits of Love and Knowledge*. Ed. Jacques-Alain Miller. Trans. by Bruce Fink. New York and London: W. W. Norton Company.

Laclau, Ernesto, and Mouffe, Chantal (1985) *Hegemony and Socialist Strategy. Towards a Radical Democratic Politics*. London and New York: Verso.

Lacoue-Labarthe, Philippe (1977) Theatrum analyticum, *Glyph*, 2, pp. 122–43.

Laing, R. D. (1974) *Knots*. Harmondsworth: Penguin.

Langer, Suzanne (1942) *Philosophy in a New Key*. Cambridge, Massachusetts: Harvard University Press.

Laplanche, Jean (1976) *Life and Death in Psychoanalysis*. (Orig. *Vie et mort en psychanalyse*, Paris: 1970). Baltimore and London: Johns Hopkins University Press.

Laplanche, Jean, and Leclaire, Serge (1972) The unconscious: A psychoanalyic study. *Yale French Studies*, 48, pp. 118–75.

Laplanche, Jean, and Pontalis, Jean-Bertrand (1973) *The Language of Psycho-Analysis*. (Orig. *Vocabulaire de la psychanalyse*, Paris, 1967). London: Hogarth Press.

Lauder, Afferbeck (1965) *Let Stalk Strine*. Australia: Ure Smith.

Lawrence, D. H. (1961a) *Fantasia of the Unconscious*. London: Heinemann.

—— (1961b) *Psychoanalysis of the Unconscious*. London: Heinemann.

—— (1962) *The Symbolic Meaning: The Uncollected Versions of Studies in Classic American Literature*, ed. Arnold Armin. Arundel: Centaur Press.

—— (1977) *Studies in Classic American Literature*. Harmondsworth: Penguin.

Lebeau, Vicky (1995) *Lost Angels: Psychoanalysis and Cinema*. London and New York: Routledge.

Lechte, John (1990) *Julia Kristeva*. London and New York: Routledge.

Leitch, Vincent B. (1983) *Deconstructive Criticism: An Advanced Introduction*. London: Hutchinson.

Lesser, Simon O. (1957) *Fiction and the Unconscious*. Chicago: Chicago University Press.

Lichtenstein, Heinz (1961) Identity and sexuality. *Journal of the American Psychoanalytic Association*, 9, pp. 179–260.

—— (1965) Towards a metapsychological definition of the concept of self. *International Review of Psycho-Analysis*, 46, pp. 117–28.

Lombroso, Cesare (1891) *The Man of Genius*. London: Walter Scott.

Lorenzer, Alfred, and Orban, Peter (1978) Transitional objects and phenomena: socialization and symbolization. In *Between Reality and Fantasy: Transitional Objects and Phenomena*, eds Simon A. Grolnick and Leonard Barkin. New York and London: Jason Aronson, pp. 472–82.

Lotringer, Sylvère (1977) The fiction of analysis. *Semiotext(e)*, 2, pp. 173–89.

Lyotard, Jean-François (1974) Au delà de la représentation ('Beyond representation'). Preface to *L'Ordre caché de l'art* ('*The Hidden Order of Art*'). *Essai sur la psychologie de l'imagination esthétique*, Anton Ehrenzweig. Paris: Gallimard.

—— (1983) Answering the question: What is postmodernism? In *Innovation/Renovation: New Perspectives on the Humanities*, eds Ihab Hassan and Sally Hassan. Madison, Wisconsin: University of Wisconsin Press, pp. 329–41.

—— (1984) The sublime and the avant-garde. Lecture at Cambridge University, 12 March.

—— (1989) Beyond representation. In *The Lyotard Reader*, ed. A. Benjamin. Oxford: Basil Blackwell, pp. 155–68.

McClintock, Anne (1993) The return of female fetishism and the fiction of the phallus. *New Formations*, 19, pp. 1–21.

Mannoni, Maud (1970) *The Retarded Child and the Mother*. (Orig. *L'enfant arrière et sa mère*, Paris: 1967). London: Tavistock Publications.

—— (1973) *The Child, his 'Illness' and the Others*. (Orig. *L'enfant, sa 'maladie' et les autres*, Paris: 1967). Harmondsworth: Penguin.

Mehlman, Jeffrey (1975) How to read Freud on jokes: the critic as *Schadchen*, *Poétique*, 6, pp. 439–61.

Meltzer, Françoise (1982) The uncanny rendered canny: Freud's blind spot in reading Hoffmann's 'Sandman'. In *Introducing Psychoanalytic Theory*, ed. Sander L. Gilman. New York: Brunner/Mazel, pp. 218–39.

Metz, Christian (1982) *Psychoanalysis and Cinema: The Imaginary Signifier*. (Orig. *Le signifiant imaginaine. Psychanalyse et cinéma*, Paris: 1977) London: Macmillan.

Miller, Jacques-Alain (1988) Extimité. *Prose Studies*, 11:3, pp. 121–31.

Mitchell, Juliet, and Rose, Jacqueline (1982) *Feminine Sexuality: Jacques Lacan and the école freudienne*. London: Macmillan.

Modleski, Tania (1989) *The Women Who Knew Too Much: Hitchcock and Feminist Theory*. New York and London: Routledge.

Muller, John P. (1979) The analogy of the gap in Lacan's *Écrits: A Selection*. *The Psychohistory Review*, 8, pp. 38–45.

Mulvey, Laura (1989a [1975]) Visual pleasure and narrative cinema. In *Visual and Other Pleasures*, Laura Mulvey. Basingstoke: Macmillan, pp. 14–26.

—— (1989b) Impending time: Mary Kelly's *Corpus*. In *Visual and Other Pleasures* (see preceding entry), pp. 148–55.

Nordau, Max (1895) *Degeneration*. (Orig. *Entartung*, Berlin: 1892–3). London: Heinemann.

Penley, Constance (1989) *The Future of an Illusion: Film, Feminism and Psychoanalysis*. New York and London: Routledge.

Phelan, Peggy (1993) *Unmarked: The Politics of Performance*. London and New York: Routledge.

Phillips, Adam (1988) *Winnicott*. London: Fontana Press.

Poizat, Michel (1992) *The Angel's Cry: Beyond the Pleasure Principle in Opera*. Ithaca and London: Cornell University Press.

Pollock, Griselda (1988) *Vision and Difference: Femininity, Feminism and the Histories of Art*. London and New York: Routledge.

Pontalis, Jean-Bertrand (1981) *Frontiers in Psychoanalysis: Between the Dream and Psychic Pain*. London: Hogarth Press and the Institute of Psycho-Analysis.

Prawer, Siegbert S. (1965) Hoffmann's uncanny guest: A reading of *Der Sandmann*. *German Life and Letters*, 18, pp. 297–308.

Rajchman, John (1977) Analysis in power: A few Foucauldian theses. *Semiotext(e)*, *Anti-Oedipus: from Psychoanalysis to Schizopolitics*, 2, pp. 45–58.

Rella, Franco (1994) *The Myth of the Other: Lacan, Deleuze, Foucault, Bataille*. Trans. Nelson Moe. Washington, DC: Maisonneuve Press.

Ricoeur, Paul (1970) *Freud and Philosophy: An Essay on Interpretation*. (Orig. *De l'interprétation: essai sur Freud*, Paris: 1965). New Haven and London; Yale University Press.

Rimmon-Kenan, Shlomith (1983) *Narrative Fiction: Contemporary Poetics*. London: Methuen.

Riviere, Joan (1929) Womanliness as a masquerade. *International Journal of Psychoanalysis*, 8, pp. 303–13.

Rose, Gilbert J. (1980) *The Power of Form: A Psychoanalytical Approach to Aesthetic Form*. New York: International Universities Press.

Rose, Jacqueline (1993) *Why War? – Psychoanalysis, Politics, and the Return to Melanie Klein*. Oxford: Blackwell.

204 References

Rosen, Charles (1996) *The Romantic Generation*. London: HarperCollins.

Rubin, Bernard (1982) Freud and Hoffmann: 'The Sandman'. In *Introducing Psychoanalytic Theory*, ed. Sander L. Gilman. New York: Brunner/Mazel, pp. 205–17.

Samuels, Andrew, Shorter, Bani, and Plant, Fred (1986) *A Critical Dictionary of Jungian Analysis*. London and New York: Routledge and Kegan Paul.

Saussure, Ferdinand de (1977 [1915]) *Course in General Linguistics*. Ed. Charles Bally and Albert Sechehaye. London: Fontana/Collins.

Schor, Naomi (1985) Female fetishism: The case of George Sand. In *The Female Body in Western Culture: Contemporary Perspectives*, ed. Susan Rubin Suleiman. Cambridge, Massachusetts and London: Harvard University Press, pp. 363–72.

—— (1992) Fetishism. In *Feminism and Psychoanalysis: A Critical Dictionary*. Oxford: Blackwell, pp. 113–17.

Segal, Hanna (1977 [1955]) A psycho-analytical approach to aesthetics. In *New Directions in Psycho-Analysis*, eds Paula Heimann and Roger Money-Kyrle. London: Maresfield Reprints, pp. 384–405.

Silverman, Kaja (1992) The Lacanian Phallus. *Differences*, 4: 1, 84–115.

Stokes, Adrian (1977) Form in art. In Heimann and Money-Kyrle eds (see preceding entry), pp. 406–20.

—— (1978) *The Critical Writings of Adrian Stokes*, 3 vols. From vol. I: The Quattrocento (1932) pp. 29–80; Stones of Rimini (1934), pp. 181–259. From vol. III: Three Essays on the Painting of our Time (1961), pp. 143–84; Painting and the Inner World (1963), pp. 209–59; Reflections on the Nude (1967), pp. 303–42. London: Thames and Hudson.

Sulloway, Frank J. (1979) *Freud, Biologist of the Mind: Beyond the Psycho-Analytic Legend*. London: André Deutsch.

Trilling, Lionel (1964a [1945]) Art and neurosis. In *The Liberal Imagination*. London: Heinemann, pp. 160–80.

—— (1964b [1947]) Freud and literature. In *The Liberal Imagination* (see preceding entry), pp. 34–57.

Walker, Steven F. (1995) Magical archetypes: Midlife miracles in *The Satanic Verses*. In Zamora and Faris, eds, pp. 347–69.

Weber, Samuel (1977) The divaricator: remarks on Freud's *Witz*. *Glyph*, 1, pp. 1–27.

—— (1978) It. *Glyph*, 4, pp. 1–31.

—— (1982) *The Legend of Freud*. Minneapolis: University of Minnesota Press.

Wehr, Demaris S. (1988) *Jung and Feminism*. London: Routledge.

Welldon, Estela V. (1988) *Mother, Madonna, Whore: The Idealization and Denigration of Motherhood*. London: Free Association Books.

Widlöcher, Daniel (1987) Interview with D. W. Winnicott. In Clancier and Kalmanovitch, pp. 143–50.

Williams, Judith (1978) *Decoding Advertisements: Ideology and Meaning in Advertising*. London: Marion Boyars.

Wilson, Edmund (1962 [1950]) A dissenting opinion on Kafka. In *Kafka: A Collection of Critical Essays*, ed. Ronald Grey. Englewood Cliffs: Prentice-Hall, pp. 91–7.

Winnicott, D. W. (1958) *Collected Papers: Through Paediatrics to Psycho-Analysis*. London: Tavistock Publications.

—— (1958a [1950–5]) Aggression in relation to emotional development. In *Collected Papers*, pp. 204–18.

—— (1958b [1953]) Symptom tolerance in paediatrics. In *Collected Papers*, pp. 101–17.

—— (1974) *Playing and Reality*. Harmondsworth: Penguin.

—— (1977) *The Piggle: An Account of the Psychoanalytic Treatment of a Little Girl*. Harmondsworth: Penguin.

—— (1979) *The Maturational Processes and the Facilitating Environment: Studies in the Theory of Emotional Development*. London: Hogarth Press and the Institute of Psycho-Analysis.

Wollheim, Richard (1971) *Freud*. London: Fontana/Collins.

—— (1973) *Art and the Mind*. London: Allen Lane. (Freud and the Understanding of Art, pp. 202–19; Adrian Stokes, pp. 315–35).

Wright, Elizabeth (1982) Modern psychoanalytic criticism. In *Modern Literary Theory*, eds Ann Jefferson and David Robey. London: Batsford, pp. 113–35.

—— (1989) *Postmodern Brecht: A Re-Presentation*. London and New York: Routledge.

Zamora, Lois Parkinson, and Faris, Wendy B. (eds) (1995) *Magical Realism: Theory, History, Community*. Durham, North Carolina: Duke University Press.

Žižek, Slavoj (1989) *The Sublime Object of Ideology*. London and New York: Verso.

—— (1990) Beyond discourse analysis. In *New Reflections on the Revolution of Our Time*, ed. Ernesto Laclau. London and New York: Verso, pp. 249–60.

—— (1991) *Looking Awry: An Introduction to Jacques Lacan through Popular Culture*. Cambridge, Massachusetts, and London: MIT Press.

—— (1992a) *Everything You Always Wanted to Know about Lacan (But Were Afraid to Ask Hitchcock)*. London and New York: Verso.

—— (1992b) *Enjoy your Symptom: Jacques Lacan in Hollywood and out*. New York and London: Routledge.

—— (1997) *The Plague of Fantasies*. London and New York: Verso.

Further Reading

The books listed below are not included in the bibliography.

Introductory material

Bennett, Andrew and Royle, Nicholas (1995) *An Introduction to Literature, Criticism and Theory: Key Critical Concepts*. London and New York: Prentice Hall/ Harvester.

Hill, Philip (1997) *Lacan for Beginners*. New York: Writers and Readers Publishing.

Lechte, John (1994) *Fifty Key Contemporary Thinkers: From Structuralism to Postmodernity*. London and New York: Routledge.

Minsky, Rosalind (ed.) (1996) *Psychoanalysis and Gender: An Introductory Reader*. London and New York: Routledge.

Molino, Anthony (1997) *Freely Associated: Encounters in Psychoanalysis*. London and New York: Free Association Books.

Nobus, Dany (1998) *Ten Key Concepts of Lacanian Psychoanalysis*. London: Rebus Press.

Vice, Sue (ed.) (1996) *Psychoanalytic Criticism: A Reader*. Cambridge: Polity Press.

Williams, Linda Ruth (1995) *Critical Desire: Psychoanalysis and the Literary Subject*. London and New York: Edward Arnold.

Part I: Classical psychoanalysis

Berman, Emmanuel (ed.) (1993) *Essential Papers on Literature and Psychoanalysis*. New York and London: New York University Press.

Bettelheim, Bruno (1976) *The Uses of Enchantment: The Meaning and Importance of Fairy Tales*. London: Thames and Hudson.

Franz, Marie-Louise von (1997) *Archetypal Dimensions of the Psyche*. Boston and London: Shambhala.

Kofman, Sarah (1991 [1974]) *Freud and Fiction*. Cambridge: Polity Press.

Mitscherlich, Alexander (ed.) (1982) *Psycho-Pathographien des Alltags: Schriftsteller und Psychoanalyse*. Frankfurt: Suhrkamp.
Person, Ethel Spector, Fonagy, Peter, and Figuiera, Sérvulo Augusto (eds) (1995) *On Freud's 'Creative Writers and Day-Dreaming'*. New Haven and London: Yale University Press.
Samuels, Andrew (1989) *Psychopathology: Contemporary Jungian Perspectives*. London: Karnac Books.

Part II: Object-relations theory

Abram, Jan (1996) *The Language of Winnicott: A Dictionary of Winnicott's Use of Words*. London: Karnac Books.
Hinshelwood, R. D. (1991) *A Dictionary of Kleinian Thought*. London: Free Association Books (revised edition).
Klein, Melanie, Heimann, Paula, and Money-Kyrle, Roger (eds) (1977) *New Directions in Psycho-Analysis*. London: Maresfield Reprints.
Mitchell, Juliet (ed.) (1986) *The Selected Melanie Klein*. London: Penguin.
New Literary History (1980): *Psychology and Literature: Some Contemporary Directions*, 12, no. 1.
Rudnytsky, Peter L. (1993) *Transitional Objects and Potential Spaces: Literary Uses of D. W. Winnicott*. New York: Columbia University Press.
Schafer, Roy (ed.) (1997) *The Contemporary Kleinians of London*. Madison, Connecticut: International Universities Press.
Wollheim, Richard (ed.) (1972) *The Image in Form: Selected Writings of Adrian Stokes*. Harmondsworth: Penguin.

Part III: Structural and post-structural psychoanalysis (and after)

Benvenuto, Bice (1994) *Concerning the Rites of Psychoanalysis, or the Villa of the Mysteries*. Cambridge: Polity Press.
Bowie, Malcolm (1987) *Freud, Proust and Lacan: Theory as Fiction*. Cambridge: Cambridge University Press.
Derrida, Jacques (1992) *Acts of Literature*. Derek Attridge (ed.), New York and London: Routledge.
Felman, Shoshana (ed.) (1982) *Psychoanalysis and Literature: The Question of Reading: Otherwise*. Baltimore and London: Johns Hopkins University Press.
—— (1985) *Writing and Madness*. Ithaca and London: Cornell University Press.
Fink, Bruce (1995) *The Lacanian Subject: Between Language and Jouissance*. Princeton, New Jersey: Princeton University Press.
Flieger, Jerry Aline (1991) *The Purloined Punch Line: Freud's Comic Theory and the Postmodern Text*. Baltimore and London: Johns Hopkins University Press.
Gilman, Sander L., Birmele, Jutta, Geller, Jay, and Greenberg, Valerie D. (eds) (1993) *Reading Freud's Reading*. New York and London: New York University Press.

Lacan, Jacques (1992 [1986]) *The Ethics of Psychoanalysis, 1959–1960: The Seminar of Jacques Lacan*. Jacques-Alain Miller (ed.). Trans. Dennis Porter. London and New York: Routledge.
Leader, Darian and Groves, Judy (1995) *Lacan for Beginners*. Cambridge: Icon Books.
Lechte, John (1996) *Writing and Psychoanalysis: A Reader*. London and New York: Edward Arnold.
Lupton, Julia Reinhard and Reinhard, Kenneth (1993) *After Oedipus: Shakespeare in Psychoanalysis*. Ithaca and London: Cornell University Press.
MacCannell, Juliet Flower (1986) *Figuring Lacan: Criticism and the Cultural Unconscious*. London and Sydney: Croom Helm.
Moi, Toril (ed.) (1986) *The Kristeva Reader*. Oxford: Blackwell.
Muller, John P. and Richardson, William J. (eds) (1988) *The Purloined Poe: Lacan, Derrida and Psychoanalytic Reading*. Baltimore and London: Johns Hopkins University Press.
Pettigrew, David and Raffoul, François (1996) *Disseminating Lacan*. Albany, New York: State University of Albany Press.
Royle, Nicholas (1995) *After Derrida*. Manchester: Manchester University Press.
Schafer, Roy (1992) *Retelling a Life: Narration and Dialogue in Psychoanalysis*. New York: Basic Books.

Part IV: Psychoanalysis and ideology

Apollon, Willy and Feldstein, Richard (eds) (1996) *Lacan, Politics, Aesthetics*. Albany, New York: State University of New York Press.
Bracher, Mark (1993) *Lacan, Discourse, and Social Change: A Psychoanalytic Cultural Criticism*. Ithaca and London: Cornell University Press.
Butler, Judith (1993) *Bodies that Matter*. New York and London: Routledge.
Donald, James (ed.) (1991) *Psychoanalysis and Cultural Theory: Thresholds*. Basingstoke: Macmillan.
Eagleton, Terry (1990) *The Ideology of the Aesthetic*. Oxford: Blackwell.
Journal for the Psychoanalysis of Culture and Society. Gardiner, New York: Critical Press/Kent, Ohio: English Department, Kent State University (particularly vol. I, no. 2, Fall, 1996).
Žižek, Slavoj (1989) The undergrowth of enjoyment: How popular culture can serve as an introduction to Lacan. *New Formations*, 9, pp. 7–29.
—— (1994) *The Metastases of Enjoyment: Six Essays on Women and Causality*. London and New York: Verso.

Part V: Feminist psychoanalytic criticism

Adams, Parveen and Cowie, Elizabeth (eds) (1990) *The Woman in Question: m/f*. London and New York: Verso.
Baruch, Elaine Hoffman, and Serrano, Lucienne Juliette (eds) (1996) *She Speaks/He Listens*. London and New York: Routledge.
Brennan, Teresa (ed.) (1989) *Between Feminism and Psychoanalysis*. London and New York: Routledge.

Garner, Shirley Nelson, Kahane, Claire, and Sprengnether, Madelon (eds) (1985) *The (M)other Tongue: Essays in Feminist Psychoanalytic Interpretation.* Ithaca and London: Cornell University Press.

Hirsch, Marianne (1989) *The Mother/Daughter Plot: Narrative, Psychoanalysis, Feminism.* Bloomington and Indianapolis: Indiana University Press.

Jacobus, Mary (1996) *First Things: The Maternal Imaginary in Literature, Art and Psychoanalysis.* London and New York: Routledge.

Merck, Mandy, Segal, Naomi and Wright, Elizabeth (eds) (1998) *Coming Out of Feminism?* Oxford: Blackwell.

Shiach, Morag (1991) *Hélène Cixous: A Politics of Writing.* London and New York: Routledge.

Sprengnether, Madelon (1990) *The Spectral Mother: Freud, Feminism, Psychoanalysis.* Ithaca and London: Cornell University Press.

Wright, Elizabeth (1992) *Feminism and Psychoanalysis: A Critical Dictionary.* Oxford: Blackwell.

Index